조기 유학생 출신 바이링구얼
뉴욕 손변의 재밌는 미국법 이야기

미주 한국일보 칼럼니스트, 카카오 브런치 작가
뉴욕 형사법원 손경락 수석변호사 지음

전체 영어 녹음 듣기

"... 인제는 돌아와 거울 앞에 선 내 누님같이 생긴 꽃이여..."

국민 시 미당 서정주 선생의 '국화 옆에서'를 읊조리며 어느덧 불혹의 나이에 접어든 내 모습을 거울에 비춰본다. 늦깎이 석사과정 유학생이셨던 부모님을 따라 중2 때 미국으로 건너왔으니 고국을 떠난 지 올해로 26년이 흘렀다. 성장기 때 한국에서 보낸 시간보다 성인이 되어 다양한 인종의 사람들과 부대끼며 아메리카합중국에서 보낸 시간이 한참 더 많아졌다.

나의 학창 시절 아버지께서는 밥상머리 교육 삼아 가끔 이런 말씀을 하곤 하셨다. "세상에는 두 그룹으로 사람을 분류할 수 있는데 성공하는 사람과 실패하는 사람이 바로 그것이다. 성공하는 사람의 특징은 일을 하다 실패했을 경우 실패의 원인을 자신의 잘못에서 찾아 고치려 하고, 남 탓을 하지 않는다. 성공했을 경우에는 주변에서 나를 도와주었기 때문에 성공했다고 생각하고 그 과실을 주변에 나눠주려 애쓴다.

이와 반대로 실패하는 그룹은 실패의 원인을 주변 탓으로 돌리려고만 하고, 성공했을 경우에는 자신이 잘났기 때문에 성공했다고 생각하고 그 과실을 혼자 독식하는 사람들이다. 결국 전자는 성공이 지속되어 행복한 인생을 살지만 후자는 한 번 성공을 끝으로 주변의 도움이 이어지지 않아 불행한 인생이 된다."는 것이었다.

가친의 말씀대로 조기 유학생 출신이었던 내가 다행히 탈선하지 않고, 현지에서 고교와 대학, 이어서 로스쿨을 졸업하고 변호사가 될 수 있었던 것은 오롯이 주위에서 음으로 양으로 나를 도와주고 보살펴준 덕분이다. 오늘의 나를 있게 한 그 한 가운데 나를 낳아주고 정신적·물질적 토양이 되어준 그리운 나의 조국 대한민국이 있다.

흔히들 미국을 '시스템과 매뉴얼로 작동되는 나라'라고 말한다. 미국의 변호사 관문인 바(Bar) 시험에 합격 후 7년간의 국선변호사에 이어 현재는 뉴욕시 형사법원 판사보좌 수석변호사로 4년째 일하고 있다. 법률 공부를 하면서 귀중한 해답을 찾은 게 하나 있다. 다름 아니라 미국으로 건너와 철들면서 늘 궁금했던 것 중의 하나는 무엇이 신생국에 불과했던 미국을 오늘날 세계 최강대국으로 만들었느냐 하는 것이 있었는데 그 답을 나름 찾은 것이다. 그것은 바로 국가와 사회의 운영 시스템으로 일찌감치 '법치주의'를 도입했다는 것이다.

신생국 U.S.A.(United States of America)의 탄생 과정이 순탄치는 않았다. 무엇보다 어제까지만 해도 자신들이 받들던 국왕과, 모국이었던 당대 최강대국 대영제국을 상대로 의용군을 꾸려 힘겨운 독립전쟁을 치러야 했던 것이다. 여기서 승리한 미국 건국의 아버지들은 자유와 평등을 건국이념으로 삼고, 삼권분립의 최신식 민주 법치 시스템으로 새로운 나라의 통치 매뉴얼을 만들었다. 중세 유럽의 왕정 시절 전제군주제에서 반복되는 절대 권력의 폐해를 직접 목도하고 체험했기 때문에 고뇌 끝에 이끌어낸 위대한 합의였다. 국가권력의 '견제와 균형'에 중점을 둔 이 법치 매뉴얼 덕분에 미국은 유럽 열강보다 한 발 앞서 보다 효율적인 국가 시스템을 갖출 수 있었다.

무릇 잘 만들어진 매뉴얼 하나가 긴급 상황에서 위기를 극복하고, 조직을 표준화하여 업무의 효율성을 높이고, 새 제품의 사용을 쉽게 하듯이 법치 매뉴얼은 누가 정권을 잡든 국가를 안정적으로 운영토록 함으로써 오늘의 미국을 만드는 데 결정적으로 기여했던 것이다.

이 매뉴얼을 통해 조성된 사회적 합의와 전통이 없었다면 훗날 전 세계에서 밀려드는 각양각색의 이민자들을 미합중국이란 용광로에 넣어 국민적 통합을 이뤄내는

데 한계에 부닥칠 수밖에 없었을 것이다.

"법은 권리 위에 잠자는 자를 보호하지 않는다."는 법언이 있다. 우리 재미교포들이 미국에서 주눅 들지 않고 당당하게 살아가려면 미국의 법치 시스템을 알아야 한다. 컴퓨터를 사용하려면 윈도우 같은 운영 시스템을 알아야 하는 이치와 같다. 그러나 내가 만난 많은 교민들은 미국 대통령 선거 과정을 제대로 이해하지 못하였고, 미국인들에겐 기초 상식인 대배심과 소배심, 헌법과 수정헌법의 차이, 사법부 우위의 미국식 삼권분립, 플리바게닝, 경찰의 면책특권 등에 대해서도 잘 모르는 것처럼 느껴졌다. 어떤 이는 왜 이처럼 강력한 경찰력이 있는데도 개인에게 총기 보유를 허용하여 툭하면 대형사고가 나게끔 만드는지 도대체 이해할 수 없다고 분개하기도 해 나를 안타깝게 했다.

이럴 때마다 '성공의 과실을 공유하라'고 했던 가친의 밥상머리 말씀이 떠올랐다. 그래서 고국으로부터 받은 은혜에 조금이라도 보답하는 마음에서 미주 한국일보에 '손경락의 법률칼럼'을 집필했던 것이다. 주로 미국 생활에 필요한 위와 같은 내용들로, 최대한 쉽고 재밌게 쓰고자 했다. 보잘것없지만 나에게 이렇게나마 재능 기부할 게 있다는 게 얼마나 다행한 일인가! 바쁜 가운데 짬을 내 격주로 시작한 게 약 3년 전 일인데 어느덧 80여 편의 칼럼이 쌓였다. 매 칼럼마다 가물가물 잊혀가는 한국말을 되새김질하며 그야말로 영혼을 끌어들여 쓴 것들인데 일회용으로 사장해버리기에는 가성비 생각이 간절했다.

병법의 대가 손자는 '지피지기면 백전불태'라고 했다. 전쟁뿐 아니라 무슨 일에 임하든 객체의 본질을 정확히 파악하라는 게 행간의 뜻일 테다. '미국 문제'라면 현지의 교포 여부를 떠나 우리 본토 국민들도 외면할 수 없는 중요 담론이다. 6·25로 혈맹의 연을 맺은 이후 우리 삶의 내밀한 구석까지 파고들어 와 한시도 지울 수 없는 그림자 같은 나라가 바로 미국 아니던가. 가친이 당신의 어린 철부지를 이곳에 남겨

두고 떠난 이유도 미국과 영어를 더 알뜰하게 배워오라고 한 게 아니었던가.

우리가 처한 지정학적 견지에서만 보더라도 수시로 핵과 미사일로 근육 자랑을 하는 불량배 북한이 지척에 있고, 우리에게 결코 우호적이지 않은 중국과 일본·러시아가 우리 한반도를 에워싸고 있다. 이처럼 험악한 국제정치의 정글 속에서 된 꼴을 당하지 않으려면 체면 불고하고 세계의 경찰 미국을 붙들고 늘어지는 수밖에 없다. 우리가 미국을 알아야 하는 절대 명제이다.

또 작금의 지구촌은 국경을 초월하여 구글의 유튜브와 메타(구 페이스북) 등을 통로로 급속하게 하나로 표준화되고 있다. 여기서도 일인 다역의 주인공 미국은 남이야 알아듣든 말든 영어를 거리낌 없이 구사하면서 세계를 쥐락펴락하고 있다.

\# 결론적으로 미국이라는 나라와 지구촌을 관통하는 영어라는 매개체는 한 세트가 되어 나의 성장기 때나, 26년이 지난 지금이나, 재미교포 사회에서나, 대한민국에서나, 국경이 없는 인터넷 상에서나, 시공을 초월하여 우리를 늘 따라다닌다는 것이다. 이 숙명적인 셈법과 연결고리들을 한 방에 정리하는 좋은 수가 없을까? 여러 날 고민 끝에 다목적 해결책으로 그간의 칼럼을 추려 책을 만들기로 용기를 냈다. 그렇게 하면 내가 영끌(영혼을 끌어들인)한 칼럼을 사장시키지 않아도 되고, 가친의 말씀처럼 태평양 너머 한국 독자들과도 소소하지만 성공의 과실을 공유할 수 있다.

그리고 기왕에 출판할 요량이라면 칼럼마다 영어 번역을 추가하는 게 하루라도 영어를 가까이하지 않으면 분리불안을 느끼는 한국 지성인들에게 도움이 될 것이다. 스토리와 함께 익힌 영어는 오래 기억되는 법-이를 출퇴근 시간에 리스닝 교재로도 활용토록 원어민 성우의 녹음파일을 곁들이자. 이것이 내가 다각적으로 고민한 출판 동기이다. 부디 이 책이 나의 의도대로 미국도 알고, 영어도 익히고자 하는 한국 독자들에게 일석이조의 도움이 되길 간절히 기대한다. 서두의 시 국화 옆에서처럼 간밤에 내린 무서리를 맞고 꽃 피우는 한 송이의 국화꽃이 되길 간절히 염원한다.

이 책이 나오기까지 도움을 주신 분들이 많다. 나의 영원한 멘토로서 영문 번역과 법리를 감수해주신 Tara Collins 판사님과 Jeffrey Zimmerman 판사님, 동료 Willoughby Jenett 변호사, 우리 집안의 이민 2세 변호사 Jane, Nancy 두 사촌 누님과 여동생 Janet 등 여러 법률가의 고마움을 잊을 수 없다.

아울러 졸필인 나에게 고정 칼럼난을 할애해 준 한국일보와 이 책이 세상에 빛을 볼 수 있도록 인도해주신 출판사 '글마당 & 아이디얼 북스' 최수경 대표님께도 깊은 감사의 말씀을 전한다. 마지막으로 나의 양가 부모님과 치과 개업의로서 바쁜 가운데 매번 싫은 기색 한 번 보이지 않고 피드백을 준 아내, 사랑스러운 두 아들과 막내딸 등과도 두루두루 이 출판의 기쁨을 같이하고 싶다.

2022. 8. 1.
뉴욕에서 손경락

직장에서 판사님, 동료 변호사들과

"Chrysanthemum! You look like my sister standing before her mirror, just back from the far gone back alleys of youth..."

I recite the famous Korean poem <Next to the Chrysanthemum> by Midang Seo Jung-ju as I approach 40 years old. It has been 26 years since I left my native land and came to America with my father. He was starting a master's degree program as a non-traditional student. I was in my second year of middle school (eighth grade in America). Now, I have spent much more time in the United States, mingling with people of different races, than in Korea.

\# When I was in school, my father used to tell me at the dinner table: "In this world, there are two types of people: those who succeed and those who fail. If successful people fail at work, they find the reason for the failure within themselves and try to fix it instead of blaming others. If they succeed, they think it is because of the help from other people around them, and they endeavor to share the fruits of their success.

On the other hand, the group defined by failure only finds the cause of failure in their surroundings. If they succeed, they think it is because of their abilities and they do not share the fruit. In the end, the successful people continue to succeed and lead happier and fuller lives but the latter group only achieves one success and as they stop receiving help from others, they live a less successful life."

As my father said, the reason why I, a young foreign student, was able to graduate from high school, college, and law school, and become a lawyer without going astray was because of the help and support of those around me. I also recognize that my motherland, Korea, provided a firm psychological and material foundation through my parents who remain there and contributed greatly to my identity today.

The United States is often referred to as a 'country of systems and manuals.' After passing the bar exam, the qualifying exam to become an attorney, I worked as a public defender for 7 years in New York City. For the past 4 years, I've been working as a principal law clerk in New York State Supreme Court, Criminal Term. As a student of law, I found a valuable answer to one of the lingering questions that I have as an immigrant. My question was this: How did the United States, as a relatively young country, become one of the strongest economic, military and cultural superpowers in the world? I found the answer in the early introduction of 'rule of law' as the operating system for the government and society.

The birth of the U.S.A. (United States of America) was not easy. Americans had to fight an arduous war by forming an all-volunteer army against the King of England, whom they had served until just a day before the war, and the British Empire, the strongest military force at that time. After achieving a hard-won victory, the framers of the Constitution made freedom and equality the foundation of the new country and adopted a democratic rule of law and separation of powers as governing principles. This great agreement was accomplished after weeks of tormenting debate, and it was only possible because the framers had a shared experience of witnessing despotism and the evils of absolute power that were perpetuated throughout the monarchies of medieval Europe.

The rule of law and the new system that focused on having checks and balances on state power allowed the United States to develop a more efficient system of governance than its European counterparts. Just as a well-written manual helps overcome crises, improve efficiency, and makes learning how to use a new product easy, the rule of law and the new system contributed enormously to making America the superpower it is today by allowing the country to maintain stability no matter who is in political control.

Without the social consensus and traditions created through this manual, it would have been impossible to place various immigrants from all over the world into a melting pot called the United States of America and achieve national unity.

There is a legal maxim, "The law assists only those who are vigilant, and not those who sleep over their rights." In order for Korean-Americans to live confidently, without being overwhelmed in America, we need to learn and understand the American legal system. It is the same reason why we should learn how to use an operating system like Windows to use a computer. However, most Korean-Americans I encountered over the years did not know, for instance, how the American presidents are elected, the difference between the grand and petit juries, the difference between the Constitution and the constitutional amendments, the separation of powers and judicial review, how plea-bargaining works, and police immunity. Not knowing the text of the Second Amendment,

some people asked why we cannot simply ban individuals from having guns given the presence of a strong police force. In my view, such knowledge is essential and indeed, elementary to understanding how American society works.

Whenever I saw and heard this, I remembered my father's dinner table lectures: share the fruits of success. As a way to pay forward, I began to write 'Attorney Son's Legal Column' in the Korea Times, which is one of the most widely circulated Korean language newspapers in America. I tried to write them without using legal jargon and include discussions about current events or stories so that readers can easily and casually pick up helpful legal knowledge. It is just a small contribution, but I am very fortunate to have the talent to share! I began writing a column biweekly, and in just three years, I have accumulated over 80 columns. Each column is a labor of love, as I struggled with my Korean, which has been regressing since I left Korea 26 years ago. I wrote my columns with all my heart and soul, so much so that I wanted to find a way to repurpose them.

Sun Tzu, the author of *The Art of War*, said, "If you know yourself and your enemy, you will not be defeated." He must have meant that we should look at the essence of our surroundings. His teachings surely rise above instructions on how to conduct a war. Understanding America is important not only for the immigrants here but also for Koreans in South Korea as well. Since forming the blood alliance during the Korean War, America has penetrated every level of Korean society and affects every aspect of our lives. Perhaps, the reason why my father left his young sons in America was for us to develop a deeper understanding of America and the English language.

South Korea is surrounded by countries like North Korea, a bully and a frequent launcher of missiles and nuclear weapons, and China, Japan, and Russia, who constantly pose military and economic threats. In this jungle of international geopolitics, we have no choice but to hold on to the United States to protect ourselves. So, it is an absolute necessity that we have a profound awareness of the United States of America: its politics, culture, and law.

In addition, thanks to various internet services like Google's YouTube and Meta (formerly Facebook), the world is rapidly becoming one global community without borders. Even in this, America plays an important role, dominating the world with its multinational companies. The English language always tags along unapologetically whether others understand it or not.

To conclude, America and English, taken together, transcend temporal and geographical boundaries. They were relevant in my youth and continue to be so 26 years later in the Korean-American community, to Koreans on the Korean peninsula, and on the internet, which has no physical borders. I thought about how to connect these different considerations with my columns. After countless days of contemplation, as a multi-purpose solution, I found the courage to combine my columns into a book. That way, I have repurposed my columns that I poured my heart into, and as my father said, I can share the fruits of my success with Korean readers on the other side of the Pacific Ocean.

I also thought that adding English translation to each column would help Korean intellectuals who feel separation anxiety if they do not read some English text even for a single day. I hired professional voice actors with the hope that listening to stories told in English will help people to remember them. Some people may benefit by listening to them during their long commute. This is my motivation for publishing the book. I sincerely hope that this book will help readers who want to know more about the United States and learn English. I hope for the book to become the chrysanthemum flower that blooms after being frosted all night long, as mentioned in the introductory poem <Next to the Chrysanthemum>.

Many people helped me with putting this book together. My mentors, Judges Tara Collins and Jeffrey Zimmerman, ensured that my explanation of the law was accurate and accessible. My colleague Willoughby Jenett as well as my cousins and fellow lawyers, Jane and Nancy nuna and Janet, have helped with proofreading and editing the book.

I also want to thank the Korea Times for giving me the space for my biweekly columns, and President Choi Su-Kyung of 'Gulmadang & Ideal Books' for making the book possible. I am deeply grateful to my parents and my parents-in-law for their support, and my wife, who was always ready with feedback despite her busy schedule running two dental offices. Finally, I would like to dedicate the book to my two sons, Aaron and Isaac, and my baby, Victoria.

August 1, 2022

From New York,
K.R. Mark Son

내가 마크를 처음 만난 것은 그가 뉴욕시 국선변호 로펌인 '리걸 에이드(Legal Aid)'의 퀸스 지사로 발령받아 온 2013년이었습니다. 우리는 둘 다 어린아이들의 아버지인 데다 가난하고 불쌍한 형사 피고인들에게 정의로운 법률 서비스를 제공하겠다는 각오로 리걸 에이드를 자원한 사람들이기 때문에 바로 호흡이 잘 맞았습니다.

우리가 형사피고인들을 지키기 위해 싸운 권리 중 하나는 이들이 경찰로부터 부당한 수색이나 구금을 당하지 않고, 신속하게 국선 변호사를 선임할 수 있도록 하는 것이었습니다. 당시 퀸스 카운티 지방검찰청은 검찰청 내규로 영장실질심사에 앞서 피고인들이 변호사와 상담하기 전 자백을 받기 위해 검사를 먼저 만나도록 강요했습니다. 우리는 이것을 CBQ 인터뷰(Central Booking-Queens)라고 불렀습니다. 우리는 이 내규가 의뢰인들의 구속을 불필요하게 연장시키고 형사사건이 시작되는 골든타임에 법률 자문을 받을 수 없게 하기 때문에 반대했습니다.

마크와 나는 수많은 CBQ 인터뷰 사건을 함께 다루면서 만나는 판사들마다 CBQ 인터뷰의 부당성을 부단하게 설득했습니다. 결국 이 내규는 우리의 끈질긴 요구와 비판 여론에 밀려 결국 2019년 새로운 검사장이 선출되면서 사라졌습니다.

마크가 현재의 판사실 재판연구관으로 이직하기 직전, 우리는 함께 강도 사건 용의자를 변호했습니다. 우리 클라이언트인 용의자는 피해자의 집에 침입해 강아지를 훔쳐 달아나다 피해자를 흉기로 찌른 혐의를 받고 있었습니다. 구속 상태였던 용의자는 잘못하면 십 년 이상 감옥살이를 해야 할 처지에 놓여 있었습니다. 우리의 변론은 강아지가 실제로 우리 클라이언트의 것이고 고소인이 그들의 잘못을 감추기 위해 사건을 조작했다는 것이었습니다.

재판을 치밀하게 준비한 마크는 공소장에 적힌 혐의 중 검사가 충분한 증거를 제시하지 못한 것들은 배심원의 심리조차 받을 필요가 없다며 기각해 달라고 요청했습니다. 재판장이 우리의 주장을 많이 수용해준 덕분에 배심원으로부터 무죄 평결을 받았고 의뢰인은 감옥에서 풀려날 수 있었습니다. 무죄 소식을 듣고 기뻐하던 클라이언트의 모습을 아직도 잊을 수 없습니다.

마크의 국선변호사 시절 무엇보다 나를 감동시켰던 것은 법과 정의에 대한 확고한 신념뿐 아니라 그의 따뜻한 인간미였습니다. 이것은 그가 변호사로서의 의무를 넘어 즐거운 마음으로 후배 변호사들을 멘토링하는 데서도 엿볼 수 있었습니다. 마크는 법정 변론이 있는 날이면 어김없이 후배들을 대동했습니다. 또한 클라이언트를 대할 때도 사무적으로 사건 파일이나 사건 번호로 접근하는 게 아니라 항상 인격적으로 대접하고 인권을 앞세워 사건을 풀고자 노력했습니다.

마크와 같이 일하던 시절 골치 아픈 사건 등을 상의하려고 그의 방에 자주 들르곤 했는데 그의 책상에 걸려있던 성경 구절(첨부)이 인상 깊었습니다. 나는 이 책을 읽으면서 이런 마크의 사람 훈기가 군데군데 살아 숨 쉬는 것을 다시금 느꼈습니다. 마치 마크가 법률 문외한인 클라이언트들을 위해 어려운 법률 내용을 이해하기 쉽게 들려주는 듯한 생각이 들었기 때문입니다.

이 책에는 더러 미국에서 태어나 변호사 생활을 하는 나도 몰랐던 실생활에 유익한 내용들도 많이 담겨 있습니다. 나는 이 책을 미국 법에 관심이 많고, 다양하고 역동적인 미국 사회에 법이 어떤 영향을 미치는지 궁금해하는 모든 사람에게 꼭 읽어

보시라고 추천하고 싶습니다.

2022.7.18
변호사 크리스토퍼 L. 힐리

잠언 31장 8~9절 "너는 할 말 못하는 사람과 버림받은 사람의 송사를 위해 입을 열어라. 입을 열어 바른 판결을 내려 불쌍하고 가난한 사람들의 권리를 세워 주어라."

 Recommendation

Mark and I met for the first time in 2013 as Staff Attorneys when he came to the Queens office of the Legal Aid Society, a public defender organization in New York City. We hit it off right away as we had much in common. We were both fathers of young children and we shared a common goal – to provide the best legal representation to indigent criminal defendants.

Among the rights we fought to protect were the individual's right to be free from unreasonable searches and seizures and the right to have an attorney. At the time, Queens County District Attorney's Office had a policy of delaying arraignment so that they could interrogate people without them having an attorney. We called these Central Booking-Queens (CBQ) interviews. We objected to this policy because it unreasonably prolonged our client's detention and deprived them of legal counsel at a critical time.

Mark and I worked on numerous CBQ interview cases together, and argued before many judges in an effort to convince them that it was violative of these individuals' constitutional and human rights. We collaborated on a memo to our colleagues laying out arguments and suggesting ways to fight against the policy in court. Due to the efforts of the defense bar and public criticism, the policy was discontinued in 2019 with the election of a new district attorney.

Before Mark left to work as a court attorney, we tried a burglary case together. In that case, it was alleged that our client broke into someone's home to steal a puppy, and injured them while fleeing from the location. Our client, who was being held pending trial, was facing more than a decade in prison. Our theory was that the puppy actually belonged to our client and that the complainant had fabricated a story to hide their own wrongdoing.

At trial, Mark's inter-personal skills and ability to judge character were critical in selecting a fair and balanced jury. After many hours of preparation, Mark's persuasive legal arguments successfully convinced the judge to dismiss several counts on the indictment based on the prosecutor's failure to present sufficient credible evidence. As to the remaining felony charges, we obtained a not guilty verdict from the jury and our client was released from jail. I still remember our client's happy face!

What impressed me about Mark is his commitment to justice and the law and his humanity. This commitment was expressed not only in his diligence in expanding his skills and knowledge but the pleasure he took in mentoring junior attorneys. He often had them as his second seats at hearings and trials. Mark's commitment was evident as well in his dealings with his clients; he treated them with respect, never as just another case file or a case number.

I often stopped by his office to talk about a troublesome case or the issues of the day. On the wall in front of his desk was this verse from the Bible (attached), which is his motto. As I was reading this book, I recognized those qualities about Mark coming to life. They reminded me of care Mark took in explaining complex legal concepts to his clients.

The book contained stories that even I, as an American-born attorney, did not know and found helpful. I recognize the value of Mark's book to everyone impacted by what goes on in America. I look forward to more interesting stories from Mark.

Christopher L. Healy

저자의 에세이는 미국의 법률 시스템에 재밌는 관점으로 접근해 누구나 쉽고 흥미롭게 읽을 수 있도록 쓰여졌습니다. 특히 미국법의 기발함이나 특이함을 잘 모르는 사람들도 말입니다. 저자는 사람들과 그들의 인간적인 이야기에 초점을 맞추어 법과 법 체계를 이해하기 쉽게 풀어줍니다. 모쪼록 이 책을 통해 많은 독자가 법과 미국 사회를 이해하는 데 도움이 되기를 진심으로 바랍니다.

포드햄 로스쿨 학장
매튜 딜러

The author's essays are interesting takes on aspects of the US legal system written in a clear manner that is understandable and engaging for a general audience - particularly for those unfamiliar with the quirks and oddities of American law.

Son accomplishes this by focusing on the human dimensions and stories about people that are so essential to understanding law and legal systems. I sincerely hope that this book will help many readers to understand law and American society.

Dean Matthew Diller
Fordham University Law School

⚖️ 일러두기

- 칼럼의 성격상 시사문제와 관련이 있는 게 대부분이기 때문에 당시 시대 상황에 대한 독자의 이해를 돕기 위해 칼럼 말미에 미주 한국일보(뉴욕판 기준)에 보도된 날짜를 명기하였다.

- 시사적 이슈가 없는 시기에는 우리 미국 교민들이 알아두면 유익한 기초 법률 상식을 다루되 흔히 딱딱하다고 여기는 법률 칼럼에 대한 거부감을 덜기 위해 최대한 쉽게 이야기식으로 꾸몄다. 이 책을 다 읽게 되면 법치로 돌아가는 미국 사회를 파악하는 데 큰 도움이 되리라 믿는다.

- 그동안 보도된 칼럼 약 80건 중에서 58건을 추려 나름대로 주제별 분류를 하긴 했으나 사건별로 연관성이 없으므로 순서대로 읽을 필요 없이 아무 데서나 관심 있는 주제부터 읽으면 된다.

- 칼럼 집필 약 3년의 세월이 흐르는 사이 칼럼에서 다룬 사건의 결말에 대해 궁금증을 느낄 독자를 위해 판결 결과나 사건의 추이를 추적하여 해당 칼럼 말미에 '결과'라 표기하고 간략하게 부기하였다.

- 신문과 달리 한정된 지면에 구애받지 않고 칼럼의 이해도와 현장감을 제고하기 위해 사진을 곁들일 수 있게 된 것은 출판과정에서 얻는 소득이었다. 다만 사진의 저작권 문제 등으로 저자 개인 사진을 다수 게재할 수밖에 없었던 점 넓은 양해를 바란다.

- 아울러 이 책에 인용된 각종 법리와 법적 해석, 개인적 견해 등은 저자가 근무하는 뉴욕시 형사법원 입장과는 무관함을 밝힌다.

■ 영어 리스닝 실력을 배양코자 하는 독자를 위해 영어 번역본을 현지 남녀 원어민 성우 7명의 다양한 목소리로 녹음하여 각 영문 칼럼별, chapter별 서두의 QR 코드로 들을 수 있도록 하였다. 전체 녹음은 책 서두에 있다. 이 번역본에 나온 영어 단어만 내 것으로 잘 소화하여도 명사, 형용사, 동사, 부사 등(대명사, 전치사, 접속사, 감탄사는 제외)이 한 칼럼당 평균 약 285 단어이므로 프롤로그와 에필로그까지 합해 약 17,000 단어를 암기하는 효과가 있다.

■ 책 편집 관련

• 외국 인명과 지명, 소송사건명 등은 한글맞춤법 외래어표기법에 따랐다.

• 고유명사 중 등장인물의 풀네임과 소송사건명은 가급적 영어를 괄호 안에 병기하였다. 다만 트럼프 대통령처럼 익히 아는 이름과 일회성 인물, 이름이나 성만 사용해도 문맥 이해에 지장이 없는 경우에는 이를 생략하였다.

• 연령 단위는 어린이라 할지라도 모두 '~살' 대신 '~세'로 통일하였다.

• 영어로 번역하는 과정에서 원문(판결문 등)에서 사용한 첫 문장의 영어 대문자를 번역문의 중간에 소문자로 인용하는 경우, 또는 시제 관계상 현재를 과거 등으로 표현해야 하는 경우에는 미국 용례에 따라 [ ](브래킷, 꺾쇠괄호)로 처리하였다.

예) President Trump said, "[t]hey've ruled and we live with the decision of the Supreme Court."

• 번역 과정에서 원어민 독자의 이해를 돕기 위해 의역이 필요한 경우에는 의역을 하였다.

예) 하나의 법을 가운데 두고 가해자와 피해자 간에 전개되는 상황 반전이 마치 새옹지마 고사를 연상케 한다(Chapter 1. 기발한 법리 '샘의 아들법'에서).

⇨ The twist in the criminals and victims' lives created by the law reminds us of the old man's story in "Saeongjima (the old man lost his horse)."

솔로몬 뺨치는 마셜의 이 명판결 하나로 사법부가 행정부에 예속되는 것을 막고,

의회의 입법 횡포도 견제함으로써 오늘날 사법부 우위의 미국식 삼권분립이 자리를 잡게 된 것이다(Chapter 2. 사법시스템 '위헌법률심판권의 시원'에서).

⇨ Marshall's Solomon-like decision prevented the judiciary from becoming a puppet institution to the executive. It also allowed the judiciary to determine the legality of the legislature's actions. It perfected the American system of checks and balances, with the judiciary on top.

내가 한국을 떠날 때가 온통 '세계화 드라이브'로 조기유학이 붐을 이루던 때였다면 몇 년이 지나 성년이 되어 다시 학원 강사로 나갈 즈음의 한국은 그야말로 '영어가 바로 계급장'인 시대라고 해도 과언이 아니었다(에필로그에서).

⇨ When I left Korea as a teenager, a huge wave of globalization had engulfed the entire country. Students were leaving en masse to study abroad. When I returned as a TOEIC instructor, English aptitude was a symbol of one's achievements.

⚖️ Introductory Remarks

- By nature, columns are written about current events. As such, to provide readers with context about what was happening when the column was written, the publication date in the Korea Times' New York edition is shown at the end of each column.

- When there was no noteworthy current event, I wrote about legal principles and court cases that would be helpful for Korean-Americans. In order to eliminate the mental barrier to reading a legal column, I tried to make it more fun to read by incorporating stories. Reading the book will help with learning how the rule of law works in American society.

- I selected 58 columns out of approximately 80 columns that have been published so far. Although they are loosely organized into different categories in the book, they are not related or written in sequential order. The reader should feel free to meander through the book and read what interests them.

- As some columns are as many as three years old, the "outcome" section was added to inform the readers who may be curious about the ultimate outcome of the case or a particular situation discussed in the column.

- Unlike with newspapers, an added benefit of publishing the columns together in a book is being able to offer photographs to provide a more comprehensive picture of the column's topic. However, in order to avoid copyright issues, many personal photographs are used throughout the book. I appreciate your understanding.

- Any views or interpretations of legal principles and court cases are mine only, and not of my employer, New York State Supreme Court.

- For those who wish to practice English listening comprehension, seven male and female native-English-speaking professional voice actors have recorded the columns' English translations. They are available through the QR code at the beginning of each column, chapter, book. Each column has about 285 English words of nouns, adjectives, verbs, adverbs, et cetera (excepting pronouns, prepositions, conjunctions, and exclamations). Reading the book cover-to-cover including the prologue and epilogue will help the reader to memorize about 17,000 English words.

⚖ 목 차

Chapter 7   정치·언론

Chapter 8   한국 재판 소식

1장 전체 영어 녹음 듣기

Chapter
1

기발한 법리
Creative Legal Theories

외국인 불법행위청구법

문명의 발달과 함께 인권이 신장하면서 인류는 대량학살, 고문, 아동학대와 같은 반인권 문제에 대해 깊은 고민을 하게 되었다. 이에 대한 해결책으로 국제사회는 U.N.헌장, 세계인권선언, 고문에 반대하는 U.N.선언 등에 국제 인권의 기준을 명시하고, 이를 위반 시 책임을 묻기 위해 국제 유고전범재판소, 국제형사재판소와 같은 국제재판소를 창설하기도 했다.

하지만 국제조약에 따라 만들어지다 보니 설치에 장기간이 소요되고, 관할권도 제한적이며 무엇보다 법적 구속력이 약해 실효성에 의문이 많았다. 그러나 세계의 경찰 나라임을 자타가 공인하는 오늘의 최강대국 미국이 미국법으로 전 세계 인류의 인권을 지켜주겠다고 보장한다면 사정은 많이 달라질 것이다.

1789년 당시 신생국가에 불과했던 미국의 첫 연방의회는 '외국인 불법행위청구법(Alien Tort Statute, ATS)'이란 것을 제정했는데 그 내용은, '지방법원은 국제관습법 혹은 미국이 체결한 조약의 위반 행위에 대해서 외국인이 제기한 손해배상 청구 소송의 관할권을 지닌다'는 짤막한 법문으로 이루어져 있다. 건국 초기 주미 외교관 상대 테러행위 등이 빈발했던 상황에 비추어 국제무대의 신출내기 미국이 국제조약과

관습을 지키겠다는 의지를 보여주기 위해 만들어진 것으로 학자들은 추정한다. 200여 년 전에 이런 법이 있었다는 것을 발견해낸 것은 인권운동가들의 업적이다.

오랫동안 유명무실했던 이 법은 1980년 '필라르티가 대 페냐-이랄라'(*Filartiga v. Pena-Irala*) 사건을 통해 급부상하게 된다. 사건의 요지는, 1976년 파라과이 독재정권하 비밀경찰이 반정부 운동가 '조엘 필라르티가'의 아들 '조엘리토'(17세)를 납치하여 고문으로 죽게 했다. 이런 연유로 미국으로 망명을 하게 된 조엘리토의 누나 '돌리'는 우연히 자신의 동생을 죽인 경찰간부 '페냐'가 뉴욕의 브루클린에서 불법체류하고 있다는 사실을 알게 되었다.

돌리는 페냐를 불법체류자로 신고하는 한편 ATS법에 근거하여 고문 및 살인 혐의로 손해배상 청구소송을 제기하였다. 소장을 접수한 뉴욕주 연방법원은 외국 정부가 그 나라의 자국민에게 가한 행위에 대해 미국 법원은 재판권이 없다는 이유로 소송을 기각했으나 항소법원은 각종 국제조약과 선언문 등을 인용해 '고문자는 이전 세대의 해적과 노예 무역상처럼 모든 인류의 적'이라고 볼 수 있기 때문에 지방법원이 관할권을 지닌다고 1심 판결을 뒤집었던 것이다.

비록 페냐는 법원이 명한 1천만 불의 배상금을 한 푼도 갚지 않고 파라과이로 추방되었지만 이 판결은 전 세계에 큰 반향을 일으켰다. 왜냐하면 이 사건을 통해 미국의 재판관할 범위가 전 세계로 확장됨으로써 미국인과 직접적으로 관련이 없다 하더라도 미국이 앞장서 세계의 도덕적 경찰 역할을 자임하겠다는 것을 알리는 의미였기 때문이다.

이 판결 이후 여러 지방법원과 항소법원은 정부 인사들뿐만 아니라 다국적 회사들에도 법의 적용 범위를 넓혀가 2008년까지 약 185건의 인권 관련 ATS 소송이 진행되었다.

사태가 점차 확대되자 교통정리가 필요하다고 판단한 연방대법원은 ATS의 해석 축소작업에 착수하였다. 우선 2004년 있었던 '소사 대 알바레즈-머체인'(*Sosa v. Alvarez-Machain*) 사건을 통해 '국제관습법'의 범주를 법안 제정 당시의 문제였던 '해적질', '대사 폭행'과 같은 악질범죄로만 국한하였고, 뒤이어 2013년 '키오벨 대 로열 더치 셸'(*Kiobel v. Royal Dutch Petroleum*) 사건에서는 외교갈등을 고려하여 미국 영토나 국익에 관계가 있어야만 미국법원에서 사법권을 가질 수 있다고 판시하였다.

그러나 미국회사가 국외에서 인권위반을 자행하거나 공모, 또는 묵인한 정황이 있다면 외국인 피해자가 그 미국회사를 상대로 미국에서 소송을 제기할 수 있는지에 대한 판단은 아직 나오지 않았다. 대법원은 12월 중에 이런 쟁점의 사건을 심리할 예정인데 과연 대법원이 국제적 인권 문제를 중시할지, 아니면 미국의 국익보호 우선 결정을 내릴지 그 귀추가 주목된다. (2020.12.2.)

결과: 대법원은 2021년, '네슬레 대 도'(*Nestle v. Doe*) 사건을 통해 미국회사가 국외에서 인권위반을 자행하거나 공모, 또는 묵인한 정황이 있다면 외국인 피해자가 그 미국회사를 상대로 미국에서 소송을 제기할 수 있는지에 대한 판단을 내려주었는데, 지금까지의 판례에 이어 미국의 국익보호 우선 결정을 내려 명맥만 유지되던 ATS는 다시 영면에 들고 말았다.

유엔본부(맨해튼, 뉴욕)
U.N. Headquarters (Manhattan, New York)

영어녹음듣기

Alien Tort Statute

As our cultural awareness grew, so did our thoughts on human rights. To deal with crimes against humanity including genocide, torture, and child abuse, the international community adopted standards for human rights such as the U.N. Charter, Universal Declaration of Human Rights, and the U.N. Convention Against Torture. In addition, international tribunals like the International Criminal Court and the International Criminal Tribunal for the Former Yugoslavia have been established to hold the human rights violators accountable.

However, such international courts are grossly inadequate. They are built on international treaties and require a long time to set up. Their jurisdiction is limited and usefulness is questionable because they cannot enforce decisions. Certainly, none of this would be the case if America, as the world's police and the strongest country, guarantees human rights everywhere.

In 1789, America was still a newly formed country. The first Congress enacted the Alien Tort Statute ("ATS"), which read, "[t]he district courts shall have original jurisdiction of any civil action by an alien for a tort only, committed in violation of the law of nations or a treaty of the United States." Legal scholars theorize that the statute was intended to show the new country's commitment to conform to the established international treaties, norms and customs because there were recurrent attacks against foreign diplomats in America. It was the achievement of human rights activists who brought this 200-year-old law back to life.

This nominal law became very relevant in 1980 through a case called Filartiga v. Pena-Irala. At the crux of the case was the killing of a 17-year boy named Joelito by the Paraguay dictator's secret police in 1976. Joelito was the son of anti-government activist Joel Filartiga. Joelito's sister, Dolly, fled the country and sought asylum in the United States. While in America, she found that Pena, a police inspector who was responsible for Joelito's death, was illegally staying in Brooklyn, New York.

Dolly reported Pena as an illegal alien to the immigration authorities and concomitantly brought a civil lawsuit under the ATS for the torture and murder of Joelito. Initially, the New York federal district court dismissed it, which determined that American courts do not have jurisdiction over acts committed by foreign governments against their citizens. However, the appellate court reversed by holding that the ATS conferred jurisdiction. After reviewing the international treaties and declarations, it determined that "[t]he torture has become – like the pirate and slave trader before him – hostis humani generis, an enemy of all mankind."

Although Pena was deported without paying a dime of the court-ordered $10 million in damages, this decision shocked the world. It showed that American courts were willing to extend their jurisdiction beyond the territorial borders. It also exhibited America's willingness to enforce its moral standards even in cases that had nothing to do with it.

Since this decision, district and appellate courts expanded the law to hold government officials and multinational companies accountable. By 2008, about 185 ATS lawsuits had been concluded or were ongoing.

As the ATS was beginning to resemble a runaway train, the Supreme Court attempted to rein it in. First, in 2004, the Supreme Court decided in Sosa v. Alvarez-Machain that the phrase "law of nations" used in the ATS was limited to piracy and offense against ambassadors as when the law was written, and did not create a legal cause of action for other wrongdoings.

미국 연방대법원 앞에서(워싱턴 D.C.2010)
U.S. Supreme Court (Washington D.C.)

Subsequently, in Kiobel v. Royal Dutch Petroleum in 2013, the Supreme Court further held that to avoid diplomatic conflicts, the district court's jurisdiction under the ATS was limited to cases relating to American territory or national interest.

However, there is still a remaining question as to whether a foreign national can bring a lawsuit against American companies that participated, conspired to commit, or were complicit in human rights violations overseas. The Supreme Court is set to hear oral arguments in December to decide this issue. It remains to be seen whether the Supreme Court will focus on international human rights or the U.S. national interest. (2020.12.2.)

Outcome: Continuing its decades-long trajectory, the Supreme Court decided in Nestle v. Doe that American companies might not be sued in district courts under the ATS based on "mere corporate presence" even though there were allegations that they committed, aided and abetted, or were complicit in, human rights violations in foreign countries. With this, the ATS fell into a long slumber again.

맨해튼 다운타운에 위치한 뉴욕주 연방법원
Federal courthouse in downtown Manhattan

반려견을 위한 법원의 배려

2020년의 미국 반려동물 제품협회 통계에 의하면 미국의 약 6,300만 가구에서 반려견을 기르고 있는 것으로 나타났다. 많은 미국인이 개를 가족으로 생각하며 온갖 사랑과 정성을 쏟다 보니 비싼 사료와 애견용품뿐 아니라 심지어 거액을 마다치 않고 호화 장례식까지 치러주기도 한다.

그러나 법적인 관점에서 엄밀히 따질 때 개는 단지 하나의 물건에 지나지 않는다. 따라서 고의나 과실로 반려견에게 상처를 입히거나 사망케 하는 사고가 발생하더라도 법원에서는 개의 시장가치만큼의 손해액만 산정해줄 뿐 개의 신체적 고통이나 견주의 정신적 위자료 같은 것은 반영해주지 않는다.

이런 일반적 통념 가운데 최근 '록시'라는 반려견의 소유권 문제를 둘러싸고 뉴욕의 한 해충방제 회사와 그 종업원 '배리 마이릭'(Barry Myrick)이 벌이는 소송에서 흥미로운 판결이 나와 소개하고자 한다.

마이릭은 5년 전, 이 회사에 취직할 때 회사로부터 해충 탐지견 핏불테리어 '록시'를 인계받아 낮에 함께 일하고 퇴근 후에도 집에 데려가 재우는 등 한 가족처럼 생활했다. 그러다 작년 초 코로나-19 여파로 회사는 마이릭을 일시적으로 해고할 수밖에 없었는데 이때 업무 차량과 법인카드, 회사의 유니폼 등만 반환 받았을 뿐 록시를 같이 돌려받지 않은 것이 분쟁의 불씨가 됐다. 해고 후 얼마 지나지 않아 마이릭에게 록시와 함께 복직할 것을 요구했으나 그는 오히려 뉴욕을 떠나 필라델피아로 이사를 가면서 이를 거절했던 것이다.

마이릭은 거절 이유로 회사 측이 고용 기간 중에는 록시 숙식비를 지급해오다 해고 후에는 이를 지급하지 않아 자비로 충당했다고 주장했다. 그리고 무엇보다 입사 당시 록시가 회사 소유임을 입증하는 법적 서류를 자신이 작성한 일조차 있어 회사 측이 분명히 록시의 소유권 문제를 인지하고 있었음에도 불구하고 해고 시 이를 일절 언급하지 않은 것은 회사 측이 묵시적으로 록시의 소유권을 자신에게 양도한 것이라고 항변했다. 결국 회사는 마이릭을 절도죄로 경찰에 신고하는 한편 민사소송까지 제기하게 된 것이다.

통상적으로 물건에 대한 소유권 분쟁의 경우 법원은 누가 그 물건을 구입하고 관리했는지, 또 선물로 준 것은 아닌지 등 재산권의 비중이 누구에게 더 큰지 여부를 판단기준으로 삼게 된다. 하지만 지난달 결정된 록시 관련 민사상 가처분명령 판결에서는 재산권 관점이 아닌, 개의 입장에서 '최선의 선택'(best interest)이라는 법리를 새롭게 적용해 세인의 눈길을 끌었다.

즉, '최선의 선택'은 흔히 이혼소송 시 자녀의 성별과 나이, 부모와의 친밀도, 부모의 건강 및 경제력, 부모와 자녀의 의사 등 다양한 요인들을 고려해 아이에게 제일 유리하도록 양육권을 결정하는 법리인데 이것을 개 소유권 분쟁에 적용한 것이다.

재판부는 뉴욕주법상 개는 재물에 불과하다고 전제하면서도 견주의 사망이나 건강상의 이유로 반려견을 돌볼 수 없을 경우에 대비해 신탁을 설정할 수 있으며 가정법원의 보호명령에 애완견도 포함시킬 수 있다는 점을 상기시켰다. 이처럼 개는 단순한 물건과 달라, 소유권은 회사에 있더라도 마이릭과 함께 있는 것이 록시에게 더 좋은 선택이기 때문에 민사소송의 본안 판결이 나올 때까지 실질적 주인인 마이릭과 함께 있으라고 배려한 것이다.

사실 반려견의 소유권 분쟁은 이혼소송에서 자주 등장하는 단골 소재이긴 했으나 이번 결정은 이혼이 아닌 재산권 소송에서 쟁점이 되었고, 이채롭게도 사람이 아닌 개에게 '최선의 선택'이라는 법리를 채택했다는 점에서 향후 이어질 본안 심리와 형사사건에도 그대로 적용될지 특히 반려가족들의 관심이 지대하다. (2021.1.27.)

펫 장례식장(뉴욕)
pet funeral house(NewYork)

저자 주: 저자는 반려견 장묘사업을 준비 중이라는 한국 고모님으로부터 "반려견 천국이라 일컫는 미국의 장묘사업 실태를 알아봐 달라"는 부탁을 받고 펫 장례식장과 공동묘지 등을 둘러볼 기회가 있었다. 위 사진은 모두 그때 촬영한 것이다. 다소 답사 시일은 경과하였지만 전통적인 반려견 장묘 방식의 기본 틀은 큰 변화가 없다고 보고, 1,500만 명이나 되는 한국 반려가족의 관심해소 차원에서 그때 작성했던 보고서도 첨부한다.

펫 공동묘지(Hartsdale pet cemetery) 방문결과 보고

1. 일시: 2015.12.9(수). 14:30~16:00

2. 장소: Hartsdale pet cemetery(www.petcem.com, 75 North Central Avenue, Hartsdale, NY 10530)

3. 상담내용

- 동 공동묘지는 지금으로부터 119년 전 1896년에 건립되었으며 3번 주인이 바뀌었는데 지금은 가족기업으로 운영

- 미국에서 제일 큰 동물 공동묘지로 2012년에 역사유적지로 지정되었으며 그 덕분에 견주들로부터 500불~1만 불 단위로 기부를 받고 있음

- 동 부지는 동물 묘지로만 지정되었기 때문에 다른 용도로 개발될 수 없고 그래서 고객들이 신뢰감을 가지고 꾸준히 많이 찾아옴

- 고객의 화장과 매장 비율은 50대 50 정도로 공동묘지 내에는 화장터도 있음(고객은 화장장 안에는 출입이 금지되어 있으며 굴뚝이 2개인 것으로 보아 2기의 화로를 운용하는 것으로 추정)

- 화장 시간은 1시간에서 1시간 30분 정도 소요되며 동물병원에서 4마리가 모이면 전화를 주는데 그때 픽업해와 소각하기도 하고

- 개별로 오는 손님은 분향소에서 잠깐 개와 마지막 시간을 보낸 뒤 관이 화장장 안에 들어가는 모습까지 참관케 함

- 화장 비용은 픽업비 150불에 세금을 합해 평균 단체 화장은 300불, 개별 화장은 400불 정도 하며 관은 종류에 따라 다르나 평균 600불

- 개 묘지 값은 위치에 따라 도로변 시끄러운 곳은 900불부터 1200, 1500, 2700불까

지 있으며 좁은 곳에 많은 개를 묻기 위해서는 땅을 깊이 파서 계단식으로 매장(개 外 고양이, 앵무새, 말까지 매장)

- 관리비는 1년에 약 72불이며, 비석 면적에 따라 차등 부과되고 관리비를 내지 않으면 계속 최고를 하다가 최종 7년 뒤에는 비석을 제거

- 비석은 대리석의 경우 20자 기본 인쇄에 보통 1천 불 정도(사진, 종교적 표시 등을 추가하게 되면 추가 부담)

- 관리비를 한 번에 목돈으로 내게 되면 JP모건 신탁회사에 위탁하여 그 이자로 대체하는 방법도 있음

- 묘지 관리인도 전체 묘지가 몇 기나 되는지 잘 모른다고 하며 대충 육안으로 전체 약 5천 평 부지에 약 2만 기 정도로 보이며 역사가 오래됨에 따라 거의 다 만석이 되었으며 도로변에 2% 정도만 비어있는 상태임

- 접견실에 걸려있는 개 모양의 원형 벽시계는 이베이에서 인터넷으로 구입했다고 하며 시간마다 견종 특유의 짖는 소리가 남(끝)

하츠데일(Hartsdale) 펫 공동묘지 입구(뉴욕)
The front entrance to the Hartsdale Pet Cemetery (Hartsdale, New York)

영어녹음듣기

Creative Legal Theories

Best Interests of a Companion Dog

According to the Pet Products Association's statistics published in 2020, approximately 63 million American households have a dog as a family pet. Many Americans consider dogs to be their family, and, as a result, they do not hesitate to buy expensive food, pet products, and in some cases, hold a luxury funeral.

As a strictly legal matter, though, a dog is merely a chattel. This is why even when a dog is killed or injured in an accident (or even intentionally), courts will only allow the owner to recover its fair market value, but nothing for its physical pain and suffering or the owner's emotional distress.

One court recently issued an interesting decision that defies this established rule. It came in a fierce legal battle between a New York extermination company and its employee, Barry Myrick, over a companion dog named Roxy.

Myrick was hired by the company five years ago. The company gave him Roxy, a pit bull terrier that could smell bed bugs. Myrick treated Roxy like family. They worked together during the day, and went home together at night. However, early last year, Myrick was furloughed because the company faced economic challenges caused by COVID-19. The company asked him to return the keys to the company car, corporate credit card, and uniform. However, Myrick was not asked to return Roxy. After a while, the company asked Myrick to return to work with Roxy. He refused, left New York and moved to Philadelphia.

Myrick argued that the company lost claim over Roxy because it stopped paying for her care when he was furloughed, and he had to pay with his own money. He further emphasized that the company never requested him to return Roxy when he was furloughed even though it could have, as it had the paperwork showing that Roxy belonged to the company. In response, the company reported Roxy as stolen to the police and filed a civil lawsuit seeking the immediate return of Roxy.

When there is a dispute over legal ownership of a personal item, courts will generally look at things like who bought it, who took care of it, and whether it was a gift to determine whose claim is greater. However, in the decision rendered last month in Roxy's case, the court did not apply property law in deciding the company's motion for a preliminary injunction. It applied a novel "best interest" standard.

Typically, courts use the "best interest" standard to decide the issue of a child's custody in divorce proceedings. The court decides what is in the best interest of the child after considering various factors, including the child's sex, age, relationship with the parent, parent's health and socioeconomic status, and the respective party's wishes. In essence, the court applied this delicate standard to an ownership dispute over a dog.

The court began its decision by acknowledging that under New York law, a dog is personal property. However, it noted that a trust could be established for a dog if the owner dies or becomes ill, and an order of protection may be issued by the family court to protect a dog. Therefore, the court held, a dog is not merely a chattel. Applying the best interest standard, the court ruled that even though the company may have the greater ownership right over Roxy, it was in Roxy's best interest to stay with Myrick while the civil case was being decided.

A dispute over who gets to keep the family pet often arises in divorce proceedings. However, this decision was unique because this was not family court and the best interest standard was applied to a dog. It will be interesting to see what, if any, effect this ruling will have on the underlying civil case and the criminal case. (2021.1.27.)

록시와 같은 핏불테리어 <출처: Unsplash>
A pitbull terrier like Roxy
<source: Unsplash>

'샘의 아들법'

뉴욕주법 중에는 범죄자가 자신의 범죄로 생긴 대중적 인지도를 이용하여 수익을 챙기지 못하도록 하는 소위 '샘의 아들법'이란 게 있다. 미 육군 출신 택시 기사 '데이비드 버코위츠'(David Berkowitz)가 이 법 배경의 주인공이다. 버코위츠는 1976년 1년간 권총을 이용한 묻지마 총격으로 6명을 살해하고 7명을 중태에 빠뜨려 뉴욕시를 공포의 도가니로 몰고 간 악명 높은 연쇄살인범이었다.

1977년 여름, 뉴욕 근처 자가에서 체포된 범인은 "악마가 나의 이웃 '샘'이 키우던 개로 현몽하여 어린 여자의 피가 필요하니 사람을 죽이라고 명령했다"며 횡설수설했다. 정신병자인 것처럼 수사당국을 속여 감형받으려던 수작이었지만 총 365년 형을 선고받고 지금도 복역 중이다.

버코위츠는 범행 현장에 자신을 '샘의 아들'이라고 소개하는 편지를 놓아두거나 추가 범죄를 예고하는 등 대담하고 기괴한 행동으로 1년 동안이나 경찰을 갖고 놀아 공포심과 더불어 대중적 인지도와 호기심 또한 상당했다. 그러다 보니 이를 상업적으로 이용코자 한 출판사가 생겨났는데 체포 후 12만 불에 범행 일대기 출간계약 사실이 알려지면서 비난 여론이 빗발쳤다.

이에 대한 대책으로 뉴욕주 의회는 범죄자로부터 이야기를 구매하는 측은 범죄자 본인 대신 '범죄피해자위원회'에 돈을 지불토록 하는 '샘의 아들법'을 미국에서 처음으로 제정했다. 이 법에 의거, 위원회는 10여 년 동안 비틀즈의 키 멤버였던 '존 레넌' 살해범 '마크 데이빗 챕맨'으로부터 압수한 8,626불을 포함하여 총 134,000불을 거둬 피해자들에게 71,450불을 나눠준 것으로 알려졌다.

정의의 기수로 칭송받던 이 법은 1991년 새로운 전기를 맞게 된다. 출판사 '사이먼 앤 슈스터'(Simon & Schuster)는 마피아에 몸담았던 '헨리 힐'과 96,000불에 그의 자전적 이야기를 '와이즈 가이'라는 제목으로 출판키로 계약했다. 이를 안 범죄피해자위원회가 중간에서 수익금을 거둬가려고 하자 '샘의 아들법'은 언론출판의 자유에 위배된다고 출판사 측이 소송을 제기했는데 연방대법원이 8대 0 만장일치로 출판사의 손을 들어준 것이다.

아무리 범행은 나쁜 것이라 하더라도 '샘의 아들법'은 범죄자들만 특별히 겨냥해 그들의 표현의 자유를 침해했으며, 범죄 피해자들을 위한 보상이라는 뉴욕주의 목적보다 범위가 더 넓게 만들어진 법이란 논리였다.

위헌 판결 이후 이 법은 범행 관련 소재로 범죄자의 수입이 1만 불을 상회할 경우 피해자에게 통지를 해주는 것으로 개정되었다. 통지를 받은 피해자들이 바로 가해자를 민사법원에 고소해 금전적 피해보상을 받을 수 있도록 해준 것이다.

한동안 잠잠하던 이 법이 지난 2.11. 가석방으로 풀려난 희대의 가짜 상속녀 사건으로 다시 세인의 주목을 받았다. 2013년 당시 약관 22세의 나이로 뉴욕 사교계에 혜성처럼 등장한 '애나 소로킨'(Anna Sorokin)은 '애나 델비(Anna Delvey)라는 가명으로 유럽 자산가의 상속녀 행세를 하며 유명세를 떨쳤다. 온갖 명품으로 치장한 자신의 호화 일상을 SNS에 올리는가 하면 뉴욕 번화가 파크 애브뉴에 고급 미술전시관을 만들겠다는 거창한 사업계획도 내세웠다.

사실 그녀의 아버지는 독일에서 조그만 냉난방 업체를 운영하는 영세업자에 불과하였고 그녀도 프랑스의 패션잡지 퍼플지의 인턴이 경력의 전부였다. 이런 4년간의 가짜 행각은 2017년 경찰에 체포되면서 막을 내리게 되었다. 그녀는 재판에서 절도와 사기, 호텔 무단숙박 등으로 27만 불의 빚을 진 혐의로 최소 4년~12년의 징역형과 손해배상금 20만 불, 벌금 2만4,000불 형을 선고받았다.

최근 출소를 앞두고 인터넷 동영상 회사인 넷플릭스가 32만 불을 주고 그녀의 스토리를 사 '애나 만들기'라는 드라마 제작에 들어갔으나 '샘의 아들법'으로 정작 본인은 땡전 한 푼 만져보지 못하고 수익금 전액을 손해배상금으로 낸 것으로 전해진다. 하나의 법을 가운데 두고 가해자와 피해자 간에 전개되는 상황 반전이 마치 새옹지마 고사를 연상케 한다. (2021.3.10.)

기발한법리

The "Son of Sam" Law

Under New York law, there is something called the "Son of Sam" law, which prevents criminals from profiting from their notoriety. This law began with David Berkowitz, an Army veteran who worked as a cab driver. He was an infamous serial killer who terrorized New York City from 1976 to 1977 by shooting and killing six and wounding seven people.

In the summer of 1977, he was arrested in front of his apartment building in a suburb of New York City. He claimed that his neighbor Sam's dog was possessed by a demon and commanded him to kill people to get blood from young women. He planned to appear insane and avoid a lengthy prison sentence. Ultimately, he was sentenced to 365 years in prison. He is still incarcerated to this day.

Berkowitz was psychotic and audacious. He left notes at the crime scene introducing himself as the "Son of Sam." He would sometimes announce his planned shootings. These bold acts and his interactions with the police for a year not only put the public in fear, but captured their imagination and curiosity as well. Perhaps naturally, a book publisher wanted to buy his story for $120,000. Public outcry ensued.

New York's legislature responded by enacting the "Son of Sam" law, the first of its kind in the country. It authorized the Crime Victims Board to seize the proceeds from book and movie deals or paid interviews. Ultimately, the Board collected over $134,000 from convicted criminals over 10 years, including $8,626 from Mark David Chapman who killed John Lennon of the Beatles. The Board has also distributed $71,450 to victims over the same period.

The law, which many praised as being justified, was challenged in 1991. Publishing giant Simon & Schuster and an ex-mafia, Henry Hill, entered a $96,000 deal to turn his biographical story into a book, Wiseguy. When the Crime Victims Board learned of this deal, it sought to confiscate the money. The publisher responded by suing the board because the "Son of Sam" law violated the First Amendment. The Supreme Court ruled in favor of the publisher. It held that even though criminal acts cannot be condoned, the law was unconstitutional because it specifically singled out speech from a particular group of people – convicted criminals – and it was not narrowly tailored to achieve New York State's objective of compensating the crime victims.

After it was determined unconstitutional, the law was amended to alert the crime victims when the proceeds exceeded $10,000 to allow the victims to sue the criminals in civil court for money damages.

This law faded in the people's memories until recently when it was catapulted into the national spotlight with the release of the "fake heiress" on February

11, 2021. In 2013, 22-year-old Anna Sorokin suddenly emerged in New York's Society. She used an alias, Anna Delvey, and pretended to be an heiress of an affluent European family. She donned expensive clothes and posted her luxurious life on social media. She also had a business plan to establish a high-end art gallery on New York's bustling Park Avenue.

However, in reality, her father ran a small heating and cooling business in Germany. Her career consisted of a short stint as an intern at the French fashion magazine Purple. Her four years of fake lifestyle came to an end with an arrest in 2017. She was ultimately convicted of grand larceny and theft of services after a trial for check fraud and failure to pay hotel bills, totaling approximately $270,000. She was sentenced to 4-to-12 years in prison, a $24,000 fine, and ordered to pay restitution for $200,000.

Before her release from prison, Netflix reportedly acquired the rights to her story for $320,000, intending to create a television series titled "Inventing Anna." However, because of the "Son of Sam" Law, it was reported that all of the proceeds were eventually given to the victims. The twist in the criminals and victims' lives created by the law reminds us of the old man's story in "Saeongjima (the old man lost his horse)."(2021.3.10.)

존 레논이 저격당한 자리에 만들어진 Strawberry Fields Memorial (뉴욕 센트럴파크)
Strawberry Fields Memorial located where John Lennon was assassinated (New York City Central Park)

'미란다 원칙'

미국의 범죄 영화나 드라마를 보다 보면 흔히 경찰관이 범죄 용의자에게 수갑을 채우면서 "당신은 묵비권을 행사할 수 있다"고 고지하는 장면이 나온다. 법적 절차에 따라 '미란다 원칙'(Miranda Warning)을 알려주는 것으로, '형사 피의자는 진술을 거부할 수 있고, 피의자의 진술이 법정에서 불리한 증거로 사용될 수 있으며, 변호사의 조력을 받을 권리가 있다'는 게 고지의 주 내용이다.

'미란다 원칙'은 1963년 애리조나주 피닉스에서 18세 소녀를 납치·강간한 혐의로 체포된 당시 22세(1941-1976) '에르네스토 미란다'(Ernesto Miranda)의 인명에서 유래하였다. 경찰은 피해자의 진술을 토대로 범행에 사용된 트럭의 번호판을 알아내고 용의자로 지목된 미란다를 경찰서로 연행했다. 이어진 2시간가량의 피의자 신문을 통해 경찰은 큰 어려움 없이 범행 전모를 자백받고 구두 진술서에 자필 서명을 받아 미란다를 재판에 회부했다. 추후 조사에서도 밝혀진 사실이지만, 신문 과정에서 강압적인 행위는 일절 없었기 때문에 미란다의 자백은 전적으로 자유 의지에 의한 것이었다.

재판에서 미란다의 국선변호사로 선임된 70대의 노익장 '앨빈 무어'(Alvin Moore)는, 당연히 피고인의 유무죄 여부에 초점을 맞춰 변론을 전개할 것이라는 검찰의 예상을 뒤집고 창조적인 논리로 검찰을 놀라게 했다. 즉 "미란다가 '자신에게 불리한 증언을 금지하고, 변호사의 조력을 받을 권리를 명시'한 수정헌법 제5조와 6조의 내용을 알 턱이 없고, 수사관들이 이를 미란다에게 미리 알려주지 않았다면 애당초 헌법적 권리가 무시된 불법 상태에서 자백이 이루어진 것이기 때문에 증거로서의 효력이 없다"고 증거력의 무효를 애써 강조했던 것이다.

미란다가 바보가 아닌 이상 자기에게 이런 권리가 있다는 것을 알았더라면 그렇게 쉽게 범행을 털어놓지 않았을 것이라는 항변이었다. 그러나 노 변호사의 재기 발랄한 변호에도 불구하고 재판부는 미란다의 자백이 강압적으로 이루어졌다는 증거가 어디에서도 발견되지 않는다며 20~30년 징역형의 유죄를 선고했다.

이 사건은 미란다 측이 연방대법원에 상고함으로써 구속상태에서의 신문이 피의자에게 미치는 심리적 영향 및 피의자의 인권문제와, 다른 한편으로는 경찰의 합리적 수사 관행 중 어느 것에 더 무게를 두어야 하는지를 놓고 미 전역에 엄청난 반향을 불러일으켰다. 4명의 소수의견 대법관은 "변호인으로부터 '진술을 거부하라'는 충고를 들은 범인이 무엇 때문에 자백을 하겠으며, 이렇게 되면 국가의 기능인 사회의 안전이 어떻게 유지되겠느냐?"고 반대론을 개진했으나 1표가 모자라 반영되지 않았다. 결국 5대4 원심판결 파기로 미란다가 석방됨으로써 그 유명한 미란다 원칙이 서두 극 중의 묘사처럼 오늘까지 이어지고 있는 것이다.

이 판결 후 기복이 심한 미란다의 인생 역정도 우리의 흥미를 끈다. 무료의 국선 변호사 한 번 잘 만난 덕에 중범죄에서 벗어날 것으로 보였던 '떠버리' 미란다는 어느 날 동거녀에게 자신의 범행에 대해 그만 떠벌리고 만다. 검사는 동거녀의 증언에다 다른 증거를 보강하여 끝내 법원으로부터 20~30년 징역형의 유죄판결을 받아내

미란다를 다시 감방으로 보내는 데 성공한 것이다.

　교도소 복역 중 1972년 가석방으로 방면된 미란다는 피닉스법원 앞에서 자신이 '미란다 원칙'에 나오는 바로 그 주인공이라고 우쭐대며 미란다 원칙이 쓰인 카드에 사인을 해주고 1불 50전씩 받으며 생계를 꾸려갔다고 한다. 그러다 1976년 술집에서 취객과 사소한 시비 끝에 칼에 찔려 살해되었는데 역설적으로 바로 이 살인 용의자 '에스키엘 모레노'(Eseziquiel Moreno)가 경찰조사에서 미란다 원칙을 내세워 묵비권을 행사했던 것이다. 에스키엘은, 자신의 묵비권 행사로 경찰이 추가 증거를 수집하는 사이에 잠적하여 오늘날까지 잡히지 않고 있다. '미란다 원칙'에 묻혀있는 아이러니한 역사의 한 토막이다. (2021.5.5.)

영어 녹음 듣기

기발한법리

Miranda Warning

In the American crime movies and shows, police officers are often portrayed saying to the suspect, "you have the right to remain silent" as they are putting on the handcuffs. They're providing the "Miranda Warning," which involves informing the arrestee that he has a right to remain silent, anything he says may be used against him in a court of law, and that he has a right to a lawyer.

The Miranda warning derives its name from Ernesto Miranda. When Miranda was 22 years old (1941-1976), he was arrested for kidnapping and raping an 18-year-old girl. Miranda became a suspect based on the victim's testimony about the license plate for the truck used during the crime. Once they took Miranda into custody, police interrogated him for about two hours. They emerged with a signed written confession from Miranda. Miranda was put to trial with this evidence. As revealed later, there was no coercion during the interrogation, and Miranda's confession was voluntarily made.

Miranda was assigned a lawyer named Alvin Moore, a public defender in his seventies. Rather than focusing on the guilt or innocence of his client, Moore surprised the prosecution by choosing to advance a creative and novel legal theory. He argued that Miranda did not know about his fifth and sixth amendment rights, such as the right to remain silent and the right to have an attorney. He further claimed that the failure by law enforcement to advise Miranda of these rights meant that his client's constitutional rights were ignored and his statement could not be voluntary. Therefore, he asserted that Miranda's written confession should not be used against him as evidence.

In other words, he averred that Miranda would not have confessed so easily if he had known about his rights. Despite Moore's creative arguments, the court concluded that his confession was not coerced. Miranda was convicted and sentenced to 20-to-30 years in prison.

Miranda appealed the decision to the Supreme Court. It was a consequential decision dealing with human rights and the psychological effects of interrogating a suspect in police custody. These concerns were weighed against the police's right to investigate by employing reasonable means. Four justices ruled against Miranda, fearing the chilling effect that it would have on public safety if the suspects were advised not to talk by their lawyers. However, their position fell short by one vote. The Supreme Court vacated Miranda's conviction in a 5-4 decision. The Miranda Warning was born. As mentioned at the beginning of this column, it continues to this day.

The ups and downs in Miranda's life after the Supreme Court decision is interesting as well. Although he was lucky to have met a competent and experienced public defender whose legal arguments put him on a path to beat the felony charge, 'chatty' Miranda had already confessed his crime to a common law spouse. Prosecutors used this confession along with additional evidence to re-secure a conviction. Miranda was sentenced to 20-to-30 years in prison yet again.

Miranda was paroled in 1972 and made a living by selling cards that had the Miranda Warning written on them for $1.50 in front of the Phoenix courthouse. In 1976, he got into an argument with a drunk man at a bar and was stabbed to death. The murder suspect, Eseziquiel Moreno, asserted his right to remain silent after being advised of the Miranda warnings. He disappeared while the police were gathering additional evidence. He still has not been caught to this day. This is the irony behind the Miranda Warning. (2021.5.5.)

'척 보면 압니다!'법

미국법 중에는 속칭 '척 보면 압니다!'라는 희한한 법이 있다. 민사상의 불법행위법(tort law)에 속한 법리 중 하나인 '레스 입사 로퀴투르'(res ipsa loquitur)를 일컫는 것인데, 법률용어로 자리 잡은 이 라틴어가 '척 보면 압니다!' 정도의 의미이기 때문에 이런 이름이 붙었다. 미국법들이 대부분 사실의 인과관계를 철저히 따져 합리적으로 구성되었다고 보면 이 법은 일종의 이단아인 셈이다.

보통 가해자의 과실로 발생한 불법행위에 대해 손해배상을 청구하기 위해서는 가해자가 주의 의무를 지키지 않아 손해가 발생했다는 것을 피해자가 입증하도록 돼 있다. 그러나 살다 보면 무언가 잘못이 있었기 때문에 사고가 난 것은 분명하지만 누가, 무엇을 잘못했는지 증명하기가 까다로운 경우가 참 많다. 이때 바로 이 '척 보면 압니다!'법이 인용되는 것이다.

이 법리는 산업혁명이 한창이던 1863년, 영국의 항구도시 리버풀에서 유래했다. 무더운 여름철 어느 날 밀가루 상점의 종업원들이 2층 창고에서 상점 앞에 세워 둔 수레에 밀가루 하역작업을 하고 있었다. 무거운 밀가루 통을 밧줄로 묶어 창문을 통해 내리다 그만, 정확하게 누군지는 모르지만, 통을 떨어뜨리고 말았다. 때마침 가게

앞을 지나가던 행인 '조셉 번'(Joseph Byrne)이 이 밀가루 통에 어깨를 맞고 쓰러지면서 문제가 되었다.

다행히 목숨은 건졌지만, 평생 절름발이 신세가 된 조셉은 가게 주인 '아벨 보들'(Abel Boadle)을 상대로 소송을 걸어 700파운드(현재 가치로 한화 약 1억 원)의 손해배상을 요구했다. 그러나 동네 유지였던 보들은 재판이 벌어지자 "현장에 있던 목격자 그 누구도 우리 가게의 종업원들이 밀가루 통을 떨어뜨리는 장면을 보지 못했고, 가게의 손님이 가해자일 수도 있기 때문에 자신은 책임질 수 없다"고 항변했다. 재판부는 원고인 조셉이 명백한 증거를 제시하지 못했다는 이유를 들어 조셉의 청구를 기각했다.

사건은 상위 법원으로 올라가 부장판사 '배런 폴락'이 항소심을 맡게 됐다. 배런은, 상식적으로 누군가의 과실 없이는 일어날 수 없는 사고가 발생한 상황에서 원고 조셉은 원인을 제공하지 않았고, 사고가 발생한 장소와 물건이 완전히 피고 보들의 통제 하에 있었다는 사실에 비추어 볼 때 증거 여부를 떠나 보들의 과실이 입증된다고 판단하고 1심 재판부의 판결을 뒤집었다. 쉽게 말해 한국 속담에 '아니 땐 굴뚝에 연기 나는 법이 없다'는 것이었다.

이 간단명료한 이치의 판결은, 이후 막심한 피해를 입었음에도 피고의 과실 입증이 어려운 사고들 - 예컨대 전신마취 도중 생긴 의료사고, 각종 형태의 낙상사고, 하늘에서 떨어진 벽돌이나 창문 등의 물건에 맞아 생긴 상해 사고와 같은 불법행위 사건들에 적용되어 많은 이들의 억울함을 풀어주는 데 크게 기여했다.

하지만 '레스 입사 로퀴투르' 원칙이 적용된다고 해서 모든 가해자에게 자동적으로 손해배상 책임이 생기는 것은 아니다. 즉 엘리베이터 낙상사고에서 피고 건물주가 사고의 원인은 자신이 아니라 엘리베이터 부품 결함에 있었다고 주장하며 비껴가는 식이다.

또 피고의 과실을 입증하려면 전문가의 증언이 필요할 경우가 있는데 이때도 적용이 애매하다. 그 예로, 환자가 마취 주사를 맞다 신경을 다쳐 의사를 상대로 제기한 소송에서 텍사스주 항소법원은 '배심원들이 전문가의 도움 없이 자신들의 경험이나 상식만으로 간호사가 부주의했는지 알 도리가 없다'고 결정했기 때문에 이런 경우 전문가의 증언 없이 '레스 입사 로퀴투르'를 적용할 수 없다고 판결했다. '예외 없는 법은 없다'는 서양 속담대로 이런 경우는 척 봐도 아는 게 아니라 척 보아서는 모르는 예외에 해당하는 경우이다. (2021.5.19.)

영어 녹음 듣기

Res Ipsa Loquitur

In American tort law, there is a concept called res ipsa loquitur, which roughly translates as "the thing speaks for itself." It stands out from the other legal concepts because it allows the factfinder to reasonably infer causation based on circumstantial evidence.

In tort law, victims must prove that their harm was caused by another person's negligence. However, there are times in life when, even though the accident occurred, it is hard to prove who did what wrong. That's when res ipsa loquitur comes into play.

This principle was invented at the height of the industrial revolution in the English port city of Liverpool. On a hot summer day, workers from the defendant's shop were lowering flour barrels from the second-floor window down to the cart in the front of the building. However, a barrel fell from the window and struck a pedestrian, Joseph Byrne, on the shoulder and knocked him to the ground.

Although Joseph survived the incident, he became disabled in his leg and sued the store owner, Abel Boadle, for 700 pounds in damages. Boadle countered by asserting that he could not be held liable because none of the witnesses from the scene saw Boadle's employee dropping the barrel. Boadle further maintained that it was possible that one of the customers pushed the barrel. The trial court dismissed Joseph's lawsuit based on his failure to establish that Boadle's negligence caused his injury.

On appeal, the case was assigned to Chief Baron Pollock of the Exchequer Court. Judge Pollock held, "There are certain cases of which it may be said res ipsa loquitur, and this seems one of them." He reasoned that an accident like this could not occur without some negligence. Since the place and object that caused the accident were within Boadle's dominion and control, and Joseph did nothing to contribute to the accident, he held that "the accident alone would be prima facie evidence of negligence" and reversed the lower court's ruling. Put another way, "where there is smoke, there is fire" as the Korean saying goes.

This common-sense approach has been instrumental in proving negligence in medical malpractice cases when the patient is under general anesthesia, personal injury cases caused by falling objects like bricks or windows, and slip and fall cases where it is difficult to know who was negligent.

It is important to remember, however, defendants do not automatically lose because res ipsa loquitur applies. For instance, in an elevator fall case, which would happen only if someone was negligent, the building owner could defend against a personal injury lawsuit by showing that he was not negligent because an elevator part caused it to malfunction and he had no way of reasonably knowing that.

Another difficulty with applying res ipsa loquitur is when expert testimony is required. For example, in a case where the patient's sciatic nerve was damaged while the nurse was making a hypodermic injection, Texas appellate court held, "[w]ithout the aid of expert testimony in this case, a jury could not, without resorting to conjecture and surmise, determine that the [nurse] failed to exercise their skill and use the care exercised by the ordinarily skillful, careful, and prudent nurse acting under the same or similar circumstances." Hence, the court held, application of res ipsa loquitur was improper under the circumstances without an expert's testimony. As the saying goes, "there is an exception to every rule." Here, the thing does not speak for itself. (2021.5.19.)

Chapter
2

사법시스템
Court System

"배심원으로 선정되었습니다"

오랫동안 미국에 거주한 독자들이라면 누구나 한두 번쯤 "배심원으로 선정되었습니다"라는 우편물을 받고 가슴 철렁한 경험이 있을 것이다. 막상 당사자가 되어 소환장을 받고 보면 속 시원히 설명해주는 사람도 없어 답답하기 마련인데 이번에는 미국 배심원 제도에 대해 간단하게 소개하고자 한다.

미국 배심원제는 크게 두 종류로 나뉘는데 먼저 재판회부에 앞서 중대 범죄사실을 따져 기소 여부를 결정하는 대배심원단(grand jury)과 기소되어 재판 중인 피고인의 유무죄를 판단하는 소배심원단(petit jury)이 바로 그것이다. 명칭에서도 알 수 있듯 대배심원단은 보통 16~23명으로, 소배심원단은 6~12명으로 구성이 된다.

많은 사람들이 검사, 변호사, 판사 같은 법률전문가들이 있는데 왜 일반인들로 구성되는 배심원단이 따로 필요한지 궁금해한다. 원래 배심원 제도는 국민들이 선거를 통해 행정부와 입법부 대표를 결정하듯이 소수의 사법 권력이 판결을 전횡하는 것을 막기 위해 국민들이 직접 재판에 참여할 수 있는 통로를 마련해준다는 취지에서 도입된 장치이다. 가령 독재 정부에서 권력자가 자신의 정적을 제거하기 위해 기소권을 남용한다든지 비공개 재판을 통해 유죄로 몰아가는 상황 등을 그려보면 배심원

제도의 당위성을 수긍할 것이다.

따라서 대배심과 소배심 제도 둘 다 미국 연방 수정헌법 5조~7조에 각각 명시되어 있을 만큼 헌법이 보장하는 중요 국민 권리 중 하나로, 검사와 판사는 각 배심원단의 결정에 따라야 한다는 점에서 재판에 미치는 영향이 막중하다.

두 제도의 주요 차이점들을 꼽아보면 대배심원단은 한 번 선정되면 2주에서 몇 개월간 임명되어 여러 사건을 심리하는 데 비해 소배심원단은 재판 사건별로 구성이 되고, 대배심에서는 모든 수사 및 증거제시가 비공개로 진행되지만 소배심이 참여하는 재판은 특별한 경우를 제외하곤 공개적으로 진행된다.

대배심원들은 검사가 제시하는 증거물을 토대로 기소 여부를 판단하는데 이때 검사들은 관련 법규를 자문해주는 법률 상담역을 겸하게 된다. 경우에 따라 대배심원단은 증인에게 소환장을 발부할 수도 있고 관공서 등에 자료 제출 요구도 가능하다.

한편 소배심원단이 구성된 재판에서의 재판장은 재판 중재와 더불어 증거채택 및 관련 법규를 해설해주며 배심원들은 이를 근거로 평결을 내리게 된다. 형사사건에서 유무죄 판단은 배심원이 내리더라도 양형은 보통 판사가 결정하지만 사형제도를 존치하고 있는 주에선 배심원단이 판사 대신 결정하기도 한다.

또 한 번에 많은 사건을 다뤄야 하는 대배심원단은 다수결로 표결하는 데 반해 소배심원들은 만장일치로 평결하는 것도 차이점이랄 수 있다. 만장일치에 실패할 경우에는 미결정 심리로 다시 새로운 배심원단을 꾸려 재판을 계속하게 된다.

배심원 제도는 법률전문가가 아닌 일반 국민의 상식과 경험에 의지하여 법을 적용하다 보니 같은 증거에 의한 범죄 혐의를 두고도 전혀 다른 결과가 나오는 경우도 허다하다. 그런 점에서 뉴욕 브롱크스의 배심원단은 특히 전국적으로 유명한데 주민 대다수를 차지하는 흑인 또는 히스패닉계 중에서 추출된 브롱크스 배심원들이 평소 뉴욕시 경찰과의 인종 차별에 따른 피해의식 때문에 감정적으로 형사피고 편

뉴욕시 퀸스 형사법원에서 배심원 소환장을 받고 줄 서있는 사람들
People who have been summoned for jury service are waiting in a line outside of Queens County Criminal Court

을 들어주는 경우가 많기 때문이다. 이는 2015년부터 2017년 사이 같은 뉴욕시 스태튼 아일랜드의 검찰청이 85%의 승소율을 보인 반면 브롱크스 검찰청은 49%밖에 승소하지 못한 통계에서도 잘 나타나고 있다.

재판의 공정성 확보와 법조인들의 배타적 판단에 대한 국민의 감시 등 장점이 많은 배심원 제도이지만 근래 들어 미국에서도 점점 사라져가는 추세이다. 형사 사건의 경우 대부분이 플리바게닝(plea bargaining)을 통해 합의처벌로 해결되고 있고 민사사건 역시 대체적 분쟁 해결 등으로 많이 해결되고 있기 때문이다. (2019.10.9.)

배심원 소환장
Summons for jury service

American Jury System 101

The readers who have lived in America for a long time must be familiar with the feeling of nervousness and anxiety that comes with receiving a jury summons. For many, there's no one to ask questions about them. So, today's column discusses basic facts about jury service.

The American jury system is made up of the grand jury, which decides whether or not to charge a person with a crime, and the petit jury, which determines whether the person is guilty after a trial. As the name suggests, grand juries are usually made up of a larger group. For example, in New York, it's somewhere between 16 to 23 people, while petit juries are smaller, typically between six to 12 people.

Some people wonder why it is necessary to have a jury composed of ordinary citizens when we already have highly educated legal professionals like lawyers, prosecutors, and judges who can decide court cases more efficiently. However, by promoting public participation in the adjudicative process, juries prevent abuse of public trust and authority by legal professionals. We can easily comprehend this justification by imagining a dictator who wields criminal indictments against their enemies and punishes them after secretly held trials.

As such, grand and petit juries provide an essential protection of one's civil rights, and their roles are etched in the fifth, sixth, and seventh amendments to the U.S. Constitution. Their importance at trials cannot be overstated because they render the verdict, not the prosecutor or judge.

There are considerable differences between grand and petit juries as well. Once selected, grand jurors serve for anywhere between two weeks to several months. They will often examine multiple cases during this time. On the other hand, petit juries are empaneled for a specific case. In addition, while the investigation and presentation of evidence occurs in a secret setting in the grand jury, trials are held publicly except in a few narrow circumstances.

The grand jury's primary function is to investigate and indict individuals against whom the prosecutor has established probable cause of criminal conduct. The prosectuors take on a double duty as a legal advisor before the grand jury. Moreover, to aid in their investigative functions, grand juries have the authority to issue subpoenas for documents and witnesses.

In contrast, judges conduct trials and make legal rulings on admissibility of evidence. Judges explain relevant law to the petit jury, who act as the "judges of facts" and determine how much weight they wish to give to each piece of evidence introduced at trial. A petit jury renders a verdict by applying the facts as they find them to the law given to them by the judge. After a guilty verdict, the sentencing decision falls on the judge. However, in some jurisdictions with the death penalty, petit jurors, and not the judge, may be called upon to decide whether to impose one as punishment.

Finally, another important distinction is that an indictment may be obtained by a majority vote in the grand jury, but a unanimous vote is required for a verdict in most jurisdictions, especially in criminal cases. If a unanimous decision cannot be reached, the court declares a mistrial and forms a new jury for the trial.

Since juries rely on common sense and their lived experiences, similar charges based on similar facts sometimes lead to entirely different results. In this regard, the Bronx juries, most of whom are pulled from the black and Hispanic communities, are notorious for their mistrust of the police in criminal cases. Thus, while the Staten Island prosecutor's office secured a guilty verdict in 85 percent of the cases it tried between 2015 and 2017, Bronx County prosecutors only won 49 percent of trials during that same period.

Although the jury system has many advantages for ensuring a fair trial, it has been gradually disappearing in recent years. It is often consuming and requires a lot of court resources. As such, many cases are resolved by plea bargaining and out-of-court settlements. (2019.10.9.)

미국의 사형제도

오늘은 좀 묵직한 주제, 미국의 사형제도에 대해 생각해보고자 한다. 국가의 형벌 가운데 사형만큼 찬반 논란이 뜨거운 주제도 드물 것이다.

사형 반대론자들은 아무리 흉악범이라 하더라도 국가가 나서 사람의 목숨을 끊을 권리는 없다는 점, 그 외에도 재판 과정에서 판사의 실수가 있을 수 있으며 사형을 시킨다 해도 범죄율이 감소되지 않는다는 점 등을 사형 반대이유로 든다. 반면 찬성론자들은 흉악범들은 타인의 생명과 존엄성을 짓밟았으므로 이들의 인권은 보호해 줄 필요가 없으며 이들을 사형시키지 않으면 평생 감방에 가두어 두어야 하는데 이들이 먹고 자는 소중한 국민 세금으로 차라리 불우이웃을 한 명이라도 더 돕는 게 낫다고 반박한다.

국제인권단체인 앰네스티 인터내셔널에 따르면 OECD 36개 회원국 중 사형제도를 유지하고 있는 국가는 미국과 한국, 일본뿐이다. 한국은 1997년 이래 사형집행을 하지 않고 있는데 비해 미국은 2018년 25건의 사형집행으로 전 세계에서 사형집행국 7위에 오를 정도로 사형집행을 활발히 하는 나라에 속한다.

미국에서 사형제를 유지하고 있는 주는 모두 29개 주인데 2018년 통계상 텍사스주가 13건의 사형집행으로 1위를 차지했으며 테네시, 앨라배마, 조지아, 플로리다 등 남부의 주들이 각각 2~3건의 사형집행으로 그 뒤를 잇고 있다. 미국 전체에는 2,673명의 사형수가 있는 것으로 추정되고 있다.

연방 체제인 미국의 특성상 연방정부 역시 사형제도를 유지하고 있는데 현재 연방정부의 사형수는 보스턴 마라톤 테러범 '조하르 차르나예프'(Dzhokhar Tsarnaev)와 흑인 교회에서 총기를 난사한 백인 우월주의자 '딜란 루프'(Dylann Roof) 등 62명이 있는 것으로 알려져 있다.

트럼프 행정부는 내년 대선을 앞두고 보수층 결집을 위해 2003년 이후 집행하지 않고 있던 사형집행을 얼마 전 다시 재개하려고 했으나 연방대법원에 의해 제동이 걸리는 돌발상황에 봉착했다.

연방정부의 사형집행은 1994년 제정된 미국 연방 사형법에 따라 '형이 부과된 주의 법에 규정된 방식'으로 집행하도록 되어 있다. 이에 따라 연방 법무부는 어떤 독극물을 사용하든 사형 방법만 같다면 이 법에 어긋나는 게 아니라며 사형집행을 재개하려 했으나 사형수의 변호사들은 사형에 사용되는 독극물의 종류나 양, 집행방식까지도 같아야 한다고 반박하며 소송을 제기한 것이다.

이 재판에서 지난달 워싱턴 DC 소재 연방 법원은 사형수들의 손을 들어주었는데 갈 길이 급한 행정부 측에서 고등법원 항소를 생략한 채 대법원에 바로 상고하자 대법원이 고등법원부터 절차를 거쳐 올라오라면서 상고를 기각했기 때문에 일이 꼬여버린 것이다.

이 소송의 배경에는 3가지의 약물을 사용해 형을 집행하는 데 따른 어려움도 큰 비중을 차지했는데 다름 아니라 사람을 치료하는 데 사용해야 할 약물을 오히려 사람을 죽이는 데 쓴다는 비난이 거세게 일자 제약회사들이 일제히 사형집행에 필요한 약물 제공을 거부한 것이다.

보스턴 마라톤 테러범 조하르 차르나예프
Boston marathon bomber,
Dzhokhar Tsarnaev

1970년대부터 사용된 3개의 약물을 사용하는 사형 방법은 먼저 진정제를 놓아 사형수를 잠들게 한 다음, 전신 근육 이완제를 주사해 사형수가 몸을 움직일 수 없게 하고, 마지막으로 염화칼륨을 투입하여 심장마비로 죽게 하는 방식인데 최근 약물 구입이 힘들어지자 텍사스와 같은 몇몇 주들은 3단계의 약물 대신 단 하나의 약물(펜토바르비탈)을 사용하는 사형방식을 택했고 트럼프 행정부 역시 이 방법의 형 집행을 시도코자 했던 것이다.

이처럼 독극물 사형이 많은 논란을 불러일으키자 유타 같은 주에선 2015년에 총살형을 다시 제정한 경우도 있다. 앞으로 연방 정부와 미국의 주들은 계속 사형제도를 유지할 것인지 그렇다면 어떤 식으로 형을 집행할 것인지 그 귀추가 주목된다. (2019.12.25.)

Court System

Capital Punishment in America

The concept of the death penalty evokes a strong reaction in most people. As such, it's one of the most debated forms of punishment.

Its opponents argue that the government doesn't have the right to take a human life, even for the worst of the criminals. They also highlight that judges and juries could make a mistake during trial, and it has no deterrent effect on crime. On the other hand, proponents say that heinous criminals who disregard other people's lives and human dignity do not deserve to live. In addition, they maintain, the precious taxpayer dollars spent to keep them alive in prison may be spent instead to help others who are more deserving of such government assistance.

According to Amnesty International, an international human rights organization, only the United States, South Korea and Japan maintain the death penalty among the 36 OECD (Organisation for Economic Co-operation and Development) member countries. Compared to South Korea, which has not carried out any death penalty sentence since 1997, the United States executed 25 prisoners in 2018 alone, making it the world's seventh largest executioner.

In the United States, 29 states maintain capital punishment. In 2018, Texas led the country by killing 13 prisoners, followed by states like Tennessee, Alabama, Georgia and Florida, each executing about two to three prisoners during the year. There are an estimated 2,673 prisoners on death row in the United States.

The federal government also maintains the death penalty. Currently, 62 people are awaiting to be executed. They include the Boston Marathon bomber, Dzhokhar Tsarnaev, and Dylann Roof, a white supremacist who perpetrated a mass shooting inside a black church.

To rally up conservative support for next year's presidential election, President Trump recently tried to restart the federal execution program, which has been in a hiatus since 2003. However, the Supreme Court put the brakes on his efforts.

Under the 1994 Federal Death Penalty Act, federal executions must be carried out "in the manner prescribed by the law of the State in which the sentence was imposed." The Justice Department interpreted the statute broadly, and argued that in a lethal injection state, an execution complies with the statute as long as lethal injection is used regardless of the drugs used to effectuate it. On the other hand, prisoners' lawyers argued that all aspects of the execution, including how the drug is administered, the type of drug used, and drug dosage, must be identical.

A federal judge in Washington D.C. rejected the justice department's argument and blocked the execution effort last month. The justice department requested an emergency hearing by the Supreme Court, skipping the intermediate appellate court. The high court rejected, telling them to follow the regular appeals process.

The lawsuit was necessitated by the difficulty of obtaining three different drugs required for a lethal injection. There has been a mounting public pressure on the drug manufacturers because the drugs they supplied to the state governments were being used to kill people and not help them. As a result, many have ceased to supply the necessary drugs for lethal injections.

The three-drug death penalty cocktail that has been used since the 1970s works by first injecting an anesthetic agent, which sedates the prisoner, followed by a muscle relaxant, which prevents the prisoner from moving. Finally, potassium chloride is injected, killing the subject by causing a heart attack. As it became increasingly challenging to obtain all three of the necessary drugs, some states like Texas have resorted to using just one drug, Pentobarbital, instead of the usual three. This is how the Trump Administration wanted to carry out the lethal injection.

In light of the controversy with lethal injection, states like Utah have gone back to execution by shooting in 2015. It remains to be seen whether the federal and state governments will keep the death penalty and how they will carry it out. (2019.12.25.)

트럼프의 판사들

역대 미국 대통령이 남기는 정치적 유산 가운데 영향력이 가장 크면서도 오래도록 미치는 것 중 하나가 바로 연방판사 임명이라고 해도 과언이 아닐 것이다. 헌법에 따르면 연방판사는 대통령이 후보자를 지명하고 상원이 인준토록 되어있다.

2018년 기준으로 연방판사 수는 총 860명으로 대법원에 9명, 13개의 항소법원 179명, 94개의 지방법원 663명, 국제 무역 재판소에 9명의 판사가 재직하고 있다. 그 외 시니어 판사, 행정 판사, 치안 판사들도 연방판사들인데 이들을 합치면 그 수가 더 늘어난다.

삼권분립이 확고하게 자리 잡은 미국에서 사법부가 가지는 힘은 실로 막강한데 그 예로 2000년 대선에서 플로리다주의 재검표를 중지시키며 부시를 대통령으로 인정해준 '부시 대 고어'(Bush v. Gore) 사건, 기업과 비영리 단체들의 정치후원금 상한선을 없애 선거 유세 방식을 바꿔버린 '시티즌스 유나이티드'(Citizens United v. Federal Election Commission) 사건, 동성 결혼을 합법화시킨 '오버게펠'(Obergefell v. Hodges) 사건 등을 꼽을 수 있다.

무엇보다 재미있는 사실은 전임 오바마 대통령이 8년의 임기 동안 2명의 대법관과 55명의 항소법원 판사를 임명한 데 비해 트럼프 대통령은 불과 임기 3년 동안 2명의 대법관과 50명의 항소법원 연방판사를 임명함으로써 두 배나 속도를 냈다는 점이다. 미국에선 지역별 항소법원이 사실상 최종심 역할을 한다고 볼 때 그만큼 빠르게 연방 사법부를 공화당 입맛에 맞게 보수화시키고 있는 것이다.

이를테면 하원의 민주당이 트럼프 탄핵에 매달려 있는 동안 상원을 장악하고 있는 공화당은 트럼프가 지명한 판사 후보들을 신속히 인준함으로써 사법부에 보수 대못을 박고 있었던 것이다. 게다가 트럼프는 미래 공화당 장기 집권의 토양을 만들어두기 위해 종신직인 연방판사 자리에 계산적으로 50세 이하의 소장 판사들을 주로 임명하고 있다.

이런 영향으로 대법원에 이어 뉴욕이 속해 있는 제2 항소법원, 뉴저지가 속한 제3 항소법원, 조지아와 플로리다가 속한 제11 항소법원, 심지어 진보 성향의 보루였던 캘리포니아가 속한 제9 항소법원까지 모두 보수 성향으로 돌아선 것으로 법조계는 분석하고 있다.

이런 결과는 트럼프와 상원 공화당 의원들의 합작품이라고 볼 수 있지만 한 발 더 깊숙하게 들어가 보면 '페더럴리스트 소사이어티'(Federalist Society)라는 보수 성향 법조인 단체가 40년간 가꿔놓은 터전이 없었다면 불가능한 일이었다.

이 이야기는 미국 40대 대통령 레이건 시절(재임기간 1981.1~1989.1)로 거슬러 올라가는데 레이건은 대통령으로 선출되자 보수 성향의 주 법원 판사 및 로스쿨 교수들을 연방판사로 임명하는 한편 1982년 예일, 하버드, 시카고대 등 명문 로스쿨 학생들로 하여금 페더럴리스트 소사이어티라는 단체를 설립하도록 측면 지원하였다.

페더럴리스트 소사이어티는 레이건의 기대대로 보수적 법 해석에 도움을 주었을 뿐만 아니라 로스쿨부터 형성되는 방대한 인적 네트워크를 통해 정치 성향이 검증된 판사 및 고위공직자 후보군의 풀 역할을 해줌으로써 오랜 기간 공화당의 든든한 동맹이 되었던 것이다. 현재 보수 성향 대법관 모두가 이 단체의 멤버였다고 알려져 있으니 가히 그 영향력을 짐작해볼 수 있다.

워싱턴D.C에 본부를 두고 있는 페더럴리스트 소사이어티는 지금도 200개 이상의 로스쿨 지부와 65,000명의 회원을 통해 미래의 보수 법조인들을 키워내는 산실 역을 하고 있다. (2020.1.15.)

저자의 모교 포드햄 로스쿨의 페더럴리스트 소사이어티 로고
The Federalist Society emblem from my alma mater, Fordham Law School

All the President's Judges

For an American president, the appointment of federal judges is one of their most significant and long-lasting political legacies. Under the Federal Constitution, the president nominates a judicial candidate and the Senate confirms them.

As of 2018, there are 860 federal judges. This consists of 9 Supreme Court justices, 179 judges on 13 appellate courts, 663 judges in 94 district courts, and 9 justices in the Court of International Trade. In addition, there are judges who take on senior status, as well as other federal judges like administrative law judges and magistrate judges.

The judiciary is a powerful, equal branch of the American government. For example, during the 2000 presidential election, the Supreme Court halted the vote recount in Florida through its decision in Bush v. Gore, which had the effect of confirming George Bush as the new president. In Citizens United v. Federal Election Commission, the Court removed restrictions on political donations by companies and non-profit organizations and reshaped how political campaigns are run. In yet another example, the Court legalized same-sex marriage through Obergefell v. Hodges.

Remarkably, in just 3 years, President Trump has appointed 2 Supreme Court justices and 50 appellate judges. This rate of judicial appointment is twice as fast as his predecessor, President Obama, who appointed 2 Supreme Court and 55 circuit court judges during his 8 years in the Oval Office. This is a significant achievement considering that appellate courts are the final resting place for most cases. Trump has quickly transformed the judiciary into a staunch protector of Republican ideas and values.

While the House Democrats were preoccupied with Trump's impeachment, the Senate's Republican majority has been confirming Trump's nominees at a dizzying speed and tipping the scales of justice a little more conservative with each new appointee. What's more, Trump is consciously appointing young candidates under 50 years of age to lifetime judgeships and ensuring a long-lasting Republican grip on the federal bench.

This resulted in conversions to a conservative majority in the following courts: the U.S. Supreme Court; the Second Circuit Court of Appeals, which includes New York; the Third Circuit Court of Appeals, which includes New Jersey; the Eleventh Circuit Court of Appeals, which includes Georgia and Florida; and the Ninth Circuit Court of Appeals, bastion of liberalism which includes California.

Taken at face value, it is a testament to the effective and efficient political collaboration between Trump and the Senate Republicans. However, this

전 뉴욕주 Jonathan Lippman 대
법원장님과 동료 변호사들(맨해
튼.2018)
With Hon. Jonathan Lippman,
former Chief Judge of the New
York Court of Appeals, and
colleagues (Manhattan)

achievement would not have been possible without the 40 years of cultivating

suitable jurists by a conservative legal organization known as the Federalist

Society.

The story of the Federalist Society goes back to the 40th president, Ronald

Reagan (1981-1989). After being elected, Reagan appointed conservative state

court judges and law school professors to the federal bench. In 1982, through

his aides, he also encouraged the establishment of the Federalist Society by law

students at Yale, Harvard and the University of Chicago.

As Reagan hoped, the Federalist Society served as a reliable ally for

conservative efforts over the years. Not only was the organization helpful with

a more conservative interpretation of the laws, but it also provided a steady

supply of proven candidates for judgeships and high-ranking government offices,

starting back in law schools. Reportedly, all the conservative justices on the

Supreme Court are now either former or current members of the organization, allowing us to glean its influence.

The Federalist Society is headquartered in Washington D.C. With more than 200 law school chapters and 65,000 members, it still serves as an active training ground for future conservative legal professionals. (2020.1.15.)

곤 회장 사건과 보석금 제도

해묵은 만성 적자로 다 죽어가던 자동차회사를 흑자로 되살린 실력을 인정받아 구조조정 귀재로 주목받았던 '카를로스 곤'(Carlos Ghosn) 전 '닛산르노 얼라이언스' 회장이 대형 음향 장비 상자에 몸을 숨겨 일본 공항을 통해 레바논으로 도주한 사실이 알려지면서 국제사회를 깜짝 놀라게 했다. 그는 금융상품거래법 위반 혐의 등으로 일본 경찰에 두 번 체포됐다가 법원에 보석금 15억 엔(약 160억 원)을 내고 석방된 상태에서 달아났다.

지금까지의 뉴스를 종합하면 곤 회장은 일본 경비업체의 감시 소홀 틈을 타 동경 자택에서 신칸센을 이용, 오사카로 도주하여 그곳에서 전세 비행기 편으로 출국한 것으로 보인다. 프랑스와 레바논, 브라질 국적을 모두 보유하고 있는 그는 합법적 여권으로 레바논의 수도 베이루트에 입국하였다고 레바논 정부는 밝혔다.

보석상태에 있던 곤 회장처럼 이런 도주 사건이 터질 때마다 사람들은 보석금을 납부함으로써 징역형을 면하게 된 것이 아니냐고 착각하곤 하는데 보석금은 어디까지나 아직 유죄판결이 나지 않은 형사피고인에게 재판 기간 동안 인신구속을 피할 수 있게 해주는 제도에 불과하다.

따라서 보석금을 내고 풀려나더라도 재판을 계속 받아야 하며 보석금은 정해진 날짜에 법원에 출석하기만 하면 재판의 유무죄 결과에 상관없이 그 돈을 돌려받게 된다. 물론 곤 회장처럼 도망간다면 보석금은 몰수되어 국고로 귀속된다. 판사에 따라서는 보석금 외 부가 조건을 달기도 하는데 곤 회장도 동경 거주와 해외 출국금지 등이 보석 조건으로 달려있었다.

미국의 경우 보석금의 액수를 정하는 것은 전적으로 판사의 재량에 속한다. 중범의 경우 개별 경제력을 감안하여 수천 불에서 수백만 불까지 그 진폭이 무척 심한 편이다. 한 예로 '미투' 운동의 진원지가 되었던 영화감독 '하비 와인스틴'(Harvey Weinstein)은 1급 강간 혐의로 구속됐다 풀려나 현재 맨해튼에서 재판 중인데 그의 보석금액은 2백만 불이다.

한 가지 흥미로운 사실은 아무리 와인스틴 같은 유명 영화감독이라 하더라도 2백만 불이란 거금을 하루아침에 마련하기가 쉽지 않은 법인데 이를 대신 지불해주는 보석금보증보험 회사가 있다는 점이다. 본드맨(bondsman)이라 불리는 이 회사는 피고인이 법원에 출석하지 않을 경우 보석금을 대납해주고 그 수수료를 챙겨 영업을 한다.

보석금 제도는 와인스틴 같은 부자들은 부담 없이 돈을 맡기고 재판에서 자유롭게 자기를 방어할 수 있는 반면 가난한 사람들은 돈이 없다는 이유로 수감되어 불리한 상태에서 재판을 받는 불공정한 제도라는 비판이 많아 뉴욕 일원에서 점차 없어지고 있다.

특히 뉴저지주는 2017년부터 보석금 제도를 아예 없애버렸다. 보석금제 폐지를 앞두고 반대론자들은 이것이 폐지되면 피고인들의 법원 출석률이 낮아지고 범죄혐의자들이 나돌아 다님으로써 그만큼 범죄가 증가할 것이라고 우려하였지만 법 시행 3년이 지난 지금 피고인들의 출석률이나 범죄율에 별 변화가 없는 반면 오히려 수감자 감소에 따른 행정력이 절감된 것으로 나타나 이 법은 성공 사례로 평가받고 있다.

뉴저지의 성공사례를 지켜본 뉴욕주 역시 올 1월 1일부터 보석금 제도를 대폭 줄이는 법을 도입했다. 새 법에 따르면 대부분의 경범죄를 비롯 중범죄 사건이라 하더라도 비폭력성 범죄의 피고인들은 보석금 없이 신병을 풀어주는 것으로 개선됐다. 신법 수혜자가 된 중범죄 전과자, 재범자, 마약범죄 혐의자 등 작년 경우에만 해도 감방에 있어야 할 사람들이 불구속 상태에서 재판을 받게 되자 검찰과 일부 지역 정치인 등 반대론자들이 걱정스러운 눈초리로 그 추이를 지켜보고 있다. (2020.1.29.)

영어 녹음 듣기

Carlos Ghosn's Escape and the Bail System

Carlos Ghosn was a corporate restructuring guru and former Nissan-Renault Alliance executive who saved the failing automaker from crumbling under a chronic deficit. However, he shocked the world when he fled to Lebanon by hiding in a large sound equipment box and sneaking out of a Japanese airport. Previously, he had been arrested twice by the Japanese police on charges of financial misconduct and was out on bail set at 1.5 billion Japanese Yen (about $ 13.5 million US currency).

According to the news reports, Ghosn escaped his Tokyo residence when the Japanese surveillance company stopped monitoring him. He traveled to Osaka onboard a Shinkansen bullet train and left the country on a private jet from there. Ghosn, a multinational with French, Lebanese and Brazilian citizenships, legally entered Lebanon's capital city of Beirut, according to the Lebanese government.

Whenever stories like Ghosn's daring escape break out, people often think posting bail allows criminal defendants to dodge jail time. Contrary to this mistaken belief, posting bail simply enables defendants in criminal cases with pending cases to avoid custodial detention while awaiting their trial.

As such, even when they are released on bail, they must continue to make court appearances. As long as they do so, the bail money is returned at the end of the case regardless of whether they are found guilty or not. Of course, bail is forfeited when a person flees as Ghosn did. In addition to cash bail, judges often impose other conditions. In Ghosn's case, as part of his release conditions, he had to reside in Tokyo and was not permitted to travel abroad.

In the United States, judges have discretion in determining the appropriate bail amount. In felony cases, the range varies greatly, from thousands of dollars to a few million dollars, depending on the charges and the defendant's economic background. For example, Harvey Weinstein, the movie mogul at the epicenter of the 'Me Too' movement, faces first-degree rape charges in Manhattan and is out on $2 million cash bail.

It is worth noting that even for a famous film director like Weinstein, it is challenging to raise $2 million overnight. This is where the bail bond companies come in. Often referred to as the "bondsman," these companies post bail for the defendant and remain liable if they fail to appear. Naturally, they charge a premium for this service.

The cash bail system is gradually disappearing in New York's Tri-state area. Many critics say it is a discriminatory system that allows rich defendants like Weinstein to remain at liberty as they defend against criminal charges while the poor must defend from their jail cell.

For these reasons, the state of New Jersey eliminated cash bail in 2017. Before the law became effective, opponents feared that this change would lower court attendance and cause a hike in the crime rate by allowing criminal suspects to roam freely. However, after three years since its passage, there has been little change in attendance or the crime rate, while a decrease in the number of inmates has reduced the administrative costs. This law is largely regarded as a success.

New York has watched New Jersey's success with much interest and enacted new legislation that would significantly reduce the use of cash bail starting January 1st of this year. Under the new law, defendants charged with most misdemeanors and non-violent felonies must be released without cash bail. Opponents of the new law, including some prosecutors and local politicians, are anxiously watching what happens as the beneficiaries of the new law – those who would have remained in jail last year like the convicted felons, repeat offenders and drug offenders – can now face trial without pre-trial detention. (2020.1.29.)

사법시스템

보수파 대법원의 진로

'진보의 아이콘'이라 불리었던 '루스 베이더 긴즈버그'(Ruth Bader Ginsburg) 연방대법관이 지난 9.18 향년 87세로 세상을 떠났다. 1993년 빌 클린턴 대통령에 의해 대법관으로 임명된 긴즈버그는 대법관 재직 27년 동안 사회적 약자와 소수자, 특히 여성들의 권익 신장에 크게 이바지했다.

그러나 대선을 코앞에 둔 시점에 진보파 대법관 자리에 공석이 생김으로써 대법원의 보수화가 불 보듯 뻔하게 되었다. 왜냐하면 후보자 지명권을 가진 대통령도, 인준 권한을 가진 상원도 모두 공화당 판이기 때문이다.

이런 호기를 놓치지 않고 트럼프 대통령은 긴즈버그의 후임으로 보수파의 거장 고(故) '안토닌 스칼리아'(Antonin Scalia) 대법관 밑에서 서기를 지낸 '에이미 코니 배럿'(Amy Coney Barrett) 제7 연방항소법원 판사를 후보로 지명했으며 이에 발맞추어 공화당의 '미치 매코널' 상원 원내대표는 11월 대선 전에 모든 역량을 총동원해 그를 인준하겠다고 화답했다.

보수 대 진보 대법관 4대 4의 팽팽한 대립 속에 스윙 보트로 대법원의 방향을 좌지우지하던 '앤서니 케네디' 대법관이 2018.7 자진 은퇴하고 그 후임으로 보수파인 '브렛 캐버너'가 임명된 데 이어 이번 공석도 보수파 소장 인사로 충원되면 종신직인 대법관 신분상 앞으로 미국 대법원은 보수 6 대 진보 3의 불균형이 오랫동안 지속될 것으로 보인다.

이에 다급해진 민주당의 펠로시 하원의장은 최근 코로나-19 확진을 받은 트럼프의 건강 상태를 놓고 대통령의 직무수행 불능과 승계 문제를 규정한 수정헌법 25조에 관해 논의할 것이라고 불을 지피는가 하면 또 다른 민주당 인사들은 2016년 오바마 대통령 시절 스칼리아 대법관이 사망했을 때 "대통령 임기 마지막 해에 대법관을 지명하는 것은 옳지 않다"며 후임자에 대한 청문 절차조차 강력 거부했던 매코널 상원대표의 과거 행적을 들춰내고, 만약 배럿 판사 임명을 강행한다면 차기 국회에서 대법관의 수를 더 늘리는 법안을 발의하겠다고 맞불을 놓고 있다.

하지만 공화당이 상원을 장악하고 있는 현실상 코로나-19로 인한 돌발사태 등 특별 변수가 생기지 않는 한 배럿 판사의 임명은 기정사실로 굳어지고 있다.

그렇다면 공화당의 그림대로 배럿이 임명되어 보수파가 수적 절대 우위를 점하게 된 미국 대법원은 어떤 방향으로 나아갈까? 우선 공화당의 숙원이었던 여성의 낙태권과 성 소수자의 권리는 축소되고 오바마케어로 불리었던 건강보험개혁법과 불법 체류 청소년 추방유예 제도(DACA)는 폐지 쪽으로 가닥을 잡을 것으로 예상된다. 그 중 임산부의 낙태권과 DACA, 성적 성향에 따른 고용차별법 등은 올해 있었던 대법원판결에서 보수파로 분류되었던 로버츠 대법원장이 잇따라 진보 성향 대법관들과 보조를 같이한 까닭에 5대 4로 아슬아슬하게 그 명맥을 유지하는 방향으로 위기를 모면하였지만 배럿이 등판하는 순간 명줄을 다하는 것은 시간문제로 보인다.

이와 달리 보수파가 옹호하는 총기 소유와 같은 개인의 전통적 권리는 배럿 판사가 작년 참여했던 '캔터 대 바'(Kanter v. Barr) 사건에 비춰볼 때 한층 강화될 것으로 예상된다. 이 사건은 메디케어에 의료비를 부당 청구한 혐의로 연방법상 중범죄인 우편사기죄로 유죄판결을 받은 캔터가 자신의 형기를 마친 후 중범죄자의 총기 소유를 금지하는 연방법과 위스콘신주 법이 수정헌법 2조에 명시된 자신의 총기 소유권을 침해한다며 제기한 소송의 항소심이다.

3명의 항소판사가 심리한 이 사건에서 2명은 합헌 결정을 내렸으나 배럿 판사는 소수 의견문을 통해 폭력과 비폭력범을 구분하지 않고 모든 중범죄자에게 일괄적으로 총기 소유를 제한하는 법은 위헌이라고 주장했던 것이다. 자신의 멘토 스칼리아 대법관이 과거의 유사 판결에서 '수정헌법 2조가 보호하고자 하는 총기 소유의 주체는 민병대가 아닌 개인'이라고 해석했던 성향 등으로 미루어보아 그의 수제자 배럿 판사는 앞으로 총기 소유권을 어떻게 넓혀 나갈지 자못 관심을 끄는 대목이다. (2020.10.21.)

The Conservative Supreme Court's Future

Justice Ruth Bader Ginsburg, a progressive icon, died on September 18 at 87. President Bill Clinton appointed Ginsburg in 1993. For the following 27 years, she fought to expand the rights of women, minorities and societally marginalized individuals.

With the vacancy left by Ginsburg right before the presidential election came an opportunity to push the Supreme Court to become more conservative. Both the White House, which is responsible for nominating a candidate, and the Senate, which will confirm or reject the nominee, are firmly within Republican control. Not one to miss such a great opportunity, President Trump has already nominated a former law clerk of conservative legal giant, late Justice Antonin Scalia: Judge Amy Coney Barrett of the 7th Circuit Court of Appeals. Republican Senate Majority Leader Mitch McConnell has vowed to do his best to confirm the nominee before the November election.

In the recent past, the Supreme Court was evenly divided into four conservative justices and four liberal justices. Case outcomes would often turn on the swing vote cast by Justice Anthony Kennedy. Justice Kennedy retired in July 2018 and was replaced by a more reliable conservative vote, Brett Kavanaugh. If another young conservative justice is confirmed this time, they will enjoy a 6-3 majority on the court – and likely for a long time, as the judges have life tenure.

In desperation, House Speaker Pelosi has threatened the use of the twenty-fifth Amendment and argued that the president could not carry out the office's duties based on his recent positive test result for COVID-19. Other Democrats reminded Senator McConnell about his comment from 2016 when President Obama tried to fill the vacancy left by Justice Scalia's death. He opposed filling the seat before the election and stated that "[t]he American people should have a voice in the selection of their next Supreme Court Justice. Therefore, this vacancy should not be filled until we have a president." Some Democrats also threatened to increase the number of Supreme Court seats if the Republicans moved ahead with Judge Barrett's confirmation.

However, in all likelihood, barring some unforeseen event caused by COVID-19, Judge Barrett will be confirmed, given the firm Republican control over the Senate.

Assuming Judge Barrett's confirmation, which path will the conservative Supreme Court take? First and foremost, women's right to obtain an abortion and the rights granted to LGBTQ will likely get reduced. They have been the goal of the conservatives for a long time. In addition, the Affordable Care Act, also known as Obamacare, and DACA, which allows illegal aliens who arrived as children to avoid deportation, will likely get terminated. Although the Supreme

앞 줄(왼쪽부터) 사무엘 알리토, 클래런스 토머스, 존 로버츠, 스티븐 브라이어, 소냐 소토마이어. 뒷 줄 (왼쪽부터) 브렛 캐버너, 엘레나 케이건, 닐 고서치, 에이미 코니 배럿 (연방대법관 9명)
Current Justices of the U.S. Supreme Court: (front left) Samuel Alito, Clarence Thomas, John Roberts, Stephen Breyer, Sonia Sotomayor (rear left) Brett Kavanaugh, Elena Kagan, Neil Gorsuch, Amy Coney Barrett

Court recently ruled to save women's abortion rights and DACA, and granted protection against job discrimination based on sexual orientation in a string of surprise 5-4 decisions (with Chief Judge Roberts casting the swing vote), that narrow margin will likely disappear with Barrett's confirmation.

On the other hand, conservative values and individual rights such as the right to bear arms are expected to be further strengthened. Kanter v. Barr, a case that Judge Barrett heard last year, provides a window into her judicial philosophy. In that case, Kanter had been convicted of mail fraud for fraudulently requesting medical payments from Medicare. Mail fraud is a felony under federal law. After completing a prison sentence, Kanter filed a lawsuit to challenge the federal and

Wisconsin state law that banned felons from owning a firearm. He claimed that these laws violated his Second Amendment right to bear arms. He lost in the trial court, and appealed the decision.

A three-judge panel heard it. Two judges held the statutes in question to be constitutional. However, Judge Barrett wrote a dissenting opinion arguing the laws restricting gun ownership to all felons without distinguishing whether they were convicted of violent and non-violent felonies were unconstitutional. Considering her mentor Scalia's interpretation that the Second Amendment gave individuals the right to bear arms, not the militia, it will be interesting to see how far his protégé can expand the individual's right to own guns. (2020.10.21.)

변호사의 비밀유지 의무

변호사가 의뢰인에게 양질의 법률 서비스를 제공하기 위해서는 무엇보다 사건의 내막을 제대로 파악하는 일이 제일 중요하다고 할 것이다. 그러려면 의뢰인은 상담 과정에서 자신의 수치스러운 비밀이나 약점, 재판에 불리한 정황까지 모두 변호사에게 솔직하게 알려줄 수밖에 없는데 대신 변호사는 이렇게 업무상 얻게 된 의뢰인의 비밀을 지켜줘야 할 의무가 생긴다.

이처럼 변호사의 비밀유지는 의뢰인에게는 직무상 의무에 해당하지만, 형사사건에서 의뢰인의 방어권과 묵비권을 지키기 위해 국가기관이나 제삼자에 대해서는 그 비밀을 공개하지 않을 변호사의 권리가 되기도 한다. 법정에서 무죄를 주장하는 피고인이 변호사에게 범죄사실을 자백한 경우에도 그 비밀은 보장되어야 한다.

비밀에 관한 정의는 나라별로 차이가 있으나 대부분 의뢰인의 신분을 비롯한 가족관계, 질병, 재산, 유언장의 내용, 범죄사실, 반윤리적인 행위 등 변호사와 의뢰인 사이에서 법적인 조력을 얻기 위한 과정에서 알게 된 정보를 포괄적으로 포함한다고 보면 되고, 비밀유지의 주체는 변호사와 사건수임을 상담한 의뢰 당사자이다. 설혹 가족이나 타인은 수임료를 대신 지불했다고 하더라도 주체가 될 수 없고, 수임계

약 체결까지 이르진 않았다고 하더라도 상담내용도 비밀로 보호되어야 한다는 것이 일반적인 이론이다.

비밀유지 의무는 법으로 정해진 특수 상황이나 의뢰인의 동의가 없다면 의뢰인의 사망 이후까지 이어진다. 단적인 예로 애리조나주에서 있었던 한 살인사건에서 진범이었던 제삼자가 죽기 전 자신의 변호사에게 자기가 살인의 진범임을 자백한 일이 있었다. 이 사람이 사망 후 그 변호사가 살인사건의 누명을 쓴 피고인에게 유리한 진술을 해주려고 했으나 법에 예외 조항이 없고 의뢰인의 동의도 없었다는 이유로 재판장은 변호사의 증언을 허락하지 않았다. 이 때문에 결국 무고한 피고인 '빌 맥엄버'(Bill MacUmber)는 2건의 1급 살인혐의로 유죄 판결을 받고 37년간을 복역하는 어처구니없는 일이 발생하였던 것이었다.

이처럼 산 사람의 억울한 사연보다 죽은 사람의 권리를 더 중요하게까지 여기는 비밀유지 의무는 무언가 형평에 맞지 않고, 비상식적으로 느껴질 수도 있겠지만 법치주의 사회의 근간이 되는 법리여서 거의 절대적이라고 보면 된다. 그렇기 때문에 미국뿐 아니라 영국, 한국 등 대부분의 민주국가에서 이를 법제화하여 실행하고 있다. 따라서 비밀유지 의무를 위반한 변호사는 자격정지나 자격박탈 같은 중징계를 받을 수 있고, 또 비밀유지 의무를 위반해 얻어진 정보는 재판에서 증거로서의 효력도 인정받지 못한다.

비밀유지 의무의 면제는 매우 제한적인 경우에만 허용된다. 그중 하나는 변호사가 의뢰인과의 분쟁에서 자신을 보호하기 위한 경우와 의뢰인이 범죄 또는 부정행위를 저지르는 데 변호사가 도움을 주는 경우(이것을 법률용어로 '범죄-사기의 예외'라고 함, crime-fraud exception)이다.

최근 들어 후자의 '범죄-사기의 예외'를 이유로 한국뿐 아니라 미국 검찰도 변호사 사무실을 압수 수색하는 일이 잦아져 변호사와 의뢰인 간 비밀의사 교환권이 심각한 위협을 받고 있다. 한국 검찰은 2016년 롯데그룹의 탈세 의혹을 수사하면서 대형 로펌으론 처음으로 법무법인 율촌을 압수 수색한 데 이어 2018년 양승태 대법원장의 '사법농단 사건' 수사에서도 한국 최대 로펌 김앤장까지 압수 수색했다. 미국에선 러시아 대선개입 의혹을 수사하던 연방 검찰이 트럼프의 개인 변호사 '마이클 코헨'(Michael Cohen)의 사무실과 호텔 방에서 수색영장을 집행함으로써 미국 법조계를 떠들썩하게 만들었다.

의뢰인과 변호사와의 신뢰를 위해선 숨김없는 의사소통이 전제되어야 하는데 이같은 신뢰를 깨트릴 수 있는 검찰의 잦은 압수 수색도 문제지만 의뢰인의 범행을 때로는 부추기기도 하는 변호사들의 윤리 의식 제고 또한 절실해 보인다. (2021.1.13.)

배심원 재판에서 무죄 판결 승소 후 후배 변호사와 함께(뉴욕 퀸스 형사법원 앞.2016)
With my junior co-counsel after obtaining an acquittal in a jury trial (Queens County Supreme Court, New York)

Attorney's Duty to Keep Confidentiality

An attorney must understand all of the facts and issues in a case to provide quality legal services. To supply the lawyer with adequate information, the client must honestly reveal personal weaknesses, embarrassing secrets, and even facts damaging her case. In return, the lawyer must keep this information confidential.

The client holds the privilege and the attorney may not waive it. In criminal cases, as an extension of the client's right to present a defense and remain silent, it can be used as a shield in response to a probe by the government or a third party. Hence, even if the client has privately admitted guilt to the attorney, the attorney is not free to divulge it in an open court.

What types of communication are protected by the attorney-client privilege varies from one country to the next. Generally speaking, though, a lawyer must keep confidential all of the information that she has learned through the attorney-client relationship including, but not limited to, whether the client has retained the attorney, information about the client's family, client's medical history and property, contents of the will, and whether the client has committed a crime or an ethical violation. This privilege exists only between the lawyer and the client even if the client's family or a third party has paid for the legal services. Also, in most cases, even when the attorney isn't retained, the privilege protects the communications made during the initial consultation.

This duty continues and even survives the client's death unless there's an exception or a client waiver. For example, in a homicide case in Arizona, the real murderer confessed to the crime to his attorney before his death. Because another individual was convicted of the murder and serving a lengthy prison term, the lawyer attempted to provide this exculpatory evidence to help the innocent prisoner. However, the court did not allow the attorney to do so, holding that there was no exception to the attorney-client privilege and the dead client never waived it. This resulted in an innocent man, Bill MacUmber, who was previously convicted of two counts of murder in the first degree, serving 37 years in prison before his release.

This extreme example makes us wonder whether it's unfair that confidentiality survives the client's death. Certainly, it seems unreasonable that we value the rights of the dead people over those living. At the same time, for the country to operate under the rule of law, respecting the attorney-client privilege is absolutely necessary. This is why this privilege exists in nearly all of the democratic countries like the United States, Great Britain, and Korea. In these countries, an attorney who breaks the duty may be disciplined, including losing their law license in extreme cases, and information obtained from violating the attorney-client relationship may not be used at trial.

The law has narrow exceptions, however. One exception allows the attorney to break the confidence to defend herself in a dispute with the client. There is also a crime-fraud exception where the attorney aids the client to commit a crime or a fraud.

Recently, Korean and American prosecutors have relied on the crime-fraud exception to search the lawyers' offices, threatening the very basic foundation of an attorney-client relationship. For example, in 2016, Korean prosecutors obtained a search warrant for a major Korean law firm, Yulchon, during the Lotte Group investigation for tax evasion. This was the first time that a large law firm in Korea was subjected to a search by law enforcement. Similarly, during the case rigging scandal investigation involving the former Chief Justice, Yang Sung-tae, in 2018, the prosecutors stormed the largest law firm in Korea, Kim and Chang. In America, federal prosecutors shocked the legal community by obtaining a search warrant for the law office and hotel room belonging to President Trump's lawyer, Michael Cohen.

The privileged communication between the attorney and the client forms the bedrock of their relationship. These frequent searches by the prosecutors are shaking up this understanding. At the same time, the lawyers must remember their ethical obligation not to aid their clients to commit a crime. (2021.1.13.)

국선변호사 사무실에서 교도소에 수감 중인 의뢰인
과 화상채팅 대기 중
Waiting to connect to a jail inmate from the
Legal Aid Society's video conference room

국선변호사의 바쁜 일상(하루만에 새로 맡게
된 사건들). 각 사건 파일 안에는 의뢰인들의 비
밀이 담겨있다.
Here is an example of a public defender's
busy schedule. I picked up these cases in
one shift. Each case file contains the client's
confidential information.

뉴욕시 변호사협회에서 Public Service Fellowship을 수상했을 때의 기사(2011)
A newspaper clip from when I received the Public Service Fellowship from
New York City Lawyer's Association

NYCLA's Public Service Awards Reception

NYCLA held its 21st annual public service awards reception on September 27, honoring seven attorneys for their outstanding record of public service. Hon. Carmen Beauchamp Ciparick, Senior Associate Judge of the New York State Court of Appeals, was the keynote speaker. In addition, NYCLA's Criminal Justice Section presented two attorneys with the 2011 Criminal Justice Fellowship, an award based on an essay competition. This year, thanks to the revenue from the New York County Criminal Justice Manual, each Fellowship winner received $2,500.

The public service award recipients' public service careers epitomize their commitment and dedication to ensure that all people – the poor; elderly; minorities, children, mentally and physically handicapped – have equal access to legal representation.

Matthew C. Williams, and **Mark Son**, staff attorney, The Legal Aid Society. With them is NYCLA President **Stewart D. Aaron**.

Pictured above (from left to right) are: honorees **Tanya Douglas**, director, Disabilities Advocacy Project, Manhattan Legal Services; **William D. Gibney**, director, special litigation unit, criminal practice, The Legal Aid Society; **Jane Greengold Stevens**, director, litigation, New York Legal Assistance Group; **Rebecca C. Martin**, deputy chief, civil frauds unit, Southern District U.S. Attorney's Office; **Alan W. Sputz**, deputy division chief, Family Court Division, Law Department; and **Barbara Zolot**, senior supervising attorney, Center for Appellate Litigation. With them are Court of Appeals Judge **Carmen Beauchamp Ciparick** and NYCLA Past President

Pictured above (from left to right) are: NYCLA Criminal Justice Section co-chairs **Keith Schmidt** and **Alison Wilkey**, who presented the 2011 Criminal Justice Public Service Fellowships to Manhattan Assistant District Attorney

Catherine A. Christian, chair of the public service awards committee. Another honoree, Marvin Bernstein, director of Mental Hygiene Legal Services, First Department, is not pictured.

플리바게닝의 거짓말 화법

2013년 6월 뉴욕 맨해튼의 형사법원, 피고인 '브라이언 프리맨'(Brian Freeman)은 동물학대 혐의로 기소되었지만 검사와 플리바게닝을 통해 동물학대죄 대신 무단침입죄에 대한 유죄를 인정하고 25일간 사회봉사를 하기로 합의했다. 실제로 남의 사유지에 무단침입을 한 적은 없었지만 동물학대범이라는 전과기록을 피하고자 검사와 협상 끝에 얻은 결과였다.

이런 사실은 검사는 물론 프리맨의 변호사와 유죄 판결을 내린 판사까지 알고 있었고, 추후 사건을 심리한 항소법원도 알고 있었지만 항소심은 피고인이 거짓을 말했더라도 플리바게닝을 통해 서로 합의한 사항이기 때문에 법적으로 아무런 문제가 없다고 판단했다. 어떻게 진실만을 추구해야 하는 법정에서 이런 '짜고치는 거짓말'이 통용되는 것일까?

우리말로 '유죄협상제도' 정도로 해석되는 플리바게닝은 수사 편의상 피고인이 유죄를 인정하거나 다른 사람의 범죄에 관련된 증언을 하는 대가로 검사가 형량을 낮추거나 가벼운 죄목으로 대체해주는 제도인데 한국에는 없고, 미국은 전역에서 이를 광범위하게 활용하고 있다. 미국의 경우 형벌제도를 운용하는 국가 입장에서 보면 굳이 유죄를 인정하겠다고 하는 사람에게까지 배심원 평결에 의존할 필요가 없다는 것이고, 아울러 수사와 기소, 재판 최종심까지 소요되는 막대한 공적 비용도 절감할 수 있다는 이유에서다.

권력형 비리 사건이나 마피아와 같은 조직범죄 수사에서 범죄를 기획하고 지시한 '몸통'을 잡기 위해선 단순 가담자나 행동대원들의 협조가 필수적인데, 이때 검찰이 제시하는 카드가 바로 플리바게닝이다. 최근 탈세 혐의로 체포된 트럼프 재단 CFO '앨런 와이슬버그'(Allen Weisselberg)가 검찰의 플리바게닝 협상에 응해 트럼프 전 대통령에 대해 불리한 증언을 할지 여부에 관심이 쏠리고 있다. 통계에 따르면 미국 형사 사건 중 97% 이상이 이 제도를 통해 해결되고 나머지 3% 정도만이 재판으로 처리된다고 한다.

하지만 아무리 수사의 효율성 측면이나 공적 비용절감 효과가 크고, 또 모든 사건이 다 그렇지는 않다고 하더라도 사법정의를 구현하기 위해 국가가 진행하는 엄정한 재판 과정에서 거짓말 화법이 공공연하게 통용되는 것은 여러 면에서 문제 소지가 많아 보인다. 미국의 플리바게닝에는 세 가지 거짓말이 존재한다는 뉴저지 럿거스 로스쿨의 '테아 존슨'(Thea Johnson) 교수의 최근 발표 논문이 이를 잘 풍자해준다.

그 첫 번째는 프리맨처럼 범죄 사실에 대한 거짓말이다. 자신이 범죄를 저지르지 않았음에도, 또는 기소 사실과 다른 범죄행위에 대해서 유죄를 인정하는 것이다. 두 번째는 법적 절차에 대한 거짓말이다.

예컨대, 변호사나 가족, 다른 이해당사자의 압력에 의해 유죄를 인정하면서도 자신이 변호사와 충분한 상담을 거친 후 자발적으로 유죄를 인정한다고 판사에게 거짓으로 말한다는 것이다. 세 번째는 죄목에 대한 거짓말이다. 즉 형법상 존재하지도 않는 범죄에 대한 유죄 인정으로, 이를테면 과실치사 미수죄와 같은 것이다.

A가 운전 부주의로 교통사고를 내 B를 사망에 이르게 하면 과실치사죄가 적용되는데, 과실치사죄는 고의성이 없는 사고 유형의 범죄라고 볼 수 있다. A에게 B를 살해하려는 범의가 없었고, 부주의 운전이 범죄행위를 위한 준비 단계도 아니기 때문에 법리상 과실치사 미수라는 것은 성립되지 않는다. 이 사건의 쟁점은 어디까지나 A의 부주의가 중대한 과실이냐 아니냐 하는 점인 것이다. 그런데도 법원은 과실치사 미수를 인정하는 모순을 스스로 만들고 있다고 지적했다.

사법정의 최고의 가치인 '진실 추구'와 정면으로 충돌하면서까지 거짓말 화법이 통용되는 플리바게닝을 어떻게 보완해 나가야 할지 미국 법조계의 시름이 깊다. (2021.9.1.)

영어 녹음 듣기

Court System

⚖️

Lies in Plea Bargaining

Inside a Manhattan criminal courtroom in June of 2013, Defendant Brian Freeman pleaded guilty to trespass and agreed to perform 25 days of community service. It was just a regular ordeal in criminal court, except, he had been charged with animal cruelty and never trespassed on another person's property. This plea was engineered through plea bargaining with the prosecutor so that he could avoid the stigma of an animal cruelty charge.

The problem is that this fact was known not only to the prosecutor and Freeman's lawyer, but to the judge who took the plea. Even the appellate court knew. Although the court found no factual basis for the plea, it was acceptable because "it was in the defendant's favor." How can the court, the institution that must pursue the truth, allow such blatant lies?

Plea bargaining allows the defendant to accept responsibility for a lesser crime than the original charge and receive a more lenient sentence. It's a preferred method of resolving criminal cases in America because it guarantees a certain outcome for both sides. It's also used to entice some defendants to provide necessary testimony in other important criminal cases. From the government's perspective with an interest in running an efficient criminal justice system, there's no reason to expend valuable resources and conduct jury trials to prosecute a person willing to accept responsibility. This system does not exist in Korea.

Furthermore, plea bargaining's importance cannot be overstated in cases involving conspiracy or fraud charges against the political establishment or organized criminal enterprises like the mafia. The prosecution needs help from low- to mid-level members to get to those at the top of the pyramid, and plea bargaining serves as an effective tool. Recently, Trump Organization's CFO Allen Weisselberg was arrested. The federal prosecutors reportedly offered to reduce his criminal exposure in exchange for his help, and are awaiting his response. According to one study, more than 97% of the criminal cases in America are resolved through plea bargaining. The remaining 3% are resolved through trials.

Even acknowledging plea bargaining's usefulness to the prosecution or cost-savings to the system, it seems problematic that lies are so prevalent in court proceedings where they must seek the solemn truth. Recently, Professor Thea Johnson at Rutgers Law School published an article about three lies in plea bargaining.

First is a lie about the facts in the case as Freeman did. In this case, people admit guilt to a criminal charge even when they're innocent or admit guilt to something other than what they did. The second is a lie about the legal process.

For example, a defendant tells the judge that he is pleading guilty voluntarily after a thorough consultation with his lawyer even though he's succumbing to the pressures of the lawyer, family members or other interested people. The third is a lie about the criminal charge. In other words, a defendant pleads guilty to a charge that does not exist in the penal code such as attempted reckless assault.

If A recklessly causes a car accident and kills B, he could be charged with reckless assault. Recklessness is closer to an accident because it excludes intentional acts. Thus, since A never intended to kill B, and recklessly driving a car is not an attempt to commit another crime, attempting to recklessly assault another person does not make any logical sense. The sole issue in this scenario is whether A's action was reckless or not. However, Professor Johnson pointed out that by accepting a guilty plea to attempted reckless assault, the court turns a blind eye to such a logical fallacy.

How can we balance the need for efficiency with the pursuit of truth? The courts are grappling with this question one case at a time. (2021.9.1.)

사법시스템

위헌법률심판권의 시원

위헌법률심판권이란 의회에서 만든 법률이 상위법인 헌법에 위반되는지 여부를 연방대법원이 심사하는 권한을 일컫는 것으로, 대법원에서 헌법에 위배된다고 판단한 법은 즉시 효력을 상실하는 게 법리이다.

최근 연방대법원은 임신 6주 이후의 낙태를 금지하는 텍사스주의 '심장박동법'과 총기 휴대의 필요성을 입증해야만 허가증을 발급해주는 뉴욕주의 '총기휴대법'이 수정헌법 제2조에 위반되는지에 대한 구두변론을 마치고 최종판결을 앞두고 있어 뜨거운 관심을 받고 있다.

흥미로운 점은, 처음부터 삼권분립 원칙에 따라 '국민의 대의기관인 입법부가 법을 만들고, 행정부의 수장인 대통령이 이를 집행하는 과정에서 문제가 드러나면 사법부인 대법원이 위헌 여부를 판단한다'고 헌법에 명문화하였으면 좋았으나 사법부의 역할을 규정해놓은 연방헌법 제3조 어디에도 이런 내용이 없다는 점이다.

연방대법원이 오늘날 위헌법률심판권의 주체로 자리 잡은 것은 건국 초기 '마버리 대 매디슨'(*Marbury v. Madison*) 사건이 그 시원이다. 1800년에 실시된 제3대 미국 대통령 선거에서 연방정부의 개입을 우선시하는 연방주의자였던 현직 대통령 '존 애덤스'(John Adams)는 주와 개인의 주권을 중시하는 반연방주의자 부통령 '토마스 제퍼슨'(Thomas Jefferson)에 패배하고 말았다. 이어 의회 권력까지 넘겨주게 된 애덤스는 남아있는 사법부만이라도 제퍼슨 행정부의 반연방 정책을 견제해달라는 요량으로 퇴임 전 정권이양 과도기를 틈타 16명의 순회판사와 42명의 치안판사를 무더기로 임명했는데 이게 사단이 되었다.

James Madison (1751-1836)

당시 각국의 외교관뿐 아니라 판사 임명장 전달 책임도 국무장관에 속해 있었는데 국무장관이었던 법률가 '존 마셜'(John Marshall)이 선거에 패배한 애덤스로부터 대법원장으로 긴급 임명을 받고 급히 짐을 싸느라 '윌리엄 마버리'(William Marbury)를 포함한 4명의 치안판사들까지 미처 임명장을 전달하지 못했던 것이다.

1801년 3월 4일 임기를 시작한 제퍼슨 행정부의 신임 국무장관 '제임스 매디슨'(James Madison)은 임명장을 받지 못한 이들 4명에 대한 임명무효를 주장하였고, 이를 수긍하지 못한 마버리는 '연방대법원이 하급법원으로 하여금 국무장관에게 임명장을 전달해줄 것을 명령할 수 있다'는 1789년 제정된 법원조직법 제13조를 인용, 하급심을 거치지 않고 바로 대법원에다 소장을 접수했다.

마버리로부터 소장을 받은 대법원장 존 마셜은 진퇴양난의 처지에 봉착하였다. 임명장을 교부하라고 명령을 내린다면 제퍼슨과 매디슨은 이런저런 구실을 붙여 판결을 무시할 게 뻔한데 그렇게 되면 사법부는 무력한 판결을 내리는 식물기관으로 전락할 것이고, 그렇다고 신임 대통령 제퍼슨 편을 드는 경우에는 사법부가 행정부 시녀임을 자처하는 모양새가 되기 때문이었다.

고심 끝에 마셜은, "대통령의 공직 임명에는 두 가지 유형이 있는데 대통령이나 행정부 각 기관장이 자신의 재량권 안에서 인사권을 행사한 경우에는 정치적으로만 평가될 수 있으나, 판사 임명과 같이 법령에 의거, 대통령의 추천을 받아 국회가 동의를 한 경우라면 대통령이 임의로 이를 취소할 수 없어 사법부의 심사 대상이 될 수 있다."고 판결문의 서두를 채워나갔다. 이 같은 법리에 따라 마버리가 제때 판사 임명장을 받지 못한 것은 국무장관의 실책이라고 지적하였다.

아울러 헌법에 규정된 연방대법원 재판권의 범위는 연방 지방법원과 주의 1심을 거쳐 올라온 항소심 사건에 국한되기 때문에 의회가 1789년, 1심의 재판권을 바로 대법원에 부여하도록 제정한 법원조직법 제13 조는 위헌이라 삭제되어야 마땅하다고 판단했다. 따라서 재판권이 없는 대법원이 하급법원에 임명장 전달명령을 내릴 수도 없다고 마무리 지었다. 다시 말해 아무리 의회가 만든 국법이라 할지라도 그것이 헌법에 위반된다고 판단되면 대법원이 무효화할 수 있다고 공언함으로써 자연스레 사법부의 위헌법률심판권을 확보한 것이다.

솔로몬 뺨치는 마셜의 이 명판결 하나로 사법부가 행정부에 예속되는 것을 막고, 의회의 입법 횡포도 견제함으로써 오늘날 사법부 우위의 미국식 삼권분립이 자리를 잡게 된 것이다. (2021.11.24.)

Court System

The Origin Story of Judicial Review

It is taken for granted: The Supreme Court has the authority to determine the constitutionality of the laws passed by the legislature. If a statute is determined to be unconstitutional, it's illegal and no longer has any effect.

Recently, the Supreme Court heard legal arguments over the constitutionality of Texas' "heartbeat" law, which bans abortion after six weeks of pregnancy, and New York's gun law, which requires the applicant to provide justification before a carry permit is issued.

Interestingly, nowhere in Article III of the Constitution – the entirety of which deals with establishing the federal judiciary – does it say that the court has such powers. Of course, it would have been clear from the beginning if the Constitution had delineated the roles of the government branches: Congress is responsible for making the laws, the president's executive branch will carry them out, and the courts will review the constitutionality of their actions.

Instead, the Supreme Court "acquired" the power of judicial review in the early days of the new republic in a landmark case called Marbury v. Madison. President John Adams, a federalist who wanted a big federal government, lost in the 1800 presidential election to a Democratic-Republican Party candidate, Vice President Thomas Jefferson, who emphasized the states and individual's rights. Adams was also set to lose Congress as well. As a last resort, he decided to pack the judiciary to keep a watchful eye over the incoming Jefferson administration's anti-federalist policies. He made the "midnight appointments" of 16 circuit court judges and 42 justices of the peace before Jefferson's inauguration. This soon caused a problem.

In those days, in addition to appointing diplomats and ambassadors, the Secretary of State was also responsible for delivering commissions to judicial appointees. Secretary of State John Marshall, a lawyer himself, failed to deliver commissions to four justices of the peace, including William Marbury, during the busy and hectic transition period (Marshall himself was confirmed as the new chief justice of the Supreme Court by Adams' administration in his last days).

Jefferson began his term on March 4, 1801. The new Secretary of State, James Madison, refused to deliver commissions to four justices of the peace who had not received them previously. Marbury brought a writ of mandamus to force Madison to deliver his commission. The writ was brought directly to the Supreme Court under Section 13 of the Judiciary Act of 1789, which provided that the Supreme Court "shall have exclusive jurisdiction over all cases of a civil nature where a state is a party . . . and shall have power to issue . . . writs of mandamus, in cases warranted by the principles and usages of law."

John Marshall, now the chief justice of the Supreme Court, was placed in an untenable position. If he ordered the commission to be delivered, Jefferson and Madison would find an excuse not to do so, making a mockery out of the judiciary. On the other hand, if he sided with Jefferson, he would be offering his court to the president on a silver platter.

After long deliberation, Marshall distinguished between a discretionary appointment by the president and

Chief Justice John Marhsall (1755-1835)

government agencies from a commission, such as a judicial appointment, which involves the president's nomination and the senate's confirmation. Marshall held that the former was "only politically examinable" while the latter may not be "annihilated" by the president and its validity was only "examinable in a court." Thus, the signing of the commission for Marbury "conferred on him a legal right to the office" and the Secretary of State's "refusal to deliver which is a plain violation of that right, for which the laws . . . afford him a remedy."

At the same time, Marshall wrote that the Constitution limits "original jurisdiction in all cases affecting ambassadors, other public ministers and consuls, and those in which a state shall be a party. In all other cases, the supreme court shall have appellate jurisdiction." He found that granting the power to bring a writ of mandamus directly to the Supreme Court under Section 13 of the 1789 Judiciary Act violated this constitutional provision and must be struck down. Because the lawsuit was brought under an unconstitutional statute, the Supreme Court may not issue a writ to Madison to deliver the commission. In other words, any law made by the legislature must be examined for its constitutionality, and "[i]t is emphatically the province and duty of the [court] to say what the law is." Thus, the principle of judicial review was established.

Marshall's Solomon-like decision prevented the judiciary from becoming a puppet institution to the executive. It also allowed the judiciary to determine the legality of the legislature's actions. It perfected the American system of checks and balances, with the judiciary on top. (2021.11.24.)

사법시스템

허드슨강 엘리스섬의 담장분쟁

미국 시인 '로버트 프로스트'(Robert Frost)의 시 <담장 고치기>에 보면 '담장이 튼튼해야 이웃 사이가 좋아진다'라는 구절이 나온다. 오늘 칼럼에선 20세기 초 유럽 이민자들이 미국에 들어오려면 첫 번째로 거쳐야 하는 관문 – 이민국 건물이 오랫동안 자리하여 유서 깊은 뉴욕 허드슨강 하구 엘리스섬(Ellis Island)의 담장에 관한 얘기를 나눠본다.

흔히 미국의 역사라고 하면 메이플라워호를 타고 영국에서 건너온 청교도들이 건국을 주도한 것으로 알려져 있지만 그 내막을 한 꺼풀 벗기고 들어가 보면 영국 왕으로부터 칙명을 받은 신하나 식민지 개척회사들이 미 동부해안선을 따라 초기 식민지 건설에 깊이 간여했다.

1609년, 이른바 대항해 시절 영국 탐험가 '헨리 허드슨'은 유럽 열강의 동인도회사 중 선두그룹인 네덜란드 동인도회사 소속으로 '반달호'를 타고 맨해튼섬 서쪽의 허드슨강을 거슬러 현 뉴욕주의 수도 알바니까지 탐험했다. 이를 계기로 뉴욕과 뉴저지 일대에 '뉴 네덜란드'라는 식민지가 건설되었다.

그러나 뉴 네덜란드는 영국과의 전쟁으로 1664년 영국의 손아귀에 넘어갔고, 당

엘리스섬(뉴욕)
Ellis Island(New York)

시 영국의 국왕 찰스 2세는 이 땅을 자기 동생 제임스 2세에게, 제임스 2세는 다시 그 일부를 자신의 충복 버클리(Lord Berkeley)와 조지 카트렛 경(Sir George Carteret)에게 하사했다. 이때 하사한 땅의 동쪽 경계를 '바다와 허드슨강'이라고 애매하게 표기한 게 1차 분쟁을 잉태한다.

이처럼 서류상의 경계 담장이 튼튼하지 못했던 탓에 뉴욕과 뉴저지주는 독립전쟁이 끝나기가 무섭게 영토분쟁에 휘말렸다. 특히 수상 무역의 요충지였던 허드슨강은 당시 주의 재정수입에 막대한 영향을 미쳤기 때문에 두 주 모두 순순히 물러설 입장이 아니었다. 뉴욕주는 뉴저지 땅의 동쪽 끝을 경계로, 뉴저지주는 허드슨강의 중간 지점을 주의 담장이라고 각각 주장했다. 그 분쟁영토 목록 가운데 상인 겸 농부 '사무엘 엘리스'가 소유한 3에이커(약 12,000㎡→약 3,600p)의 섬도 포함되었다. 이게 바로 현재 자유의 여신상이 위치한 리버티섬에서 800m 떨어진 엘리스섬이다.

수십 년간 이어진 지루한 분쟁 끝에 1829년 1차 소송이 제기되었으나 1834년 뉴욕과 뉴저지는 물밑 협상을 통해 허드슨강과 뉴욕만 중앙을 두 주의 경계로 하되 뉴욕이 강 전체를 독점적으로 관할하고, 엘리스섬 역시 뉴욕이 갖는 것으로 합의했다.

이후 엘리스섬은 미 육군이 포병 진지로 개축하여 사용하다가 19세기 후반부터 맨해튼에서 대대적인 지하철 공사가 시작되며 나온 흙을 매립하여 원래 3에이커에서 27.5 에이커(약 3만 5천 p)까지 면적이 늘어나게 되었다. 이렇게 확장된 땅에 연

118

방정부는 유럽에서 오는 이민자들의 수속을 위해 서두에 언급한 이민국과 이민병원 등을 설치했다. 이곳 이민국 입국심사장을 통해 1892.1.1~1954.11.2까지 62년간 1,200만여 명의 이민자가 아메리칸드림을 품고 거쳐 갔다.

　이후 유럽 이민자의 감소로 이민국은 폐쇄되었지만 섬의 활용방안 검토과정에서 간척사업으로 확장된 땅의 소유권 문제가 또 불거져 2차 담장 분쟁이 시작됐다. 뉴저지는 1834년 두 주의 경계선 합의에 따라 확장된 지역이 허드슨강 중앙에서 서쪽 뉴저지 쪽에 있기 때문에 자기들 것이라고 우기고, 뉴욕은 자신들의 섬에 간척사업을 통해 새로 생긴 땅이니 뉴욕 소유가 되어야 당연하다고 맞대응했다.

　1998.5.26. 엘리스섬을 둘러싼 상고심에서 대법원은 6대3의 판결로 '1834년 두 주의 합의에 따라 당시 뉴욕의 소유였던 3에이커는 뉴욕주, 이후 간척사업으로 얻어진 24.5에이커는 뉴저지주의 소유'라고 담장을 정리해 주었다. 대법원이 법의 권위를 빌려 두 이웃의 담장을 사이좋게 고쳐준 판례이다. (2022.1.19.)

엘리스섬 지도
　<출처: City Experiences>
Map of Ellis Island
<Source: City Experiences>

*지도상 간이 다리가 놓여있으나 페리 관리 직원용이라 관광객은 이용할 수 없다.
*Although the map shows a bridge between Ellis Island and New Jersey, it is not for tourists. Only the ferry company's employees may access it.

영어 녹음 듣기

Fence Disputes on Ellis Island

In a poem by American poet Robert Frost, Mending Wall, it is written, "Good fences make good neighbors." In today's column, we discuss the fence dispute on Ellis Island, located at the mouth of the Hudson River. It was home to the immigration office that served as a gateway for the Europeans who arrived in the early twentieth century.

It is commonly said that America was founded by Pilgrims who came from England on the Mayflower. However, underneath that veil of historical myth lies the truth that the eastern seaboard of the United States was colonized by individuals and companies that arrived with colonial charters granted by the King of England.

In 1609, at the height of the Age of Exploration, English explorer Henry Hudson arrived as a member of the East India Company, one of the most influential colonization companies. He sailed his ship, Half Moon, up the modern-day Hudson River along the west of Manhattan Island to Albany, the modern-day capital of New York State. As a result, a new colony called New Netherland was established over the New York and New Jersey regions.

However, following a war in 1664, New Netherland fell into the hands of the English. The King of England at the time, Charles II, granted the newly acquired territory to his brother, James II. James II, in turn, gave part of the colony to his loyal followers and proprietors, Lord Berkeley and Sir George Carteret. The clause in the colonial land grant vaguely outlined the territory as being "bounded on the east by the main sea, and part by Hudson's river." It gave birth to the first conflict.

Poor fences on paper led to a real-life land dispute between New York and New Jersey when the American Revolutionary War was over. The Hudson River was a major trade route and controlling it would have a huge impact on the state's revenue. Neither state was willing to back down easily. New York argued that the clause in question set the line at New Jersey's shore and gave New York sovereignty over the entire river. New Jersey claimed that it was entitled to a boundary in the middle of the river. Among the disputed area was a three-acre island owned by a merchant and a farmer, Samuel Ellis. This is Ellis Island, which sits 800 meters from Liberty Island, home of the Statue of Liberty.

After decades of uncertainty and dispute, the first lawsuit was filed in 1829. However, in 1834, both states reached an agreement. The interstate compact set the boundary line as the middle of the Hudson River while giving New York exclusive jurisdiction over the entire river and Ellis Island.

Then, Ellis Island was taken over by the U.S. Army, which fortified it with artillery guns. In the nineteenth century, as massive subway construction projects began in Manhattan, the soil from the construction site was taken to Ellis Island. Through the reclamation process, the island grew from 3 to 27.5 acres. Here, the federal government erected an immigration office to process the entry of European immigrants and a hospital for them as well. From January 1, 1892 to November 2, 1954, over 12 million immigrants that arrived with the American dream passed through this office.

The immigration office closed its doors due to a decreasing number of European immigrants. As the government contemplated various proposals for the use of the island, a second fence dispute arose over the reclaimed portion of

뉴욕 첫 방문 가족여행(1997)
My first visit to New York with family

the island. New Jersey claimed that the boundary between the two states follows the high-water mark of the original island with the balance belonging to New Jersey as the island sits on the westside of the midpoint of the Hudson River. On the other hand, New York argued that it had sovereignty over the entire island because the original compact said that the island belonged to New York without describing its land mass.

On May 26, 1998, the Supreme Court finally settled the fence dispute in a 6-3 decision. According to the 1834 compact between the two states, the Court held that the balance of the island other than the original three acres belonged to New Jersey. It's an excellent example of how the Supreme Court used its legal authority to mend the wall between neighbors. (2022.1.19.)

미필적 고의에 의한 과실치사죄

법률용어로 '미필적 고의'란 게 있다. 자신의 행위로 인하여 반드시 어떤 결과가 발생하는 것은 아니지만 발생 가능성을 미리 알고 있었고, 또 그 결과가 발생해도 상관없다고 생각하는 심리상태를 일컫는 말이다.

예컨대 민가와 가까운 데서 엽총으로 사냥을 하면 자칫 행인이 맞을지도 모른다고 생각하면서 발포하고 보니 역시 사람이 맞아 사망하였을 경우이다. 이럴 경우 사냥꾼에게 살인의 고의가 없었던 것은 분명하다고 하더라도 상식적으로 충분히 발생 가능한 결과를 무시하고 행동을 했기 때문에 법적으로 책임을 묻게 되는 것이다.

미필적 고의는 확정적 고의와 과실의 중간단계 정도로 볼 수 있기 때문에 과실범보다는 미필적 고의범을 더 엄하게 처벌하는 게 형법의 원칙이다.

최근 매사추세츠주에서 남자친구에게 '자살 강요'를 한 여학생에게 미필적 고의에 의한 과실치사죄가 적용되어 주의를 끌고 있다. 2019년, 보스턴칼리지에 재학 중이던 한인 유학생 Y양이 18개월간 사귄 필리핀계 남자친구에게 지속적으로 가학적인 문자 폭탄을 보내 우울증에 걸린 남자친구가 끝내 주차빌딩 옥상에서 투신자살한 사건이 그 배경이다.

검찰조사 결과 남자친구가 사망하기 전 2개월간 두 사람은 7만 5천 건 이상의 문자 메시지를 교환했던 것으로 밝혀졌다. Y양은 문자 등으로 남자친구의 자살을 요구했을 뿐만 아니라 자살 현장에도 함께 있었던 것으로 드러났다. 보스턴 검찰은 Y양에게 과실치사법을 적용해 체포했다.

매사추세츠주의 과실치사법은 '타인이 죽을 수 있는 확률이 높은데도 불구하고 죽어도 상관없다'라는 정도의 미필적 고의에 의한 행동도 처벌하는 것을 골자로 하고 있다. 2년간의 법정 투쟁 끝에 Y양은 작년 12월, 유죄를 인정하고 30개월 집행유예와 사회봉사 300시간을 선고받았다.

매사추세츠 주 검찰은 이번 사건 외에도 이미 2014년, 전화 통화와 문자메시지를 통해 남자친구 '콘래드 로이'(Conrad Roy)의 자살을 요구하여 죽음에 이르게 한 17세 '미셸 카터'(Michelle Carter)를 재판에 회부시켜 과실치사 유죄 판결을 이끌어낸 전력이 있다. 피고 미셸은 표현의 자유를 내세우며 연방대법원까지 상고했지만 받아들여지지 않아 결국 2년 6개월의 징역형을 선고받고 형기를 마쳤다.

전국 최초로 매사추세츠 주 검찰이 이처럼 '자살 강요' 사건을 과실치사법으로 적용한 것을 두고 법조계 일각에선 우려의 목소리도 만만치 않다. 아무리 상대방을 죽음에 이르게 했다 하더라도 표현의 자유가 철저하게 보장된 미국에서 단지 '자살해라', 죽어버려라'와 같은 말만으로 과연 과실치사죄가 성립되느냐는 것이다.

이게 성립된다면 앞으로 상대방을 자살에 이르게 하는 유사 성격의, 인터넷상 언어폭력이나 학교에서 이뤄지는 '왕따'(집단 따돌림) 같은 사건에도 과실치사죄가 적용될지 눈여겨보겠다는 입장이다. 실제로 미국에서 가해자들로부터 '너는 언제쯤 자살할래?'와 같은 놀림과 학대를 견디지 못해 2017년 '말로리 그로스맨'을 시작으로 2018년 '가브리엘라 그린', 2019년 '케빈 리스' 등 해마다 어린 학생들이 극단적 선택을 한 바 있고, 이런 불상사는 케빈 리스를 끝으로 다시 일어나지 않는다는 보장이 없기 때문이다.

　Y양 사건 이후 과실치사죄가 너무 폭넓게 적용되는 것을 우려한 매사추세츠 주의회는 다른 사람의 '자살적 충동'에 대해 알면서도 '의도적으로 그 사람에게 자살을 강요하거나 부추기는 행위'를 할 경우 최고 5년 이하의 징역형을 받게 하는 이른바 '콘래드 법'의 법제화를 추진하고 있다. 하지만 코로나-19사태로 2년 넘게 아직도 의회에서 발목이 잡혀 진행은 지지부진한 실정이다.

　좋은 말만 하고 살아도 짧은 인생살이에서 왜 나쁜 말로 사람을 괴롭히는지, 불현듯 '말 한마디로 천 냥 빚을 갚는다'는 우리 속담이 생각난다. (2022.2.2.)

영어 녹음 듣기

Recklessness and Involuntary Manslaughter

Legally speaking, a person acts recklessly when she, while being aware of a substantial and unjustifiable risk that a particular result will occur, consciously disregards it.

A classic example would be a hunter who fires a shotgun in a residential area. If he kills someone, he can be held criminally accountable for being reckless because he disregarded a high chance that someone would get hit. Indeed, the hunter did not intend to kill anyone but he consciously disregarded a substantial and unjustifiable risk.

Being reckless falls somewhere in between being intentional and being negligent. Thus, generally speaking, it's punished more severely than negligent acts but not as severely as intentional acts.

By applying the recklessness standard, Massachusetts prosecutors recently got a conviction for involuntary manslaughter against a female student who coerced her boyfriend to commit suicide. In 2019, 'Y', a Boston College student from

Korea, incessantly sent abusive text messages to her Filipino-American boyfriend during their 18-month relationship. Finally, the boyfriend, who was suffering from depression, jumped to his death from a parking garage.

Police investigators discovered that they exchanged more than 75,000 text messages with each other in the last two months before the boyfriend's death. Inyoung demanded that her boyfriend commit suicide and was present when it happened. Boston's Suffolk County District Attorney's Office charged her with involuntary manslaughter.

Under Massachusetts' law, involuntary manslaughter is defined as "an unlawful killing unintentionally caused by wanton or reckless conduct." Two years after her arrest, Inyoung pleaded guilty last December. She was sentenced to 30 months in jail, which is suspended, and 300 hours of community service.

Another prosecutor's office in Massachusetts had already obtained a guilty verdict after trial in 2014 in the case involving 17-year-old Michelle Carter who demanded her boyfriend, Conrad Roy, to commit suicide. She coerced him through multiple phone calls and text messages. Carter appealed her conviction to the U.S. Supreme Court, claiming that her phone calls and messages were protected speech. The Court did not accept her argument. She served two and a half years in prison.

Some critics point out that Massachusetts prosecutors' use of involuntary manslaughter to prosecute "coerced suicide" cases, which are novel and appear to be the first in the nation, is problematic. They argue that even if a person's words lead to another person's suicide, they must be protected as free expression unless some other unlawful action accompanies them.

They question, if mere words can be used to bring involuntary manslaughter charges, can similar acts, such as cyber or school bullying, be prosecuted under the same statute? Unfortunately, many young students in America choose to end their lives because of verbal abuse like "when will you kill yourself?" Such students include Mallory Grossman in 2017, Gabriella Green in 2018, and Kevin Reese in 2019, and it is likely to grow.

Concerned with the prosecutors' broad use of involuntary manslaughter, as in Inyoung's case, some members of the Massachusetts legislature are pushing to pass the "Conrad Law." If passed in its current form, it would require the perpetrator to know about the victim's "propensity for suicidal ideation" and to "intentionally coerce[ ] or encourage[ ] that person to commit or attempt to commit suicide." It would be punishable by up to five years in prison. However, the proposed legislation has been held up for two years, in part because of the COVID-19 situation.

Our life is too short even for words of encouragement and love. I am reminded of the Korean proverb, "one word can be used to repay an enormous debt."(2022.2.2.)

사법시스템

트럼프와 소환장

뉴욕주 법원은 지난 2월 17일 트럼프 전 대통령 측으로부터 "뉴욕주 검찰이 조사를 받으러 오라고 소환장을 보내왔는데 이는 민주당 소속 '레티샤 제임스'(Letitia James) 뉴욕주 검찰총장이 정치적인 이유로 부당하게 수사를 벌이고 있는 것이니 소환되지 않도록 해달라"는 신청을 받고 이를 기각했다.

트럼프는 퇴임 후 부동산 관련 탈세 및 금융사기 혐의로 현재 2건의 소송에 연루돼 조사를 받고 있다. 하나는 맨해튼 검찰청에서 똑같은 사건을 형사문제로 수사 중인 사건이고, 나머지 하나는 민사로 진행되고 있는 이번 사건이다.

전국적으로 일원화된 검찰조직이 형사사건만 취급하는 한국과 달리 미국은 연방, 주, 카운티마다 각 검찰조직이 따로 있다. 연방검찰은 연방법 위반 형사사건을, 카운티 검찰청은 주법 위반 형사사건을 처리한다. 주 검찰청은 각 카운티 수준에서 다루기 힘든 대형 형사사건과 이번 트럼프 그룹 조사처럼 민사 사건을 다루기도 한다.

대통령 재직 시절부터 3년간 진행돼 온 민사 사건의 요지는 '트럼프 그룹'이 세금을 낼 때는 맨해튼 소재 트럼프 호텔 등 그룹 소유 부동산의 자산가치를 축소 신고하는 수법으로 탈세를 했고, 반대로 은행 대출이나 보험심사 과정에선 시세보다 가치를 부풀렸다는 혐의다. 트럼프 그룹은 트럼프 전 대통령을 비롯 장녀 이방카, 장남 도널드 트럼프 주니어 등 트럼프 가족 소유의 회사이다.

트럼프 측은 뉴욕주 검찰이, 맨해튼 검찰청의 형사사건은 자신들이 묵비권을 행사하면 소환해봤자 별 소용이 없다는 것을 알고 대신 묵비권이 인정되지 않는 민사 건으로 먼저 엮어 나중에 형사 건에 이용할 증언을 확보하려는 목적이 다분하기 때문에 소환에 응할 수 없다고 주장해왔다.

그러나 뉴욕주 법원의 담당 판사 '아더 엔고론'(Arthur Engoron)은 "주 검찰총장이 트럼프 그룹에 대한 조사를 통해 금융사기 관련 증거를 많이 찾아냈기 때문에 트럼프 가족 중 여기에 관련된 주모자가 누구인지를 가려내려면 신문절차가 필요하다"고 밝히고 트럼프 가족은 3주 안에 검찰의 신문에 응하라고 명령했다.

뉴욕주 검찰청에 따르면 트럼프 그룹은 현재까지 약 900,000건의 서류를 제출했으며 12명이 넘는 직원들이 증인으로 호출됐다고 한다. 아무튼 트럼프 측은 항고할 것으로 알려져 신문이 당장 이루어지진 않고 법적 공방이 계속될 것으로 보인다.

이번 사건의 쟁점이 된 소환장 제도는 증인을 강제로 법정에 불러 증언을 듣는 절차로 크게 두 종류가 있다. 증인에게 영장에 적시된 문서를 가지고 나오도록 명령하는 '문서제출명령'과 대배심이나 재판정, 데포지션(deposition, 법정 외 신문제도로, 주로 변호사 사무실에서 이루어짐) 등에서 증언을 요구하는 '증인호출장'이 바로 그것이다.

대부분의 경우에는 법원의 개입 없이 검사나 변호사가 증인에게 직접 소환장을 발부하는 게 관행이다. 가령 증인이 정당한 사유 없이 출석에 불응할 경우 변호사는 법원에 소환장의 집행을 요구하고, 법원은 이의 수리 여부를 결정한다. 증인이 법원의 명령에도 따르지 않는다면 법원은 법정모독죄로 과태료를 부과하거나 사안에 따라 구인도 가능하다.

그러나 이번 사건처럼 소환장 자체의 적법성에 대한 다툼이 생기면 소환장 관련 개인이나 법인의 쌍방 변호사는 법원에 이의를 제기할 수 있다. 법원은 이해당사자의 변론을 들은 후 소환장 집행 여부를 결정한다.

우리도 만약 일상생활 중 뜻하지 않게 법원으로부터 소환장을 받게 되면 어떻게 해야 할까? 아무리 소환 이유가 부당하다고 생각하더라도 소환장을 묵살하는 것은 나중에 더 큰 문제를 야기할 수 있으므로 변호사와 상의해서 대책을 강구할 것을 추천한다. (2022.3.2.)

Trump and Subpoena

A New York Supreme Court justice denied Trump's motion to quash the subpoena on February 17, rejecting the former president's argument that the Democratic New York Attorney General, Letitia James, was engaging in "selective prosecution" for political reasons.

Since leaving the White House, Trump has been the subject of two separate investigations for tax evasion and financial fraud involving his real estate. Currently, the Manhattan District Attorney is conducting a criminal investigation while the AG's office is pursuing a civil case. Unlike in Korea, which has a centralized prosecutor's office that only handles criminal matters, the American system has a separate prosecutor's office representing the government at the federal, state, and county levels. The federal prosecutors prosecute federal law violators while the county-level district attorney's offices bring charges based on state penal law offenses. The AG's office typically handles larger criminal cases involving multiple counties or civil matters, as in the Trump Group investigation.

At the crux of the three-year investigation by the AG's office, which began while Trump was still in office, is whether the Trump Group minimized the value of its real estate holdings for tax purposes while inflating it for bank loans and insurance claims. The Trump Group is jointly owned by the former president's family members, including his eldest daughter, Ivanka, and eldest son, Donald Trump Jr.

According to Trump's lawyers, the AG's office would try to circumvent his client and his family's right not to make incriminating statements since they would not be able to assert this right in a civil matter. They argued that the AG's office will give the depositions to be used in the parallel criminal investigation by the Manhattan DA.

However, Justice Arthur Engoron of the New York State Supreme Court held, "In the final analysis, a state attorney general commences investigating a business entity, uncovers copious evidence of possible financial fraud, and wants to question, under oath, several of the entities' principles, including its namesake. She has every right to do so." Under his ruling, Trump's family members must appear for deposition within three weeks. According to the AG's office, the Trump Group has turned over approximately 900,000 documents, and 12 of its employees have been deposed. At any rate, Trump vowed to appeal the decision, so the deposition is likely to be postponed while the legal battle continues.

A subpoena is a writ issued by the court to compel a witness' testimony. There are two kinds of subpoenas. The first is subpoena duces tecum, which compels the witness to appear with the documents specified in the subpoena. The other is subpoena ad testificandum which requires the witness to appear in the grand jury, trial, or deposition to give testimony.

In most cases, prosecutors and lawyers will issue a subpoena, and it is complied without the court's intervention. However, if the witness doesn't comply, the lawyer may file an order to show cause to enlist the court's help. The court can choose to enforce, modify, or deny it. If the witness still doesn't comply after the court order, he may be held in contempt and be fined or detained. As shown in the Trump case, if there's a dispute over the subpoena's legality, the opposing counsel or the individual served with the subpoena may move to quash it. The court would then conduct a hearing with all interested parties and make a ruling.

What should we do if we get a subpoena from the court unexpectedly? Even if it seems unreasonable or unfair, one must seek legal advice because simply ignoring it could lead to a bigger problem. (2022.3.2.)

가족들이 보는 앞에서 취임선서를 하는 제 45대 트럼프 대통령(2017)
Trump, the 45th President of the United States of America, takes the oath of office as his family watches

3장 전체 영어 녹음 듣기

Chapter
3

경제·사회
Economy and Society

마리화나의 경제학

대표적 마약의 하나인 대마초(마리화나) 합법화를 둘러싸고 미국 전역이 들썩거리고 있다. 이미 의료용 대마초의 사용은 절반 이상의 주에서 허용되고 있으며 매사추세츠와 콜로라도 같은 10개 주에선 기호용 대마초까지 합법화되었다.

불과 몇 년 전 대마초의 재배와 유통, 판매, 소지 행위를 범죄로 엄히 다스려 대마초 사범이 미국 전체 체포 사건의 40%나 차지하던 시절을 상기해볼 때 격세지감을 느낀다.

법안 지지자들에 의하면 대마초의 합법화는 대마범들을 체포나 기소하지 않음으로써 이들을 전과자로 양산하지 않을 뿐 아니라 경찰과 검찰, 법원의 업무경감에 따른 예산 절감, 역으로 대마 판매세 등을 통한 주 정부의 세수 증대와 일자리 창출에도 획기적으로 기여한다고 주장한다.

이를 뒷받침하듯 대마 사업은 미국 내 가장 급성장하는 고용시장 중 하나로 떠올라 작년 그 종사자 수만도 이미 211,000명에 이르렀다. 미국 전역 통틀어 셰프가 131,430명, 항공 엔지니어가 65,760명인 것에 견주어보면 폭발적 증가세가 금세 피부에 와닿는다. 시장조사 기관들은 대마 시장이 내년에는 134억 달러(약 14조 4천억 원) 규모까지 성장할 것으로 전망했다. 그야말로 볼품없는 풀 쪼가리 하나를 에워싸고 천문학적인 돈이 돌고 있는 셈이다.

이 같은 변화 무드는 뉴저지의 한인 커뮤니티 주위에서도 감지되고 있다. 의료용 대마초가 합법인 뉴저지주의 보건당국은 의료용 대마 환자수요가 작년 17,000명에서 올해 47,000명으로 276% 폭증한 것으로 추산하고 있다.

이에 비해 의료용 대마 배급소는 현재 6곳밖에 되지 않아 턱없이 부족한 실정이기 때문에 주 정부는 의료용 마리화나 재배 및 유통, 판매 라이선스를 추가 발급할 계획이라고 한다. 이의 일환으로 2017년 한인 밀집 지역인 '시카커스 메도우랜드 파크웨이'(Secaucus Meadowland Parkway)에 이어 최근 또 다른 한인 밀집 지역인 '리지필드'(Ridgefield)에도 마리화나 재배시설 건립이 허용되었다.

하지만 대마초 사업 전망이 모두 장밋빛인 것만은 아니다. 어디까지나 대마초는 엄연한 향정신성 마약으로 이를 합법화함으로써 야기되는 많은 부작용도 간과할 수 없기 때문이다. 대마초 흡입 후 환각 상태에서의 근무, 상대방 위해가 뻔히 예견되는 운전행위, 마약중독 예방교육과 치료에 따르는 비용문제 등도 무릇 사회적 합의가 필요한 부분들이다.

또 반대론자의 우려대로 대마초를 징검다리 삼아 더 강력한 마약으로 옮겨 탈 개연성과 대마초 남용으로 인한 연쇄 범죄 가능성도 배제할 수 없다.

연방법과의 충돌 문제도 시급히 풀어야 할 과제이다. 연방 정부는 주 정부의 합법화와 상관없이 여전히 대마초를 가장 강력한 규제가 적용되는 1등급 마약으로 규정하고 대마초의 재배, 수출입, 제조, 유통, 소지를 모두 엄격하게 금지하고 있다.

따라서 주 정부 승인을 받아 합법적으로 의료용 대마초를 재배하더라도 연방법상으로는 중범죄에 해당하여 법적 처벌이 불가피한 것이다. 다만 현재로서는 연방 법무부장관이 주 정부 승인 대마 사업자는 기소하지 않기로 결정함에 따라 문제 삼지 않는 것일 뿐 향후 정치환경에 따라 언제든지 변경될 수 있다고 보면 임시방편에 지나지 않는다.

사정이 이렇다 보니 상부 행정기관인 주 정부에서 허가한 사항을 카운티 및 시 정부 공무원들이 연방법에 배치된다며 사업부지 및 건물 사용 허가를 내주지 않는다든가 건물주가 임대 계약을 거부하는 등 혼선이 일선 현장에서 왕왕 일어나고 있다.

대마초 사업자들이 당면한 더 절박한 문제는 시중은행 거래가 원천 봉쇄돼있다는 점이다. 즉 연방법에 의해 규제를 받고 있는 은행들이 연방법상 불법인 대마초 관련 사업에 당연히 돈을 빌려주지도, 예금조차 받아주지 않기 때문이다. 대마초가 허용된 워싱턴이나 캘리포니아 같은 주에선 대마초로 번 캐시를 은행에 맡기지 못해 개인금고에 넣어두고 무장 경호원들이 지키고 있는 웃지 못할 진풍경이 그래서 벌어지는 것이다. 연방국가인 미합중국에서 일어날 법한 한 단면이다. (2019.8.12.)

마리화나 재배시설 <출처: Unsplash>
Marijuana greenhouse <source: Unsplash>

Economy and Society

The Marijuana Economics

An active debate about legalizing marijuana is taking place across the country. Medical marijuana is currently legal in more than two dozen states. In ten of them, including Massachusetts and Colorado, recreational use is permitted as well.

This new trend stands in stark contrast to the situation just a few years ago when cultivation, distribution, sale, and possession of marijuana were strictly forbidden, and marijuana offenders accounted for more than 40 percent of all arrests in the United States.

Proponents argue that legalization could help reduce the crime rate and the number of people arrested or prosecuted. This, in turn, will allow the governments to save the money it spends on police, prosecutors, and courts. In addition, by changing how we view marijuana, they claim that we could even create jobs and increase tax revenue.

Indeed, the marijuana industry has emerged as one of the fastest-growing job markets, employing about 221,000 people in 2018. The explosiveness of this job growth becomes readily apparent when we consider the fact that in the United States as a whole, the number of chefs and aircraft engineers are tabulated at about 131,430 and 65,760, respectively. Market researchers forecast that the marijuana market will be worth approximately $13.4 billion by 2020. An astronomical sum of money is being traded over some "weed."

These changes are felt around New Jersey's Korean-American community as well. For instance, in New Jersey, where medical marijuana is legal, the state's health department estimated that demand for medical marijuana has grown from 17,000 patients in 2018 to 47,000 in just one year – a 276 percent increase. With only six dispensaries in the state, there is a huge shortage and the state plans to issue more licenses for the cultivation, distribution, and sale of medical marijuana. They have issued permits to build a marijuana cultivation site in Secaucus Meadowland Parkway in 2017 and more recently, in Ridgefield as well. Both locations have a sizable Korean-American population.

However, not all marijuana business prospects are rosy. Critics worry that marijuana is a hallucinogen and its legalization could have many undesirable side effects. For example, there could be more incidents of working or driving while high, leading to more accidents. The cost of education and prevention will not be negligible, either. The opponents also point out that there is a possibility that marijuana use could lead to abusing other drugs or lead to other criminal activity.

There are conflicts with the federal law which must be resolved as well. Apart from the states' attempts to legalize it, the federal government still maintains marijuana on Schedule 1 of the Controlled Substances Act.

As such, it is subject to the strongest regulations. Under federal law, cultivating, importing, exporting, manufacturing, distributing, and possessing marijuana is strictly prohibited. Thus, even if marijuana is cultivated legally under the state law, it still constitutes a serious crime under federal law and criminal charges may be brought. Currently, such a scenario is unlikely as the Attorney General has decided not to bring charges against marijuana businesses that operate with the state government's approval. However, it is only a temporary measure and may change depending on the political climate.

Because of this conflict between the federal and state laws, marijuana businesses must deal with the confused county and municipal officials who sometimes refuse to give necessary building or business permits, saying that doing so would violate federal law. Some landlords refuse to enter into a lease for the same reason.

Perhaps a more pressing concern for marijuana business operators is the fact that they cannot engage in commercial banking transactions. Since federal law regulates banks, they cannot lend money or accept deposits from marijuana-related businesses, considered money generated from the illicit drug trade. This is why marijuana businesses in states where it is legal like Washington or California must put their cash in a private vault and keep it protected with armed guards. Marijuana economics highlights one of the limitations of federalism. (2019.8.12.)

콤마로 야기된 혼란

텍사스와 오하이오에서 발생한 연쇄 총기참사로 온 미국이 침통하다. 올 들어서만도 벌써 17번째 총기사건이라고 한다. 이런 사건이 터질 때마다 무슨 공식이나 되는 것처럼 민주당에선 총기 규제를 외치고, 공화당에선 헌법에 명시된 개인의 무기 소유권을 제한해서는 안 된다고 팽팽히 맞선다.

'전미총기협회'의 이야기를 듣거나 미국 독립전쟁이나 서부 개척시대 시절의 영화나 소설들을 보다 보면 마치 수정헌법 2조가 조지 워싱턴 때부터 개인의 무기 소유 및 휴대를 보장해주었던 것으로 오해하기 십상이지만 사실은 불과 10여 년 전 처음 '해석된 권리'라는 점이다.

수정헌법 2조는 "A well regulated Militia, being necessary to the security of a free State, the right of the people to keep and bear Arms, shall not be infringed"라는 짧은 한 문장으로 이루어져 있다. 우리가 잘 아는 "국민의 무기를 소유하고 휴대할 권리는, 침해될 수 없다"라는 문장 앞에 "잘 규율된 민병대는, 자유로운 주의 안보에 필수적이므로,"라는 구절이 있는데 세 번이나 사용된 콤마 때문에 법 조항의 해석이 쉽지 않다. 도대체 "침해될 수 없다"라는 술부의 주어가 "잘 규율

된 민병대"인지 "국민의 무기를 소유하고 휴대할 권리"인지 헷갈리기 때문이다.

따라서 이 문장의 주체를 '민병대'로 보게 되면 총기를 보유할 권리는 주의 안보를 위해 민병대에 속한 시민에게만 부여된 권리로 볼 수 있고, '국민의 권리'에 무게를 두고 해석하게 되면 폭압적인 정부에 맞서 민병대를 꾸릴 수 있도록 국민들은 무기를 소지할 권리를 갖는다고 볼 수도 있는 것이다.

미국 건국 이후 200여 년간 수정헌법 2조는 민병대에 속한 시민의 권리를 보장한다는 것이 법학자들 간의 다수학설이었는데 국가형태가 자리를 잡아가면서 군대가 민병대를 대체하자 이 권리 또한 점차 희미해져 갔던 것이다. 그러다가 이 조항은 2008년 결정된 '워싱턴 DC 대 헬러'(Washington D.C. v. Heller) 사건으로 일대 전환점을 맞게 된다.

워싱턴의 '카토 인스티튜트'(Cato Institute)의 변호사 '로버트 레비'(Robert Levi)는 총과는 별 상관없는 사람이었지만 평소 권총과 엽총 등 워싱턴의 총기류 규제법이 수정헌법 2조에 명시된 권리에 위배된다는 신념을 갖고 있었다. 헌법에 보장된 자유를 국가권력이 침해하여서는 안 된다고 믿는 열혈 자유당원이었던 그는 이 문제를 제기할 만한 적당한 소송 원고 당사자를 물색하던 중 중년의 백인 남성 '딕 헬러'(Dick Heller)와 만나게 된다.

당시 헬러는 연방대법원 별관에서 무장 경비원으로 일하던 사람이었는데 낮에는 권총을 휴대하다 워싱턴 법상 총을 개인적으로 휴대할 수 없어 매일 퇴근 시에는 총기와 탄환을 반납해야만 했다.

그는 레비 변호사가 원고를 찾아다니던 시점에 마침 총기 소유 신청을 했다가 거부당하고 자신의 사건을 맡아 줄 변호사를 찾고 있었던 것이다. 절묘한 타이밍에 양측의 이해가 딱 맞아떨어진 셈이었다.

미국의 '민속촌' Colonial Williamsburg에서 재연된 미국 독립전쟁 당시 민병대 행사(버지니아.2013)
Actors re-enacting Revolutionary War American militiamen at Colonial Williamsburg (Virginia)

헬러의 소송은 워싱턴 지방법원에서는 기각이 되고 연방대법원까지 올라가게 되었다. 연방대법원은 5대 4로 결국 국민의 권리에 무게를 둔 쪽으로 기울어졌는데 다수판결문은 뉴욕 퀸스 출신 '안토닌 스칼리아'(Antonin Scalia) 대법관에게 맡겨졌다.

사냥 마니아로 널리 알려진 스칼리아 대법관은 헌법 도입부의 민병대에 관한 내용은 '국민의 권리'에 대한 프롤로그에 해당한다고 해석했다.

따라서 총기 소지권은 민병대의 권리에 국한되지 않기 때문에 개인적 신변보호나 동물사냥 등 목적으로도 총을 소지할 수 있으며 자신과 가족을 보호하기 위해 가장 절실한 때인 집에 있을 때조차 권총과 엽총 등 총기 소지를 규제하는 워싱턴의 법은 위헌이라고 판단했다. 이렇게 해석함으로써 비로소 개인의 총기 소지권이 권리로 정당화된 것이다. (2019.8.28.)

Economy and Society

A Constitutional Confusion Caused by Commas

America is mourning the loss of life from the mass shootings in Texas and Ohio. In this year alone, there have been 17 mass shootings already. Politicians regurgitate a formulaic response when it happens: Democrats call for gun control, and Republicans don't want to see our constitutional right diminished.

When we listen to the National Rifle Association's propaganda, hear or read about the gunfights in the Western movies or how readily the volunteers brought their rifles during the Civil War, it is easy to believe that the Second Amendment has protected an individual's right to keep and bear arms since the time of George Washington. However, this right was interpreted for the first time only a decade ago.

The amendment is made up of a short sentence, "A well-regulated Militia, being necessary to the security of a free state, the right of the people to keep and bear Arms, shall not be infringed." In front of the well-known phrase, "the right of the people to keep and bear arms, shall not be infringed," is the phrase, "A well-regulated Militia, being necessary to the security of a free State." It is difficult to fathom the exact meaning of the constitutional amendment because three commas are sprinkled in random places. Is the subject of the phrase "shall not be infringed," a "well-regulated Militia" or "the right to keep and bear arms"?

In other words, if the subject of this confusing sentence is a "militia," then the right to bear arms belongs to the militiamen who maintain the state's security. If it's "the right of the people," then individuals would have the right to bear arms so that they may form a militia against a tyrannical government.

For more than 200 years since the founding of this nation, most legal scholars believed that the Second Amendment guaranteed the rights of militiamen. As the federal government became stronger, the right naturally faded into history as militias were replaced by a standing army. However, this amendment was given a new life through the 2008 case of Washington D.C. v. Heller.

Robert Levi, a lawyer for the Cato Institute in Washington, was a man who had little interest in guns. However, he believed that Washington D.C.'s gun laws regulating the possession of pistols and shotguns violated the Second Amendment. Levi was a passionate Libertarian who believed that the government should not infringe upon rights guaranteed by the Constitution. Thus, he set out to find a plaintiff for his cause and met a middle-aged Caucasian man named Dick Heller.

Heller worked as an armed guard at the Supreme Court Annex. Although he carried a gun during the day, he had to return it at the end of his shift because he was not allowed to have a gun in his home under Washington's laws. As Levi was searching for a plaintiff, Heller's application for a gun permit was rejected and he was looking for a lawyer who could file an appeal on his behalf. The timing was impeccable for both men.

Heller lost in the district court in Washington D.C. and the case was appealed to the Supreme Court. Ultimately, in a 5-4 decision, the Supreme Court interpreted the amendment as protecting an individual's right. Justice Antonin Scalia, a New Yorker from Queens, wrote the majority opinion.

Scalia, widely known to be a hunting enthusiast, found that the amendment's opening clause about militia was a prefatory clause that merely announced the purpose of the right. Since it was unconnected with service in a militia, he ruled that the right to keep and bear arms must be protected for traditionally lawful purposes, such as self-defense or hunting. He held that D.C.'s statute was unconstitutional since it improperly prevented people from keeping pistols and shotguns, even inside their own homes, arguably when the right is at its maximum strength. Based on this Supreme Court decision, an individual now has a constitutional right to bear arms, protected by three commas. (2019.8.28.)

총기 공개휴대를 금지하는 안내문(텍사스의 놀이공원에서)
Public announcement prohibiting open carry of a firearm (water park in Texas)

뉴욕시의 노숙자 주거지 지원법

지난 10월 5일 새벽 맨해튼 차이나타운의 바워리 스트리트 군데군데서 흩어져 자던 노숙자들이 묻지마 폭행을 당해 모두 4명이 숨지고 1명이 중상을 입은 끔찍한 사건이 발생했다. 이들에게 쇠 파이프를 휘두른 것으로 알려진 살인 용의자는 '로드리게즈 랜디 산토스'라는 20대 청년인데 그 역시 두 달 전 감옥에서 출소 후 바워리 지역에서 노숙자 생활을 해왔던 것으로 알려졌다. 그는 현재 구속되어 재판을 기다리고 있는 상태다.

이 사건은 날로 심각해져 가는 뉴욕시의 노숙자 문제를 다시 한번 상기시켜 주는 계기가 되었는데 통계에 따르면 2019년 8월 현재 뉴욕시 관할 노숙자 보호소에는 약 62,000명의 노숙자가 투숙하고 있다고 한다. 이 숫자는 50,287명을 수용하는 양키스 구장을 채우고도 남는 숫자로 1930년대의 경제대공황 이후 최고치라고 한다. 보호소가 아닌 길거리에서 잠을 청하는 노숙자의 수도 3,600명 정도 되는 것으로 '홈리스연대'는 추정하고 있다.

미국 전체에서 노숙자 수는 캘리포니아주가 제일 많으나 대도시 단위에서는 뉴욕시가 단연 으뜸이다. 두 지역에 유독 노숙자가 많은 이유는 두 곳 다 집세 등 기본 생활비가 비싸 실직 등으로 수입이 끊어질 경우 쉽게 길거리로 내몰릴 수밖에 없는 환경인 데다 사람들이 붐비는 대도시여서 구걸 행위가 용이한 것도 한 원인으로 추측된다.

특히 뉴욕시는 혹독한 겨울이 있어 노숙하기에 매력적인 곳은 아니나 오래전에 만들어진 노숙자주거지지원법 때문에 사람들이 몰려오는 것으로 보고 있다.

이 지원법은 이번 노숙자 살인 사건으로부터 정확히 40년 전, 1979년 10월 '칼라한 대 캐리'(*Callahan v. Carey*) 사건을 계기로 제정되었다.

당시 26세의 '로버트 헤이스'(Robert Hayes)는 NYU 법대를 졸업하고 월가의 유명 로펌에서 일하던 전도유망한 변호사였다. 헤이스는 NYU 재학 당시 학교 앞 워싱턴 스퀘어 공원의 많은 노숙자를 보고 그들을 도와줄 방법이 없을까 궁리하던 중 마침 같은 문제로 고민하던 두 명의 콜럼비아대생 동지를 만나게 되었다.

의기투합한 이들 3명의 청년들은 노숙자들과 인터뷰 등을 통해 그들을 돕는 가장 확실하고 항구적인 방법은 법률에 바탕을 둔 제도적 지원 방법이라 판단하고 세 명의 노숙자를 앞세워 맨해튼 소재 주 법원에 당시 뉴욕주지사 '휴 캐리'(Hugh Carey)를 상대로 소송을 제기하게 된다. 대표 원고는 53세의 '로버트 칼라한'(Robert Callahan)이었는데 공교롭게도 칼라한 역시 이번 살인 사건이 일어난 바워리 출신의 노숙자였다.

뉴욕주 헌법 17조 1항은 "어려운 사람들에 대한 보살핌과 지원은 공적 관심사이기 때문에 의회 결정에 따라 뉴욕주 및 그 하위 기관은 보호책을 마련하여야 한다"라고 명시하고 있는데 뉴욕시가 노숙자들에게 거주지를 제공하지 않는 것은 이 조항에 위배되는 것이라고 헤이스 변호사는 주장했다.

그는 뉴욕주지사와 시장에게 바워리의 노숙자들을 위한 침대 750개 규모의 보호소를 제공할 것을 요구하는 한편 재판장에겐 추운 겨울이 오기 전까지 신속하게 판결을 내려줄 것을 주문했다.

최후 변론이 끝나고 본격적인 겨울을 앞둔 12월 5일, '앤드루 타일러' 판사는 뉴욕주 헌법에 따라 뉴욕시는 바워리의 노숙자들에게 숙식을 제공할 의무가 있다는 판결을 내리게 되었고, 이 판결은 이후 뉴욕 시민들의 주거권을 보장하는 중요한 지침으로 자리 잡게 되었다.

인간의 주거 문제는 세계인권선언문에도 명시된 주요 인권 중 하나이지만 미국에서 이처럼 법적으로 그 권리를 보장해 주는 곳은 워싱턴 D.C.와 매사추세츠주, 뉴욕시 등 세 곳밖에 없다. (2019.11.6)

NYU 캠퍼스
N.Y.U. Campus

Economy and Society

NYC's Homeless Housing Law

In the early hours of October 5, four homeless men sleeping around Bowery Street in Manhattan's Chinatown were found dead. A fifth was found seriously injured. The murder suspect is Rodriguez "Randy" Santos, and he is alleged to have wielded an iron pipe in his killings. A man in his twenties, Santos was reportedly living on the streets around Bowery since his release from jail two months ago. He is in custody and awaits trial.

This incident was a somber reminder of the ever-growing homelessness problem in New York City. According to data, as of August 2019, approximately 62,000 people are staying in the city's homeless shelters. This is more than enough people to fill up the Yankee Stadium, which accommodates 50,287 people. It's reported to be the highest number since the Great Depression in the 1930s. There is an estimated number of an additional 3,600 people sleeping on the street.

California has the largest homeless population in America. However, New York City tops the list among the large metropolitan areas. Such a high number of homeless people in both places may be explained by the expensive living and housing costs. If there's a sudden loss of income, people can quickly lose the roof over their heads. Also, there are more people in these areas, making panhandling more convenient for some. Finally, although New York City is a harsh place to be without a home compared to California because of its cold weather, it may still be a popular destination for the legal right to shelter recognized a few decades ago.

This right stems from Callahan v. Carey, a case decided precisely 40 years before the Bowery Street murders, in October 1979.

Robert Hayes, an NYU Law graduate, was a promising 26-year-old lawyer working at a prominent Wall Street law firm. When Hayes was a law student, he saw many homeless people at Washington Square Park in front of the NYU campus and often wondered if there were ways to help them. Then, he met two students from Columbia University who had the same question.

The trio conducted numerous interviews with the homeless and decided that the most concrete and permanent way to help them was to provide institutional support based on the law. On behalf of three homeless men, they filed a lawsuit against New York's governor at the time, Hugh Carey, in Manhattan Supreme Court. The lead plaintiff was Robert Callahan, 53, who was also a homeless man from Bowery Street.

New York State Constitution's Article 17, Clause 1, states, "The aid, care and support of the needy are public concerns and shall be provided by the state and by such of its subdivisions, and in such manner and by such means, as the legislature may from time to time determine." Hayes argued that the failure to provide shelter to the homeless amounted to violating this constitutional right. Accordingly, he asked the court to mandate the governor and New York City mayor to provide a 750-bed shelter for the homeless from Bowery. He also requested an expedited ruling from the judge before winter.

Following legal arguments, Judge Andrew Tyler rendered his ruling on December 5 before the cold winter set in. He held that the government was obligated to provide adequate shelter to the homeless people from the Bowery section under the New York State constitution. This was a watershed moment for ensuring the New Yorkers' housing rights.

The right to housing is a major human right and recognized in the Universal Declaration of Human Rights. However, only three cities in the United States, Washington D.C., Boston and New York, legally guarantee it. (2019.11.6)

악플처벌 vs. 표현의 자유

지난 10월 14일 한국의 걸그룹 f(X) 출신 탤런트 설리가 25세의 꽃다운 나이에 세상을 떠났다. 인터넷의 악플(악성 댓글)이 그녀가 극단적 선택을 한 직접적 원인이었던 것으로 알려졌는데 이 악플들은 제삼자 입장에서 읽어보더라도 차마 견디기 어려운 인격 모욕적 표현들이라 당사자가 받았을 정신적 고통에 연민의 정을 느낀다.

악플로 인한 우울증으로 생을 마감한 한국 연예인들로는 설리 말고도 한때 국민배우 반열에 올랐던 최진실과 가수 유니, 탤런트 정다빈, 그룹 샤이니의 종현 등이 더 있다. 설리의 죽음을 계기로 더 이상 악플에 의한 희생을 막기 위해 한국에선 인터넷 실명제 및 악플 처벌을 골자로 하는 일명 '설리법' 제정 움직임이 확산되고 있다고 한다.

미국 역시 인터넷의 혐오 발언뿐 아니라 한발 더 나아가 학살 차원의 끔찍한 인종 혐오 범죄도 빈발하고 있다. 백인우월주의를 자처하는 중년 남성이 작년 10월 피츠버그시의 유대인 회당에서 총격전을 벌여 유대교인 11명을 숨지게 한 사건이나 올 8월 또 다른 백인 청년이 텍사스주 엘파소 월마트에서 히스패닉계 쇼핑객을 상대로 무차별 총기를 난사한 사건 등이 다 이런 범주의 혐오 범죄라고 볼 수 있다.

총기범들의 행적을 거슬러 올라가 보면 처음에는 페이스북이나 트위터 같은 사회적 네트워크나 8Chan과 갭 등의 인터넷 커뮤니티에서 올라오는 혐오 글들을 동질감에서 읽기 시작했다. 그러다 사용자 취향을 근거로 전산 알고리즘에 의해 자동 생성되는 가짜 뉴스나 악플 등에 중독되어 차츰 균형감각과 이성을 잃고 급기야 나하고 다른 부류의 사람에 대한 증오심으로 변해 범행에 이른 것으로 알려지고 있다. 결국 인터넷의 혐오 발언들이 범행의 발단이었던 것이다.

이처럼 혐오 글들이 문제가 되자 검열을 실시하라고 페이스북이나 트위터에 사회적 압력이 가중되고 있지만 큰 기대를 걸기에는 한계가 있어 보인다. 왜냐하면 미국 연방 수정헌법 1조에 "연방의회는 종교의 자유를 비롯 언론, 출판의 자유나 국민이 평화로이 집회할 수 있는 권리 등을 제한하는 법률을 제정할 수 없다"고 규정하고 있기 때문이다.

이 수정헌법 1조는 영국 왕실의 폭정에 맞서 독립을 이끌어 내고 현대식 민주주의를 꽃피워낸 미국인들에게 목숨만큼이나 중요하게 생각하는 권리 중의 하나이기도 하다.

궁여지책으로 페이스북의 CEO '마크 저커버그'(Mark Zuckerberg)는 올해 4월 혐오 표현들을 어떤 식으로 검열해야 할지 기준법을 제정해달라고 미국 의회에다 공을 넘기려 했다가 대중의 격렬한 항의를 받고 불과 몇 달 후인 지난 10월엔 "정부는 표현의 자유를 규제해선 안 된다"고 태도를 바꾸고 있다.

표현의 자유는 시대상에 따라 그 적용기준이 조금씩 변천되어왔는데 건국 초창기에는 공공의 안녕에 '나쁜 영향'을 끼칠 수 있는 표현들을 주로 규제대상으로 삼았다. 그러다가 1900년대 두 차례의 세계대전 시에는 병역기피 조장을, 미국 내 공산주의 확산 과정에서는 공산화 지지 등 공익에 실질적인 폐해가 예상되는 '명백한 현

총격이 일어난 엘 파소 월마트에 세워진 십자가(텍사스 주)
Crosses at the El Paso Walmart where the mass shooting occurred (Texas)

Tree of Life 유대인 회당 앞에 놓여진 헌화(피츠버그)
Flowers in front of the Tree of Life synagogue (Pittsburgh)

재의 위험성'에 대한 규제로 법이 바뀌었다.

　이 법은 다시 1969년부터 '임박한 무법 행동'에 대한 선동으로 적용 대상이 바뀌어 오늘날까지 내려오고 있다. 즉 이 법에 따르면 "흑인들을 아프리카로 돌려보내야 한다"든가 "미국을 백인들만의 나라로 만들어야 한다"는 식의 표현 등은 임박한 무법 행동을 부추기는 표현으로는 볼 수 없어 제재나 처벌을 할 수 없다는 게 사법당국의 판단인 것이다. 따라서 악플 부류의 혐오발언들에 대한 처벌도 현행법상으로는 불가한 실정이다.

　영리적인 인터넷에 자정 능력을 기대할 수 없다면 시대에 따라 탄력적으로 변해온 수정헌법 1조에 대한 해석이 나날이 도를 더해가는 혐오 표현과 혐오 범죄 양상에 부응하여 새로운 판례로 바뀔 때가 된 것은 아닌지 생각해 본다. (2019.11.20)

Economy and Society

Regulating Online Hate Speech vs. Freedom of Expression

Sulli, a 25-year-old South Korean actress and former member of the girl group f(X), died on October 14, 2019. She reportedly committed suicide as a result of online hate speech. Personal insults hurled at the actress online were so nasty that it would give anyone the shudders. One can only imagine the horrible mental pain and anguish she must have endured.

Other than Sulli, many other Korean celebrities took their own lives because of online hate speech: actress Choi Jin-sil, singer U;Nee, actress Jung Da-bin and Jonghyun of boy band Shinee. The so-called "Sulli Act" has been proposed to prevent suicides and is gaining momentum in Korea. It eliminates anonymity on the internet and provides a way to punish people who post malicious comments online.

Online hate speech poses a serious threat in the United States as well. What's more, it has also arguably led to racially-motivated massacres. For instance, in October 2018, there was a shooting by a middle-aged white man at a Jewish synagogue in Pittsburgh, which resulted in 11 people being killed. The Walmart shooting in El Paso, Texas, in August 2019 by a young white man also appears to fall into that category.

From the police investigations behind the shooters' motive, it was revealed that they were reading hateful posts on social media networks like Facebook and Twitter or internet boards like 8Chan and Gab. It also appeared that they were eventually consumed by poisonous hatred towards the people who were different from them. Hateful online comments destructively affected these gunmen's actions.

As online hate speech has become a major social issue, pressure is mounting on companies like Facebook and Twitter to conduct self-censorship. However, censorship is unlikely to result because of the First Amendment, which provides, "Congress shall make no law respecting an establishment of religion, or prohibiting the free exercise thereof, or abridging the freedom of speech, or of the press; or the right of the people peaceably to assemble." This is one of the key rights of the Americans who won independence from the oppressive British crown and established the modern democracy.

To avoid public pressure, Facebook's CEO, Mark Zuckerberg, tried to pass the responsibility to Congress in April of this year by asking it to enact laws establishing the standard on how to censor hate speech. However, it was met with harsh public criticism. A few months later, he changed his position and urged the government to "respect people's right to express themselves."

It is also worth noting that freedom of expression has undergone several transformations throughout the years, depending on the pressures of the time. In the Republic's early days, speech that had a "bad tendency" to cause or incite illegal activities could be restricted. This standard changed to the "clear and present danger" test in the 1900s. It was brought about in part by the two world wars and the red scare. Any speech that encouraged draft dodging or sympathy towards Communists needed to be regulated.

The law changed again in 1969. Under the latest iteration, incitement for "imminent lawless action" is regulated. Under this law, statements like "we should send all black people back to Africa" or "America must be a white country" cannot be regulated as they do not incite an "imminent lawless action." Similarly, most of the hateful comments on the internet cannot be punished under the standard.

If the tech companies cannot weed out hate speech, then it may be time for another transformation of the First Amendment to deal with the ever-increasing number of hate crimes and hateful comments. Indeed, this critical right has proven its resilience by adapting to the changing times. (2019.11.20)

'뜨거운 담론 낙태'

법률적 관점에서 본다면 사람이라는 생명체는 과연 어느 시점부터 사람이라고 봐야 할까? 엄마 뱃속에서 심장 박동이 감지되는 순간부터일까? 아니면 엄마의 자궁 밖에서 자생능력이 부여되는 순간부터일까?

상원에서 자신의 탄핵 재판이 한창 진행 중임에도 불구하고 트럼프 대통령은 태연스럽게도 지난 1월 24일 현직 대통령으로선 최초로 워싱턴 D.C.에서 개최된 '생명을 위한 행진'(March for Life)에 참석해 낙태 반대 연설을 했다.

이 행사는 미국 최대 규모의 낙태 반대 운동으로 1973년 '로 대 웨이드'(*Roe v. Wade*) 사건을 통해 낙태를 허용한 대법원의 판결에 반발해 1974년부터 매년 1월에 열리고 있다.

로 대 웨이드는 지금으로부터 50여 년 전 당시 임신 상태였던 21세의 '노마 맥코비'(Norma McCorvey)가 텍사스의 낙태금지법이 연방헌법에 보장된 '사생활의 권리'에 어긋난다며 댈러스 지방검사 '헨리 웨이드'를 상대로 제기한 위헌소송 명칭이다. 맥코비가 첨예하게 대립하고 있던 낙태 반대자들로부터의 신변보호를 위해 '제인 로'라는 가명을 사용했기 때문에 이런 명칭이 붙게 됐다.

소송 결과 대법원은 임신 6개월까지는 임산부에게 중절 수술을 선택할 수 있는 권리를 헌법에서 보장해준 것이라고 해석하고 맥코비의 손을 들어주었다.

다만 7개월부터 출산까지의 기간인 임신 3기부턴 그 권리가 제한된다고 봤는데 이유는 출산 직전 3개월간은 태아가 자궁 밖에서도 생존 가능성이 높기 때문에 그때부터는 태아를 독립적인 생명체로 보아 모태와 따로 보호되고 존중되어야 한다는 것이었다.

지난 50여 년 동안 그 어떤 대법원 판례보다 거센 풍파를 견뎌낸 로 대 웨이드였지만 트럼프가 2018년 '브렛 캐버너'(Brett Kavanaugh)를 대법관으로 임명함으로써 풍전등화와 같은 처지에 놓이게 되었다.

그간 미국의 대법원은 보수 대법관 4명과 진보 대법관 4명 사이의 팽팽한 균형과 대립 속에 캐버너의 전임자인 '앤서니 캐네디' 대법관의 사건별 태도에 따라 대법원의 방향이 결정되었으나 확실한 보수성향인 캐버너의 등장으로 대법원이 보수 쪽으로 기울게 됨으로써 50년 만에 비로소 로 대 웨이드도 뒤집힐 수 있는 전기가 마련된 것이다.

캐버너의 등판을 손꼽아 기다리고나 있었다는 듯이 로 대 웨이드를 뒤집기 위한 낙태금지 입법 움직임이 미국 전역에 요원의 불길처럼 번지고 있다. 한 통계에 따르면 캐버너로 대법관이 교체된 이후 공화당 우세의 많은 주에서 낙태를 금지하거나 여성의 낙태권을 제한하는 법안이 무려 400여 개나 상정되었다고 한다.

그중 조지아와 켄터키 주에서 제정된 법이 특히 눈길을 끄는데 이는 태아의 심장 박동이 감지되는 순간 즉 임신 6주 경부터 낙태를 금지하는 것으로 돼 있다. 50년 전과 달리 사람이란 생명체의 태동을 태아의 심장이 뛰기 시작하는 시점부터로 시기를 훨씬 앞당겨 법으로 정의한 것이다.

이런 움직임 가운데 낙태와 관련하여 캐버너 대법관이 가장 먼저 심리하게 될 사건으로 '준 메디컬 대(對) 기'(June Medical Services v. Gee) 사건이 기다리고 있다. 올 봄쯤 대법원의 판결이 나올 예정인 이 사건은 2014년에 제정된 루이지애나주의 낙태병원 입원 시설 확충관련법이 여성의 낙태권 보장에 크게 미흡하다고 해서 낙태 옹호론자들이 주 정부를 상대로 제기한 소송이다.

캐버너 대법관의 낙태 성향을 가늠할 수 있는 첫 판결이 어떻게 나올지 이미 법안을 통과시켜놓고도 로 대 웨이드 판결에 배치된다는 이유로 집행금지 명령 상태에 놓여있는 조지아, 켄터키를 비롯 앨라배마주 등 미국 전역에서 뜨거운 관심을 가지고 그 결과를 지켜보고 있다. (2020.2.12)

결과: 2020.6.29. 결정된 '준 메디컬' 사건에서 연방대법원은 많은 사람들의 예상을 뒤엎고 5대4로 루이지애나 주법이 여성의 낙태권을 침해한다며 낙태 찬성론자들의 손을 들어주었다. 예상대로 캐버너 대법관은 낙태 반대편에 섰지만 보수 성향 대법원장 로버츠가 진보 성향 대법관 편에 가담함으로써 낙태 금지 시도는 무위에 그쳤다.

그러나 2022.6.24. 연방대법원은 '돕스 대 잭슨 여성보건기구'(Dobbs v. Jackson) 사건에서 6대 3으로 " '로' 사건을 위시한 낙태권 사건들이 사법적 권한 남용에 해당할 정도로 치명적 오류가 있어 반드시 기각되어야 한다"고 밝히고, 낙태 불법화 여부를 각 주의 판단에 맡기도록 결정함으로써 엄청난 후폭풍을 예고했다.

'생명을 위한 행진'(워싱턴D.C.2020)
'March for Life' (Washington D.C.)

Economy and Society

The Abortion Debate

Legally speaking, when can we say that a fetus is a living human being? Is it when its heart begins to beat or when it can survive on its own outside of the mother's womb?

While his Senate impeachment trial was in full swing, President Trump appeared nonchalantly at the "March for Life" rally in Washington D.C. on January 24, 2020, to give an anti-abortion speech. It is the nation's largest anti-abortion event, held every January since 1974 to protest the Supreme Court's 1973 decision Roe v. Wade that allowed abortion. This was the first time that a sitting president spoke at the event.

Roe v. Wade began its life almost 50 years ago when a 21-year-old pregnant woman, Norma McCorvey, filed a lawsuit against Henry Wade in his capacity as the Dallas County District Attorney. McCorvey claimed that Texas' abortion ban violated the "right to privacy" guaranteed by the Federal Constitution. McCorvey used the alias "Jane Roe" to protect her identity from pro-life activists.

The Supreme Court ruled in McCorvey's favor and held that the Constitution guaranteed pregnant women a right to choose abortion until the end of the second trimester. However, the Court limited this right in the last trimester, as the fetus was more likely to survive outside the womb. At this point, the Court held, the fetus' life should be protected and respected separately from the mother.

Since then, Roe v. Wade has withstood harsher treatment than just about any other Supreme Court decision in the last 50 years. But its fate looks dismal after President Trump's appointment of Brett Kavanaugh to the Supreme Court in 2018.

Before Justice Kavanaugh's appointment, the high court maintained a delicate balance between four liberal and four conservative justices. The swing vote cast by Justice Anthony Kennedy, Kavanaugh's predecessor, often decided the cases. With Kavanaugh's elevation, there is a reliable conservative vote and the stage has been set for the first time in 50 years to overturn Roe.

Unsurprisingly, since Justice Kavanaugh's appointment, countless anti-abortion laws aimed at overturning the Supreme Court's precedent have sprung up throughout the country. According to one estimate, more than 400 laws banning or curtailing women's abortion rights have been introduced in Republican-controlled state legislatures.

Among them, the laws passed in Georgia and Kentucky are particularly noteworthy. They make it illegal to obtain an abortion in the state once the fetus' heartbeat can be detected, which may be as early as six weeks into pregnancy.

This is a marked departure from the 50-year-old ruling and recognizes a human life at a much earlier stage in the pregnancy.

Against this background, June Medical Services v. Gee is poised to be the first case to be heard by Justice Kavanaugh. In this case, pro-choice activists have filed a lawsuit alleging that Louisiana's state law requiring doctors to have admitting privileges at medical facilities unjustifiably restricted women's abortion rights. The Supreme Court's decision is expected in the spring.

How Justice Kavanaugh decides this case will shed light on his judicial philosophy on abortion issues. For obvious reasons, many are anxiously awaiting the result, including in states like Georgia, Kentucky and Alabama – where temporary injunctions have prevented their anti-abortion laws from becoming effective because they violate Roe v. Wade. (2020.2.12)

Outcome: June Medical was decided on June 29, 2020. Contrary to many people's predictions, the Supreme Court held in a 5-4 decision that Louisiana's law illegally violated the women's right to obtain abortion. Justice Kavanaugh dissented in the decision, as expected, but Chief Justice Roberts joined the progressive wing of the Court and the attempt to ban abortion failed.

However, in a different case decided on June 24, 2022, the Supreme Court ruled in a 6-3 decision that Roe and its progeny "must be overruled" because they were "egregiously wrong" and so "damaging" that they amounted to "an abuse of judicial authority." The Court left the issue of banning abortion to state governments, setting the stage for yet another set of court cases.

우주시대 개막과 국제조약

미국의 민간기업 '스페이스X'가 제작한 유인 우주선 '크루 드래건'이 지난 5월 30일 플로리다주 케네디 우주센터에서 트럼프와 미국우주위원장인 펜스 부통령이 참관한 가운데 성공적으로 발사되었다. 스페이스X는 전기차로 유명한 테슬라의 창업자 '일론 머스크'(Elon Musk)가 2024년을 시작으로 장차 인류 100만 명을 화성에 이주시킨다는 원대한 꿈을 내걸고 2002년에 설립한 우주기업이다.

두 명의 비행사를 태운 크루 드래건은 19시간을 날아 지상 400km에 설치된 축구장 크기의 국제우주정거장(ISS)에 안전하게 도킹하였고, 비행사들은 여기서 수개월 정도 연구업무 등을 수행하다 지구로 귀환할 예정이다.

크루 드래건의 발사 성공은 러시아와 미국, 중국 등 3개국 위주로 국가 차원에서만 독점해오던 우주사업 영역이 민간으로까지 확대된 것을 의미한다. 아울러 9년 전 미국의 우주왕복선 퇴역 이후 미국 우주인과 화물을 우주정거장에 날라준 운송료로 연간 5천억 원씩을 챙기던 러시아의 주요 수입원이 미국기업 금고로 자연스레 이전되는 것을 뜻하기도 한다.

스페이스X 외에도 항공기 제조사 보잉과 아마존 창업자 '제프 베이조스'가 이끄는 '블루 오리진', 영국의 우주회사 '버진 오빗' 등 세계 굴지의 기업들이 우주사업에 본격적으로 뛰어들고 있다고 보면 공상과학 영화에서나 나옴 직한 우주시대 개막이 그리 멀지 않은 것으로 보인다.

이를 반영하듯 소행성에 매장된 천문학적 규모의 백금 등 광석을 채굴하기 위해 '플래니터리 리소시스'와 같은 신종 광물회사가 몇 년 전 미국에 생겨났는가 하면 작년 12월 트럼프 대통령은 세계 최초로 미 우주군을 창설하기도 했다.

이처럼 우주 환경은 급변하고 있지만 관련 국제법규는 까마득한 과거에 머물러 있는 것으로 보인다. 왜냐하면 기존의 우주 법규가 유인 우주선이나 인공위성을 발사할 정도의 경제력과 기술력을 겸비한 극소수 나라에만 해당되다 보니 여기에 끼지 못하는 다른 나라들은 아예 관심조차 없었기 때문이다.

따라서 지금까지 마련된 국제조약이라곤 '닐 암스트롱'이 1969년 인류 최초로 달에 착륙하기 전에 체결된 우주조약(1967년)을 비롯하여 우주항공사의 구조 및 외기권에 발사된 물체의 회수에 관한 협정(1968년), 우주물체에 의하여 발생한 손해에 대한 국제책임에 관한 협약(1972년), 외기권에 발사된 물체의 등록에 관한 협약(1976년), 달에 관한 협정(1979년) 등 5개 조약이 전부다. 이들 조약의 요지는 천체를 포함, 외기권의 탐색과 이용은 모든 국가의 이익을 위하여 행해져야 하며 어떤 국가도 독점적 영유권을 주장할 수 없다는 것이다. 또 달을 비롯 모든 천체는 평화적 목적을 위해서만 이용되어야 하며 군사적 이용은 일절 금지된다.

이 조약을 바탕으로 우주 강국들은 지난 반세기 동안 별다른 분쟁 없이 소위 그들만의 리그를 맘껏 누려왔지만 민간 우주시대가 성큼 다가옴으로써 새로운 우주 질서를 위한 국제사회의 합의가 시급하게 됐다. 왜냐하면 민간기업과 개인이 소행성 자원을 채굴하고 소유할 수 있도록 미국이 2015년에 제정한 '상업적 우주발사 경쟁력법'(CSLCA)이 독점적 우주 영유권을 배척키로 한 조약에 어긋난다며 다른 나라들이 시비를 걸고 있기 때문이다.

　하지만 개인 재산권의 보장 없이 어느 누가 천문학적인 돈과 목숨을 걸고 우주를 개발할 것인지 입장 바꿔 생각해보면 미국만 탓할 수도 없는 노릇이다. 이런 문제해결과 더불어 우주법 위반자를 단속할 국제기구와 국제기업 간의 각종 분쟁 해결을 위한 국제법원 설치, 우주여행과 소행성 개발에 따른 환경오염과 같은 문제들도 지구촌 모든 나라가 모여 우주적 합의를 끌어내야 할 부분이다. (2020.6.17.)

우주선　발사 장면 (NASA)
Spacecraft launch

Economy and Society

Birth of the Space Age and International Treaties

On May 30, 2020, a manned spaceship named the Crew Dragon was successfully launched from the Kennedy Space Center in Florida. The spacecraft was manufactured by a private space exploration company, SpaceX. President Trump and Vice President Pence, who also serves as the head of the U.S. National Space Council, were in attendance. SpaceX was established in 2002 by Elon Musk, the founder of Tesla, a leading electric car company. SpaceX's mission is to transport 1 million people to Mars and colonize it starting in 2024.

With two astronauts onboard, Crew Dragon flew for 19 hours. Then, it docked successfully with the International Space Station, a station that is the size of a soccer field flying at about 400 km above the ground. The astronauts are expected to perform research for several months before returning to Earth.

The successful launch of Crew Dragon means that the business of space travel, which has been monopolized by Russia, the United States, and China, has been expanded into the private sector. It also means that Russia will not be collecting

500 billion won each year from the United States. It has been a lucrative business for Russia to transport American astronauts and cargo to and from the space station since the American space shuttle's retirement nine years ago. Now, with the new capabilities, income from this business will naturally be transferred to the coffers of American corporations.

Besides SpaceX, other major corporations from around the world have jumped two feet into the space business. There are Blue Origin, led by the airplane manufacturer Boeing and Amazon founder Jeff Bezos, and a British space company, Virgin Orbit. Also, a few years ago, a space mineral company called Planetary Resources was created in America to mine astronomical amounts of minerals like platinum buried in the asteroids. Finally, President Trump established the world's first Space Force. With these new developments, the space age that we've only imagined in sci-fi movies doesn't seem distant.

Although our relationship with space is rapidly changing, governing international treaties and regulations have stayed behind in the years past. In many ways, this is natural because only the countries with enough wealth and technology to launch manned spacecraft and satellites would care about what happens up there. The other countries are more concerned with what happens down here.

As such, there are only five international treaties in existence: the Outer Space Treaty (1967), which was signed before Neil Armstrong took "one small step for man" on the moon in 1969; the Agreement on the Rescue of Astronauts, the Return of Astronauts and the Return of Objects Launched into Outer Space (1968); the Convention on International Liability for Damage Caused by Space Objects

(1972); the Convention on Registration of Objects Launched into Outer Space (1976); and the Agreement Governing the Activities of States on the Moon and Other Celestial Bodies (1979). The main aim and goal behind these treaties is to ensure that exploration of space and use of celestial bodies must be done for all humankind. No country should be allowed to stake an exclusive claim of property or sovereignty. In addition, these treaties further provide that all celestial bodies, including the moon, must be used for peaceful purposes. Military use is to be strictly prohibited.

Certainly, these treaties have provided relative peace among the space-faring superpowers for the past half a century. However, now that the age of private space travel has come, there is an urgent need for a new international agreement. For instance, several countries are already claiming that the U.S. Commercial Space Launch Competitiveness Act (CSLCA), enacted in 2015 by the American government to allow private companies and individuals to engage in asteroid mining, violates the treaty that bans exclusive ownership.

At the same time, without any guarantees of personal ownership and pecuniary benefit, who will risk unimaginable sums of money and human lives to develop the celestial resources? In that sense, it's hard to fault the United States. In addition to finding solutions to these problems, there must be international agencies to prosecute violators of space laws, courts to adjudicate international corporate disputes, and an agreement on how to mitigate and manage environmental pollution caused by space travel and the development of asteroids. It is time for a cosmic agreement. (2020.6.17.)

반독점법과 마주한 4 빅테크

     지난 7월 29일, 연방하원 법사위 소속 반독점소위는 아마존과 애플, 페이스북, 구글의 CEO들을 상대로 청문회를 열었다. 대형 정보기술(IT) 기업을 '빅테크(Big Tech)'라 칭하는데 부득이 코로나-19로 인해 각자 사무실에서 온라인 화상채팅 형식으로 진행하긴 했어도 이들 빅테크 CEO 4명을 의회로 한자리에 불러 모은 것은 처음 있는 일이다.

  이번 청문회는 지난해 6월 반독점 주무 기관인 미국 법무부와 연방거래위원회(FTC, Federal Trade Commission)가 공동으로 빅테크의 위반행위 조사에 착수했다는 보도 이후 1년 넘게 진행해 온 의회 차원에서의 반독점법 입법 마무리 단계로 보인다.

  이번 청문회에 소환된 회사들은 공통적으로 막강한 시장 지배력을 무기로 공정한 경쟁을 저해했다는 비판을 받고 있다. 대표적 불공정행위로, 아마존은 온라인 상점에 입점한 판매업자의 인기 상품을 자체 브랜드로 바꿔 우선적으로 노출시킨 게 도마 위에 올랐고, 페이스북은 경쟁사인 인스타그램을 인수한 게 의혹을 샀다. 애플은 앱 개발자들로부터 30%의 높은 수수료를 받았다는 점이, 구글은 검색 결과에 경쟁사보다 자신들의 광고가 먼저 나오게 했다는 점 등이 각각 문제점으로 부각되었다.

오랜 시장자본주의 역사를 가진 미국의 반독점 관련 법률은 130여 년 전으로 거슬러 올라간다. 1890년에 독점행위를 규제하기 위해 처음으로 제정된 '셔먼법'(Sherman Act)을 시작으로 1914년에 '클레이턴법'(Clayton Act)과 '연방거래위원회법'(Federal Trade Commission Act)이 제정되었다. 이들 법에 의하면 경쟁업체를 약화시키는 카르텔 형성과 인수합병 제한, 시장을 왜곡시킬 수 있는 가격 담합행위 등을 금지하고, 위반 시 민사소송뿐 아니라 과징금 부과와 형사처벌, 경우에 따라 기업의 강제 분할도 명령할 수 있다. 이를 감시·감독하기 위한 연방거래위원회도 이때 설치되었다.

석유왕 록펠러의 스탠더드 오일을 비롯 아메리칸 토바코 담배회사, 통신기업 AT&T 등 미국 굴지의 회사들이 이 법에 희생되어 강제로 분할되거나 역사의 뒤안길로 사라졌다. 빌 게이츠의 마이크로소프트사도 1990년대 윈도우에 웹브라우저 익스플로러를 끼워 팔다 여기에 해당하여 1심에서 회사분할 명령을 받았다가 항소심에서 기각됨으로써 가까스로 회사를 지켜낼 수 있었다.

반독점법 적용은 시대 상황이나 사안을 대하는 판사들의 가치관 등에 따라 일률적으로 기준을 정하기 어렵다는 데 고민이 있다. 이러한 이유로 셔먼법 제정 초반에는 불합리한 경쟁제한 행위만을 불법으로 간주하는 '합리의 원칙'을 적용하다가 과연 '합리적인' 기준이란 게 무엇이냐 하는 것을 두고 설왕설래 여러 부작용이 나타나자 1970년대에 소위 '소비자 복지'의 침해 여부가 판례에 등장했다. 즉 기업의 독점행위로 인해 소비자가 피해를 입었는지를 판단기준으로 삼는 것이다.

청문회에 나온 CEO들은 이런 법적 기준을 염두에 두고, 자신들은 독점적 기업이 아니며 국내외 시장의 무한경쟁에서 살아남기 위해 끊임없는 혁신으로 미국의 경제

발전뿐 아니라 미국인들의 삶도 윤택하게 만들어 주었다고 주장했다. 예컨대 애플 사의 CEO '팀 쿡'(Tim Cook)은 삼성전자와 LG, 화웨이 등과의 경쟁을 거론하며 개발자들의 앱도 많이 수용해주었기 때문에 애플은 독점행위와 상관이 없다고 항변했고, 구글의 '순다르 피차이'(Sundar Pichai) 회장은 트위터, 인스타그램 등과의 치열한 경쟁으로 광고수익이 40%나 줄어들었다고 읍소했다.

이에 비해 페이스북의 '저커버그'(Zuckerberg)는 페이스북은 자랑스러운 미국기업이라는 취지로 애국심에 호소했으며, 아마존 CEO '제프 베이조스'(Jeff Bezos)는 17세에 자신을 임신한 어머니와 쿠바 출신 양아버지 등 어려웠던 성장환경 소개로 본인이 아메리칸드림의 상징임을 부각시켜 의원들의 반감을 누그러뜨리려 애썼다.

소비자 입장에서만 본다면 이들 CEO의 주장처럼 4빅테크가 우리의 복지에 과연 어떤 피해를 주었는지 실상 피부에 와닿는 게 없어 보인다. 과연 연방하원 반독점소위는 어떤 보고서를 내놓을지 세인의 관심이 무척 뜨겁다. (2020.8.12)

결과: 2020.10.6. 반독점소위는 400쪽 분량의 보고서를 통해 4 빅테크는 독점적 시장 지배력을 남용했다고 지적했다. 하지만 미국의 반독점 관련법을 정비해야 한다고 권고하면서도 어떤 기업에도 분할 요구까진 하지 않았다.

반독점소위에서 의원들의 질문에 대답하는 빅테크 CEO 4인방 <출처: YouTube 캡처>
CEOs of 4 Big Techs answering questions at the Antitrust Subcommittee hearing <source: YouTube screenshot>

4 Big Techs Facing Antitrust Challenges

The Antitrust Subcommittee of the House of Representatives' Judiciary Committee held a public hearing on July 29 with the CEOs of Amazon, Apple, Facebook, and Google. These mega-companies are sometimes referred to as "Big Tech." Although it was conducted over a video chat platform with each CEO being connected from their office because of the COVID-19 pandemic, it was the first time that they were brought together before Congress.

The hearing follows a year-long investigation by the U.S. Justice Department and the Federal Trade Commission into whether these tech companies have engaged in illegal anti-competitive business practices. The subcommittee will make recommendations for new or modified antitrust legislation.

The companies summoned at the hearing were at the center of criticism for hindering fair competition by abusing their enormous power over the market. For example, Amazon is accused of using its access to data on popular products sold by the third-party vendors on its platform, and creating and highlighting their competing products. In addition, Facebook bought out its competitor, Instagram, and Apple charged a 30 percent commission from app developers for selling their programs on its app store. It's also alleged that Google engaged in deceptive search advertising such as giving preference to its pages in search results.

American capitalism has a long history, and American antitrust laws also go back about 130 years. The U.S. Congress passed the first antitrust legislation, Sherman Act, in 1890, followed by the Federal Trade Commission Act and the Clayton Act in 1914. According to these laws, unfair business practices that can weaken competition and disrupt a healthy market economy such as the formation of cartels and price-fixing are banned. The companies that engage in such illegal activities may be sued civilly, or criminally prosecuted and fined. In extreme situations, they can also be ordered to be split up. The Federal Trade Commission was established to monitor and supervise this activity.

Major American companies such as Rockefeller's Standard Oil, American Tobacco Company, and telecommunications giant AT&T were forced to break up under the antitrust laws and faded into memory. Bill Gates' Microsoft was also on the verge of a breakup in the 1990s when they imposed restrictions on Windows users from uninstalling the web browser Internet Explorer. The district court ordered the company to be split as a remedy. The appellate court ultimately reversed this decision, and Gates was able to save his company.

The challenge with enforcing the antitrust laws is finding the right standard that can be applied consistently. For instance, at the beginning of the Sherman

Act's enforcement, the "rationale principle" test was used. Under this test, only unreasonable anti-competitive restrictions were illegal. However, the test proved too challenging to apply as it varied significantly depending on the court's perception of the current events and what constituted reasonable business practices. As a result, the "consumer welfare" standard appeared in the 1970s. Under the new standard, the court must examine whether the company's antitrust behaviors harmed the consumer.

With this legal standard in mind, the CEOs at the hearing denied that they had a monopoly over the market. Also, they claimed that they survived fierce domestic and international competition by endlessly innovating, which, in turn, improved the quality of consumer welfare and the American economy. For instance, Apple's CEO Tim Cook argued that his company has competitors such as Samsung, LG, and Huawei. He also maintained that Apple's app store was not monopolistic. Google's Chairman Sundar Pichai complained that his company's advertising revenue decreased by 40 percent due to competition with Twitter and Instagram. Taking a slightly different tone, Facebook's Zuckerberg appealed by claiming that Facebook is a proud American company, while Amazon's Jeff Bezos tried to soften up the lawmaker's antipathy by talking about his challenging childhood, including being born to a 17-year-old single mother and being raised by a Cuban stepfather.

If, as these CEOs argue, there is no harm to the consumers, should these big companies not be regulated by the antitrust laws? It will be interesting to see the report that the subcommittee will issue after the hearing. (2020.8.12)

Outcome: On October 6, 2020, the subcommittee issued a 400-page report pointing out that 4 Big Tech companies abused their monopolistic market power. Although the report recommended several concrete proposals, it did not demand these companies to be divided up.

종교와 실정법의 간극

코로나-19가 좀처럼 진정되지 않고 계속 기승을 부리자 쿠오모 뉴욕주지사는 궁여지책으로 지난 10.9. 확진자 발생률에 따라 레드, 오렌지, 옐로우 존을 지정하고 각 구역별로 종교시설의 예배 인원을 각각 10명, 25명, 건물 수용인원의 50% 이하 등으로 제한하는 행정명령을 발동했으나 연방대법원으로부터 불가 판정을 받고 말았다.

대법원은 레드 존에 위치한 가톨릭 브루클린 교구와 오렌지 존의 아구다트 유대교 회당이, 주지사의 행정명령은 종교의 자유를 침해한다며 법원에 일시적 명령 금지처분을 신청한 사건에 대해 '예배 참석 규제는 종교의 자유를 보장한 수정헌법 제1조를 위반한 것'이라고 판단했다. 종교집회가 코로나-19 확산에 직접적 원인이 되었다는 증거가 없는 데다 슈퍼마켓이나 주류판매점과 같은 사업장에 대해서는 규제가 없음에도 종교시설의 예배 참석자 수를 제한하는 것은 문제가 있다는 것이다.

이번 대법원의 판결은, 공익과 대중을 위해서라면 사소한 개인의 희생쯤은 당연시되는 동양 정서와는 달리 전례 없는 팬데믹 상황이라고 하더라도 정부가 개인의 종교적 자유를 침해한다면 '그것이 아무리 짧은 기간이라도 의심할 여지없이 회복할 수 없는 상처'라고 보는 미국인들의 정서를 반영한 것으로 보인다.

달리 말해 미국인들에게 종교 문제는 정교분리 원칙에 따라 신성불가침의 영역이기 때문에 정부의 개입은 법원의 엄격한 심사를 거쳐야 한다는 것이다. 이 원칙에 의거, 공립학교 교육과정에 성경을 읽거나 함께 기도하는 과정 같은 것은 만들 수 없고, 공공장소에 십계명 조형물과 같은 특정 종교 관련 장식물의 설치 등도 금지된다. 한때 루이지애나주 의회가 창조론과 진화론을 수업시간에 공평하게 가르치도록 법을 제정한 적이 있었는데 이를 두고 연방대법원이 '특정 종교의 교리를 전파하는 것'이라며 철회토록 제동을 건 것도 같은 맥락이다.

또 종교기관에 대한 연방 노동법의 적용 여부도 정교분리 원칙의 논란이 뜨거운 분야이다. 이 사건 발단의 주인공은 미시간에 위치한 루터란 교회 부속학교의 선생이었던 '세릴 페리치'(Cheryl Perich)이다. 학생들에게 종교학을 가르쳤던 그녀는 2004년, 불행히도 밤에 충분히 잠을 자도 갑자기 낮에 졸음에 빠져드는 기면증에 걸려 치료에 전념하기 위해 휴직계를 내야 했다.

이듬해 의사로부터 복직 허가를 받고 교직에 돌아가려 했던 페리치는 학교에서 이미 다른 사람을 고용했다는 충격적인 답변을 듣고 연방 장애인법 위반으로 학교를 고소하기에 이르렀다.

하지만 대법원은 '성직자 예외법'(ministerial exception)이라는 법리를 내세워 페리치의 소송을 기각시켜 버렸다. 이 법리에 의하면 종교단체의 성직자 채용 문제는 정교분리 원칙에 따라 정부가 개입할 수 없기 때문에 부당해고와 같은 연방 노동법 위반 소송 대상도 될 수 없다는 것이었다.

더구나 페리치는 루터란 교육위원회의 구술시험 통과 및 공동의회의 투표를 통해 목사 안수까지 받은 성직자인데 이런 사람이 교회 부속학교를 상대로 소송을 제기하는 것은 가당찮은 것으로 판단했다.

성직자 예외법은 올해 7월 결정된 '과달루페 성모학교 대 모리시-베루'(*Our Lady of Guadalupe School v. Morrissey-Berru*) 사건을 통해 그 적용 범위가 더욱 넓어졌다. 즉 가톨릭계 초등학교 교사 두 명이 고용상 연령과 의학적 이유로 차별을 받았다며 제기한 소송에서 대법원은, 그 직원이 성직자인지 아닌지의 기준은 직함이나 종교 교육 이수 같은 형식적인 요건보다 담당하고 있는 일의 성격이 무엇보다 중요하다고 해석했다.

이 기준에 따르면 종교 교육은 성직자의 업무 중 가장 핵심적인 일에 해당하므로 가톨릭 학교의 일반 교사들 역시 '성직자'에 해당한다고 보고 원고들의 소송을 기각시켰던 것이다.

이 결정으로 종교단체 직원들은 실정법의 사각지대에 놓이게 됐는데 뾰족한 구제책은 없는지, 또한 이러한 신앙 세계와 현실과의 조화로운 접점은 어떤 것인지 법률가들의 고민이 깊다. (2020.12.16.)

영어 녹음 듣기

Distance Between Religion and Secular Law

As the infection rate of COVID-19 spiked up, New York's governor issued an executive order on October 9 restricting various kinds of gatherings depending on the zone designation. For places of worship, the attendance at services was limited to 10 people, 25 people, and 50 percent of maximum capacity for red, orange, and yellow zones, respectively. However, it was ruled unconstitutional by the U.S. Supreme Court.

In a suit for preliminary injunction brought by the Roman Catholic Diocese of Brooklyn in a red zone and Agudath Israel of America in an orange zone, the Supreme Court held that the governor's executive order unconstitutionally infringed upon the religious freedom protected by the First Amendment. The Court found that religious services did not directly cause the spread of COVID-19, and that the executive order unconstitutionally targeted religious services when there were no such restrictions on "essential businesses" like supermarkets or liquor stores.

This ruling highlights the clear contrast between the traditional Asian sentiment, in which individual sacrifices are tolerated for the common good and public safety, and the American view that "[t]he loss of First Amendment freedoms, for even minimal periods of time, unquestionably constitutes irreparable injury."

To Americans, any government involvement in regulating religious activities must endure strict judicial scrutiny based on the deep-rooted constitutional principle of separation of church and state. Under the establishment clause, no prayers or bible readings are allowed in public schools. Nor can the Ten Amendments or other religious emblems be displayed in public space. Once, the Louisiana legislature passed laws to require public schools to teach creationism side-by-side with evolutionism. The Supreme Court struck it because it advanced doctrinal teachings of a particular religion.

Another area where an intense legal debate is happening is whether federal labor laws must apply to the employees of religious institutions. It started with Cheryl Perich's case. Perich was a teacher at Hosanna-Tabor Evangelical Lutheran Church and School in Michigan, where she taught several classes, including religion. In 2004, Perich took a medical leave when she was diagnosed with narcolepsy, which caused her to fall asleep during the day even on a full night's sleep. Although she received medical clearance to return to work the following year, she was told that the school had already hired someone else to replace her. So, she brought a lawsuit under the Federal Americans with Disabilities Act.

However, when the case reached the Supreme Court, it was dismissed under the "ministerial exception." The Court held that secular courts could not judge whether "ministers" were illegally fired because the establishment clause prohibited the federal government from determining how religious organizations may operate. Furthermore, the Court found Perich to be a "minister" because she passed an oral examination by a Lutheran college's faculty committee and was commissioned as a minister upon election by the congregation. The Court determined that the case fell outside of its adjudicative powers.

In July, the ministerial exception was expanded through the holding in Our Lady of Guadalupe School v. Morrissey-Berru. In a job discrimination lawsuit brought by two teachers at Catholic schools claiming age and medical discrimination, the Supreme Court held that whether one is a "minister" or not depends on the employee's function than the formal requirements like a job title or religious education. Applying this standard, the Court dismissed the case because providing religious education is arguably the most essential task of a minister. Hence, the Court held, teachers must also be considered "ministers."

With this ruling, teachers in religious schools have been placed into the blind spot of the federal labor laws. Courts will need to ponder how to find a middle ground and protect those who are stuck in between these two worlds. (2020.12.16.)

수정헌법 제5조, 공용수용의 허실

도로나 철도, 발전소 건설과 같은 공익사업을 추진하려면 정부가 됐든 민간기업이 됐든 사업 주체는 개인의 토지나 건물 등을 소유주 의사와 상관없이 강제로 수용할 필요성이 생긴다. 이와 관련 미국 수정헌법 제5조에 '사유재산권은 정당한 보상 없이는 공공의 용도로 수용되어서는 아니 된다'라고 명시돼 있다.

공용수용의 가장 핵심은 헌법 조항에 명시된 그대로 과연 무엇이 '공공의 용도'이며, 어느 정도의 수준이 '정당한 보상'인지에 대해 정의를 내리고 판단하는 것인데 이것은 법원이 해야 할 몫이다. 특히 공용수용은 '공공의 용도'가 분명한 공익사업뿐 아니라 도시 재개발에도 폭넓게 적용되어 많은 논란이 있는데 이번에는 이에 대해 조명해본다.

도시개발 문제로 대법원까지 법적 논쟁이 되었던 첫 사례는 1954년에 있었던 '버먼 대 파커'(*Berman v. Parker*) 사건이다. 미국 연방의회는 1945년, 워싱턴 D.C.의 낙후 지역을 재개발하기로 하고 사업추진 주체로 'D.C. 토지재개발청'을 설립했다. 토지재개발청은 사전 조사를 통해 워싱턴 D.C. 남서쪽 지역 주택가 64.3%가 보수 불가능할 정도로 노후도가 심각하다고 결론짓고 재개발에 착수했다.

버먼은 당시 이 지역에서 백화점을 운영하고 있었는데 아직 멀쩡한 자신의 건물을 지방정부가 강제로 수용하여 부동산 재개발 사업자에게 주는 것은 '한 사업가의 이익을 다른 사업가에게 주는 것'일 뿐 공공의 용도에 해당하지 않는다고 주장하며 수용에 응하지 않았다. 하지만 대법원은 버먼처럼 일일이 개인 사정들을 다 들어주다 보면 전체적으로 사업추진이 요원하다고 판단하고 8대0 만장일치로 정부 편을 들어주었다. 주민의 안전과 편익, 도시미관 등이 공익의 가치라고 본 것이다.

대법원의 이 같은 결정은, 보스턴시의 경우 웨스트엔드 빈민가에 살던 약 2만 명의 이민자들을 이주시키고 대규모 재개발을 통해 현대식 빌딩 숲으로 바꾸는 데 성공하는 등 미국 전역에 재개발 열풍을 몰고 와 낙후된 구도심을 오늘의 도시 모습으로 바꾸는 데 크게 일조했다.

그러다 2005년 '켈로 대 뉴런던시'(Kelo v. City of New London) 사건으로 공용수용 문제가 또 한 번 도마 위에 올라온다. 코네티컷 주의 뉴런던시 테임즈 강가 작은 집에서 남편과 함께 오랫동안 살던 '수젯 켈로'(Susette Kelo)는 어느 날 청천벽력 같은 통지를 받게 된다. 다름 아니라 거대 제약회사인 화이자가 자기 동네를 재개발하여 화이자 사옥과 그에 따르는 부대시설을 짓기로 한다는 것이었다.

뉴런던시 당국은, 켈로가 살던 동네는 낙후지역이라 도시 재생 사업이 필수적인데다 대형 제약회사를 유치하게 되면 일자리 창출과 시의 세수 증대에도 크게 기여한다며 켈로의 집에 대한 공용수용을 승인했다. 켈로를 비롯한 주택 소유주 몇 명은 만족스럽지 못한 보상가에 반발하며 소송을 불사했지만 결국 대법원은 고용창출 문제와 세수증대는 공익에 해당한다고 판단하고 강제 이주를 명령했다.

그러나 아이러니하게도 소송이 진행되는 동안 화이자는 기업 인수합병에 따라 이미 완공된 뉴런던시 사옥을 떠나 다른 도시로 이전하였기 때문에 당초 기대했던 일자리 창출과 세수 증대에 별로 기여하지 못하였고, 재개발 사업 또한 부동산 시행업자의 자금난으로 계획대로 진척이 되지 못한 채 오늘날까지 황량한 공터로 남아 있다.

어차피 개발을 통해 이익이 남는 장사라면 가만히 두어도 민간에서 자발적으로 참여할 텐데 이처럼 행정기관이 나서 민간에게 이익을 보장해주는 게 과연 '공공의 용도'로 볼 수 있는지, 아울러 시세보다 더 많은 돈을 준다면 당연히 팔고 나갔을 가격이 자연스럽게 형성된 시장에서의 주택 가격이라고 본다면 여기에 미치지 못하는 공용수용 보상가를 '정당한 보상'이라고 볼 수 있는지, 도심재개발 문제가 대두될 때마다 회자되는 과제이다. (2021.2.10.)

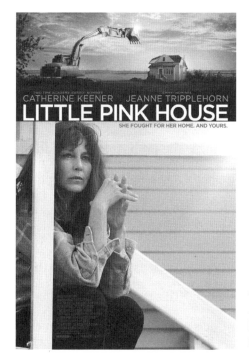

수젯 켈로의 법정 투쟁을 그린 2017년 작 <리틀 핑크 하우스> 영화의 포스터
Poster from the 2017 movie <Little Pink House> based on Susette Kelo's legal struggle.

영어 녹음 듣기

Economy and Society

The Fifth Amendment: Truth Behind Eminent Domain

To build public infrastructure such as roads, railroads and power plants, there often arises a need by the government or private agencies to forcefully acquire private land and buildings. The Fifth Amendment to the Constitution provides, "nor shall private property taken for public use, without just compensation."

The central question in these eminent domain cases is what constitutes "public use" and how much is "just compensation." This task falls squarely on the courts. The court's definition of "public use" has gradually expanded from clear examples of public works to the more controversial urban redevelopment. This column traces this history.

The first Supreme Court case that decided the legality of using eminent domain for urban redevelopment was Berman v. Parker in 1954. In 1945, Congress passed a plan to redevelop the "blighted areas" in Washington D.C. It established the D.C. Redevelopment Land Agency to lead this effort. The Agency concluded after the initial survey that 63.4% of the dwellings in Southwest Washington D.C. were beyond repair and began to make plans to redevelop the entire area.

Berman owned a department store in the targeted redevelopment zone. He argued that taking his building, which was not blighted, and transferring it to the redevelopers under eminent domain amounted to "a taking from one businessman for the benefit of another businessman," not public use. However, in an 8-0 decision, the Supreme Court rejected Berman's argument. It held, "[i]f owner after owner were permitted to resist these redevelopment programs on the ground that his particular property was not being used against the public interest, integrated plans for redevelopment would suffer greatly." It was clear that the Court considered the residents' safety, convenience, and attractiveness of the neighborhood to be "public use."

The Supreme Court's decision spurred further redevelopment efforts and contributed to the modernization of the skyline in cities across America. One of the most famous examples was turning West End, Boston's working-class neighborhood, into a hubbub of commercial activity with several high-rise buildings. About 20,000 immigrants were relocated during the eminent domain and urban renewal phase.

Eminent domain once again made the national headlines in 2005 with the Supreme Court's decision in Kelo v. City of New London. Susette Kelo lived in a small house with her husband on the banks of Thames River in New London, Connecticut. One day, she received a shocking notice saying that a giant pharmaceutical company Pfizer would redevelop her neighborhood and build a hotel-retail-condo.

The City of New London approved eminent domain after concluding that Kelo's neighborhood was blighted and in need of revitalization. The city hoped to create new jobs and increase tax revenue by allowing the pharmaceutical company to build there. Several homeowners, including Kelo, were dissatisfied with the proposed compensation and brought a lawsuit against the city. However, the U.S. Supreme Court ruled against them by finding that job creation and increased tax income for the city constituted "public use," and ordered their homes to be condemned.

Ironically, Pfizer did not contribute much in the expected job creation or tax revenue. While the case was working its way through the court system, it abandoned the plan and relocated to another city after a corporate merger. The developer could not secure financing and had to give up the redevelopment plan. The land where Kelo's house used to sit is empty and desolate to this day.

The normal market operation allows businesses to buy blighted private property, fix up, and sell it at a profit. However, when the government takes the lead to ensure profit for businesses at a cost to people like Kelo, can it be defined as "public use"? Also, if a fair market value is the price point where most people will sell voluntarily, can it be called "just compensation" if they don't wish to sell at the amount offered? These are two challenging questions that come up repeatedly every time eminent domain is discussed for urban renewal. (2021.2.10.)

자율주행차 사고책임

AI(인공지능) 기술이 나날이 발전하면서 불과 얼마 전까지만 해도 공상과학 영화에서나 볼 수 있었던 자율주행 자동차가 현실 세계로 성큼 다가왔다. 이에 따라 자연스레 교통사고에 대한 법적 책임 문제가 사회문제로 등장하였다.

자율주행차 사고로 희생된 첫 번째 보행자는 49세 여성 '일레인 허즈버그'로, 2018.3.18. 애리조나주 템피에서 자전거를 끌고 길을 건너다 우버의 자율주행 시험 차량에 치여 변을 당했다.

'보행자가 어두운 곳에서 걸어 나와 자동차의 센서가 제대로 감지하지 못했고, 너무 순식간에 일어난 일이라 운전자 역시 손을 쓸 수 없었던 것으로 보인다'는 템피 경찰의 초동 조사보고가 있었으나 우버는 경찰조사에 아랑곳하지 않고 사고 발생 10일 만에 피해자 측과 손해배상에 합의하고 사건을 서둘러 봉합하였다. 이로써 외부적으로는 자신들 차량에 문제가 있었음을 인정한 모양새가 되었다.

민사문제와 별도로 경찰당국은 교통안전국과 함께 18개월간의 조사를 통해 운전자 '라파엘라 바스케즈'가 사고 당시 전방을 주시하지 않고 휴대폰으로 TV를 시청하고 있었다는 사실을 밝혀내고 바스케즈를 과실치사 혐의로 기소했다. 그녀는 자신이 운전자 신분이 아니었기 때문에 형사책임을 질 수 없다고 항변하고 있어 올해로 예정된 재판에서 자율주행차에 대한 법적 시비가 처음으로 가려질 전망이다.

자율주행 차량사고의 법적 문제를 이해하려면 우선 SAE(Society of Automotive Engineers, 미국자동차 기술학회)에서 정한 레벨 0에서 레벨 5까지 총 6단계 분류방법부터 알아야 한다. 레벨 0은 운전자가 주행의 모든 것을 통제하는 고전적 단계이고, 레벨 1은 크루즈 컨트롤, 차선 유지 기능과 같이 컴퓨터가 단순 도움을 주는 단계를 일컫는다. 레벨 2는 부분 자동화로 특정 조건 내에서 일정 시간 동안 컴퓨터가 차간 거리나 차선 유지 등을 제어하는 단계. 0~2단계에서 생긴 사고는 전적으로 운전자 책임이라는 데 이론이 없다.

문제는 현재 대부분의 메이저 자동차 회사가 만들고 있는 레벨 3 수준의 자율주행차이다. 레벨 3은 평상시엔 컴퓨터가 주행을 담당하다가 위험시에만 운전자가 개입하는 '조건부 자율주행' 시스템 단계인데, 이 단계에서 발생하는 사고대책이 바로 우리가 풀어야 할 현안인 셈이다.

예컨대 차량 결함으로 사고가 났다면 기계장치 부분은 GM과 테슬라, BMW, 현대자동차 같은 자율주행 자동차 제조사가, 주행 프로그램 부분은 구글이나 애플, 우버와 같은 IT업체가 책임을 져야 한다. 설혹 자동차에 결함이 있었다 하더라도, 앞의 바스케즈의 경우처럼, 운전자가 충분히 대응할 수 있었음에도 주의의무를 지키지 않아 사고를 막지 못했다면 운전자 역시 법적 책임에서 자유로울 수 없다는 게 법조계 중론이다.

그러나 문제는 현재의 기술 수준으로는 사고발생 원인을 정확하게 규명하는 일과 운전자가 주의의무를 다했는지를 밝혀내기가 쉽지 않다는 데 딜레마가 있다. 그래서 차선책으로 누구에게 과실이 있는지를 따지지 않고 지정 보험회사가 피해보상을 전담하는 노폴트 보험 등이 거론되고 있다.

SAE 레벨 4는 택시같이 특정 지역 내에서 운전자의 어떤 개입도 필요 없이 AI가 주행 제어를 담당하는 단계를 말한다. 최고단계인 레벨 5의 자동차는 '완전 자율주행'이 가능하기 때문에 이 단계에서는 음주운전도 문제가 되지 않고, 사고가 나더라도 운전자가 아닌 자동차 제조사나 프로그램 개발사가 전적으로 책임을 져야 할 것으로 보인다.

하지만 레벨 5의 자동차는, 아직까지는 여전히 공상과학 영화에서나 나올 법한 먼 나라 얘기라고 보면, 올해 진행될 바스케즈 재판에서 레벨3의 자율주행차를 법원은 어떻게 판단할지 귀추가 주목된다. (2021.6.2.)

Liability of Self-Driving Cars

As Artificial Intelligence continues to advance, the world of self-driving cars, which we had only dreamed about in sci-fi movies, is nearer than ever. Naturally, the question of who is responsible when an autonomous car gets into an accident needs to be resolved.

The first pedestrian killed by an autonomous vehicle was a 49-year-old woman, Elaine Herzberg. She was crossing the street with her bike in Tempe, Arizona, on March 18, 2018 when she was fatally hit by a self-driving Uber test vehicle.

The initial report by the Tempe police department stated that the accident was unavoidable because Herzberg suddenly emerged out of the darkness and the car's sensors did not have sufficient time to respond. They further claimed that the human driver could not help avoid the accident because of how quickly it happened. However, in an apparent acknowledgement of potential legal liability, Uber entered into a settlement with the victim's family within 10 days of the accident.

Apart from the settlement, the police department continued to investigate for 18 months with the National Transportation Safety Board. Ultimately, they learned that the human driver, Rafaela Vasquez, was not paying attention to the road at the time of the accident, and was instead watching a TV show on her phone. She was indicted for negligent homicide. Vasquez pleaded not guilty and claimed that she could not be held liable because she was not driving. The trial is scheduled to take place later this year, and it will be the first time that a court tackles this issue.

To appreciate legal liability with autonomous vehicles, understanding the levels established by the Society of Automotive Engineers (SAE) is a good starting point. The scale consists of 6 levels starting from Level 0 to Level 5. At Level 0, the driver has full control of the vehicle. At 1, the automated system provides simple assistance to the driver to get better control of the car. Some examples include cruise control and lane centering. At level 2, the computer can help maintain distance between cars or keep the car in the center of the lane, and cars can drive themselves for a while under certain conditions. There's no question that when Level 0, 1 or 2 cars get into an accident, the fault lies with the human driver.

Level 3 is "partial automation." The automated system drives the car at this level and will alert the driver when it requires human intervention. Major automakers are manufacturing Level 3 cars now. Accordingly, the question of liability in accidents involving these cars is the current problem that we must solve.

It seems logical that if a mechanical issue causes the accident, then car manufacturers like GM, Tesla, BMW, or Hyundai would be liable. If it's caused by self-driving software, then the liability would fall on the IT companies like Google, Apple and Uber. Even with faulty mechanical parts or software, however, if the human driver could have avoided the accident, then the driver may not be able to escape from liability, as the Vasquez case shows.

Another problem that we're facing is that with current technology, it's not easy to know exactly what caused the accident and whether it was preventable by a human driver. No-fault insurance, in which the insurance company will cover the damage regardless of who is at fault, is being discussed as the second-best option.

Cars at SAE Level 4 do not need human intervention as long as they stay within a geographic boundary like a robotic taxi. At the highest level, Level 5, cars are fully automated. It would not even matter if the "driver" is drunk. If there's an accident, it would be the manufacturer or the self-driving software company's fault.

However, Level 5 cars are still only in sci-fi movies. Back in reality, it will be interesting to see how Vasquez's trial unfolds with a Level 3 car. (2021.6.2.)

다시 점화된 '뜨거운 담론 낙태'

연방대법원은 지난 9월 1일, 낙태 찬성파들이 "태아의 심장 박동이 감지되는 임신 6주 이후의 낙태를 금지하는 텍사스의 '심장박동법' 시행을 금지해달라"며 낸 가처분신청에 대해 소송대상 선정 오인 이유를 들어 대법관 5대 4로 신청을 기각했다.

대법원의 이 같은 결정은, 비록 본안소송이 아닌 가처분신청 사건이라고 하더라도, 태아가 자궁 밖에서 생존 가능한 시기 전까지 여성의 낙태권을 폭넓게 인정한 현재까지의 판례 태도와 배치되는 것이어서 비상한 관심을 불러일으키고 있다.

낙태 문제는, 필자의 작년 칼럼(2020.2.12)에서도 '뜨거운 담론 낙태' 제하로 한 번 다룬 바 있지만, 1973년 결정된 '로 대 웨이드' 사건부터 비롯된다. 이 사건에서 대법원은 여성의 임신기간을 3 분할한 후 임신초기부터 6개월까지는 임산부가 중절 수술을 선택할 수 있고, 7개월부터 출산까지의 기간에는 태아가 자궁 밖에서도 독자적으로 생존 가능성이 높기 때문에 그 권리가 제한된다고 연방헌법을 해석했다.

이 삼분법은 1992년 '플랜드 페런트후드 대 케이시'(*Planned Parenthood v. Casey*) 사건을 통해 의료기술의 발전을 고려, 태아의 생존 가능성 시험결과에 따라 융통성 있게 낙태허용 기간을 정하는 것으로 판례가 일부 대체되어 오늘에 이르고 있다.

낙태 금지는 공화당의 오랜 숙원사업 중 하나였는데 트럼프 대통령이 2017년 '닐 고서치'에 이어 2018년 '브렛 캐버너', 2020년 일곱 아이의 엄마인 '에이미 코니 배럿'을 대법관에 앉혀 보수파 6 대 진보파 3으로 대법원 구도가 완성됐을 때 그 초석이 다져졌다고 볼 수 있다.

대법원의 보수화가 완성되자 이를 기다렸다는 듯이 공화당 우세의 많은 주에서 낙태를 금지하는 법안이 우후죽순처럼 상정되었다. 이중에서도 텍사스가 제정한 '심장박동법'은 대부분의 여성들이 임신 사실을 자각하지 못하는 6주부터 강간이나 근친상간에 대한 낙태까지도 금지할 정도로 가장 까다롭고 제한적인 것으로 알려졌다.

텍사스법은 '로 대 웨이드'라는 거대 장벽을 비껴가기 위한 하나의 해법으로 소송 주체를 정부가 아닌 개인으로 명시한 것이 특징이랄 수 있다. 즉, 지금까지는 정부가 앞장서 불법 낙태 시술을 받은 여성이나, 시술을 행한 의료진을 상대로 민·형사 소송을 담당해왔는데 텍사스법은 정부 대신 시민을 앞세워 일차 민사소송을 제기토록 하고, 성공할 경우 1만 달러의 보상금 지급 조항을 마련한 것이다. 소송 피고는 낙태 시술 의료진뿐 아니라 환자를 병원에 데려다준 우버 운전기사, 낙태 비용을 지원한 자선단체, 심지어 가족까지도 모두 그 대상이 된다.

이렇게 해놓으면 낙태 찬성파들이 도대체 누구를 상대로 소송을 제기해야 할지 주적 개념을 희석시킬 수 있고, 기존 판례도 정면으로 비껴갈 수 있다고 본 것이다. 아니나 다를까 텍사스 당국의 예측대로 낙태 병원이 텍사스의 재판부 판사들을 상대로 낸 가처분신청에 대해 연방대법원은 소송 대상이 잘못 선정됐다며 신청을 기각시켰던 것이다.

한편 시술 주체인 의사나 낙태 비용을 지원한 자선단체 등의 입장에서 보더라도 1회 시술당 1만 불의 보상금이 걸려있다면 '현상금 사냥꾼'들의 감시망을 도저히 피하기 어렵다고 보고 낙태 시도를 체념할 것으로 판단했을 것이다. 이를 방증하듯 텍사스 소재 24개의 낙태시술 병원은 임신 6주 이후의 중절수술을 모두 중지했다고 뉴욕타임스는 보도했다.

대법원은, 이번 사건이 긴급 현안을 시급하게 처리하기 위한 가처분신청 사건이라는 점을 감안하여 기존 판례를 계속 유지할지에 대해선 결정을 내리지 않았지만, 이번 심리 회기 내에 텍사스법과 비슷한 미시시피의 낙태금지법 위헌 여부에 대해 심리할 것이라고 밝혔기 때문에 낙태 문제에 대한 보수화 대법원의 입장이 조만간 가닥을 잡을 것으로 보인다. (2021.9.15.)

텍사스 주청사
Texas State Capitol

The Abortion Debate: Rekindled

On September 1, the Supreme Court declined to act on a request brought by pro-abortion-rights groups to enjoin Texas state actors from enforcing the "heartbeat law" which bans abortion after six weeks of pregnancy. Instead, in a 5-4 decision, the justices ruled that the lawsuit was brought against the wrong parties.

Although it was not a decision on the merits, it was shocking because the Texas law runs in the face of the existing Supreme Court precedent that guarantees the pregnant women's right to obtain an abortion until fetal viability.

I wrote about the issues relating to abortion in my previous column titled, The Abortion Debate, published on February 12, 2020. The controversy began with Roe v. Wade in 1973. In that case, the Supreme Court decided that the Constitution provided women with a right to obtain an abortion in the first and second trimesters, but not during the third-trimester because the fetus may survive outside of the mother's womb at that point.

This holding was affirmed with a slight modification in Planned Parenthood v. Casey in 1992. To account for medical and technological advances, the Court moved away from the rigid third-trimester test and opted instead for the fetal viability test.

Eliminating or reducing women's abortion rights has been one of the core political goals of the Republican Party. President Trump succeeded in appointing to the Supreme Court Justices Neil Gorsuch in 2017, Brett Kavanaugh in 2018, and Amy Coney Barrett, mother of 7 children, in 2020. The Trump administration cemented a solid 6-3 conservative control over the Court, paving the way for the new fight over abortion rights.

With a conservative majority in the Supreme Court, many Republican-dominated state legislatures began to enact laws that effectively banned abortion. The Texas law in question bans abortion after 6 weeks, before when most women realize that they're pregnant, and even in pregnancies caused by incest and rape. It's known to be one of the most restrictive.

One of the defining characteristics of this statute is granting a cause of action to private citizens rather than the government. It was specifically designed to avoid the holding in Roe v. Wade. Thus far, state governments have been responsible for bringing civil or criminal actions against women and the medical staff involved with abortion. Texas law allows a private citizen to bring civil lawsuits, and authorizes $10,000 in bounty if they're successful. The law targets the medical staff who perform abortion procedures, and Uber drivers who provide transportation to the patient, abortion groups that provide funding for the procedure, and even family members if they provide any assistance.

Texas legislature designed this new law to withstand the Supreme Court's scrutiny and confuse pro-abortion groups from figuring out whom they must enjoin. The theory proved accurate when the Supreme Court denied an injunction sought by pro-abortion groups because the lawsuit named the wrong defendants.

Moreover, the legislature correctly calculated that $10,000 bounty would prove to be too much for the medical staff and pro-abortion groups that provide funding for abortion procedures. The New York Times reported that all 24 abortion clinics in Texas announced that they will no longer provide abortion in cases where more than six weeks have elapsed since conception.

Because the lawsuit concerned whether an injunctive relief must be granted, the Supreme Court did not engage in a detailed analysis of the underlying law and whether it violated the Constitution. However, the Court is slated to hear about a similar ban in Mississippi. We will know soon how the "conservative" Supreme Court decides. (2021.9.15.)

경제·사회

교도소 단상

뉴욕시 이스트강에 있는 라이커스섬은 섬 전체가 교도소로 이루어져 있는데 여기에는 주로 기소자 중 보석금을 내지 못 한 사람들과 1년 이하의 가벼운 형을 받은 사람들이 수감되어 있다. 1932년 건립될 당시에는 세계 최대 교정시설로 유명세를 떨쳤지만 최근에는 시설 노후화로 인한 열악한 환경과 교도관의 재소자 폭행, 재소자끼리의 유혈 난투극 등으로 올 들어서만도 10명의 수감자가 사망할 정도로 악명이 높다.

지난 9월 4일에는 이곳에 수감 중인 세 명의 남성이 다른 재소자 한 명을 잔인하게 폭행하는 장면과 감방 안에서 대여섯 명의 재소자들이 음악을 켠 채 담배를 피우며 파티를 하는 모습이 동영상 플랫폼 틱톡에 올라와 또 구설에 휘말렸다.

'빌 드블라지오' 뉴욕시장은 이처럼 재소자들의 관리가 제대로 되지 않는 근본 이유는 코로나-19로 인한 교도관 부족에 기인한다고 보고, 앞으로는 하루 이상 병가를 쓰는 교도관에게 의사 소견서를 제출할 것과 당분간 부족 인력을 뉴욕시 경찰관으로 보강 투입할 것이라고 발표했다. 뉴욕타임스에 따르면 코로나-19로 인해 올 7월 한 달간 9,000여 명의 교도관 중 약 1/4인 2,300명 정도가 병가를 내고 출근을 하지 않은 것으로 나타났다.

이 같은 뉴욕시의 조치에 부응하여 '캐시 호컬'(Kathy Hochul) 뉴욕주지사도 9월 17일 라이커스 재소자 중 통금시간과 음주 금지 위반 등 가벼운 가석방 조건을 어겨 재수감됐던 191명을 즉각 석방하고, 약 200명은 뉴욕주의 다른 교도소로 이송을 명령했다.

교도소 사건이라고 하면 미국 건국 후 최악의 폭동사건으로 평가되는 아티카(Attica) 사건을 빼놓을 수 없는데 올해는 때마침 그 50주년이 되는 해이기도 하다. 1971년 9월 9일, 뉴욕주 버펄로와 로체스터 사이에 위치한 아티카 교도소에서 일어난 이 폭동으로 교도관 11명을 포함한 43명이 군인의 총에 맞아 죽고, 100여 명이 부상을 당했다.

아티카 교도소 1,200여 명의 죄수들은 '하루에 한 번 샤워하게 해달라', '한 달에 한 통씩밖에 지급되지 않는 화장실 휴지의 배급을 늘려달라'는 등의, 지금으로 봐선 너무나 당연한 기본권 보장을 요구하며 교도관 20명을 인질로 잡고 교도소를 점거했다. 그러나 당시 주지사였던 '넬슨 록펠러'는 수감자들의 요구를 무시하고 군대를 동원, 무자비하게 진압을 감행했던 것이다.

50년이 지난 지금은, 비록 죄수라고 하더라도 기본적인 인권은 보장해주어야 한다는 데에는 이견이 없는 세상이 되어 격세지감을 느낀다. 특히 2015년 유엔총회에서 채택한 '넬슨 만델라 규칙'에 수감자의 처우에 대한 최소한의 가이드라인을 제시였기 때문에 전 세계 모든 국가가 이를 준수할 의무가 있다.

이 규칙은 반정부운동으로 종신형을 선고받고 27년간 복역 후 남아프리카공화국 대통령으로 당선된 '넬슨 만델라(1918~2013)'의 사망 2주기를 맞아 그를 추모하기 위해 채택한 결의안이다.

'처벌과 교화'가 교도소의 역할이라고 하지만 이는 동전의 양면과 같아서 어디다 더 비중을 두어야 할지 여전히 어려운 숙제로 남는다. 처벌에 중점을 두면 아티카 폭동사건처럼 수감자들의 처우가 문제될 위험이 있고, 반대로 교화에 중점을 두어 편의시설과 다양한 프로그램을 제공하면 국민의 혈세를 낭비한다는 비판이 생기기 마련이기 때문이다.

이런 상황에서 최근 '조이스 스미스' 뉴욕주 낫소카운티 검사장 대행이 "사람을 구금하는 것만이 범죄 재발을 방지할 수 있는 방법이 아니라고 생각하기 때문에 앞으로 비폭력 경범죄자들에 대해서는 불기소하겠다"고 검찰의 방침을 밝힌 것처럼 상식적 범위 내에서 최대한 재소자 수를 줄여나가는 것도 교화를 위한 하나의 대안이 될 것으로 보인다. (2021.9.29.)

문제가 된 라이커스 아일랜드 재소자들의 틱톡 비디오 캡처
Screenshots of Tiktok video clips posted by inmates at Rikers Island

영어 녹음 듣기

Economy and Society

The Prison Story

Rikers Island in New York's East River comprises several detention facilities. The inmates there are people with pending criminal cases who cannot post bail or who have been sentenced to less than one year in jail. When the facilities were first erected in 1932, they were notorious for being one of the world's most extensive correctional facilities. Several decades later, however, the buildings show their age and the housing conditions are poor. In this year alone, 10 inmates have died from various causes. There are also reported incidents of correctional officers abusing an inmate or inmates fighting with each other.

On September 4, a video clip of three inmates at Rikers Island savagely beating another inmate was posted on TikTok, a video-focused social networking service. There was another video of five to six inmates partying while listening to music and smoking a cigarette.

New York City's mayor, Bill de Blasio, concluded that the inmates cannot be controlled because of the staffing shortage caused by COVID-19. To remedy the problem, he announced that staff must submit a doctor's note for any medical absence that lasts for longer than a day. He also announced plans to have officers from the New York City Police Department fill in the empty posts. According to The New York Times, in July alone, 2,300 out of approximately 9,000 officers, or about a quarter, were out for medical reasons.

In response to the mayor's actions, New York Governor Kathy Hochul also signed an order on September 17 immediately releasing 191 inmates who were detained at Rikers Island for relatively minor parole violations like breaking a curfew or alcohol ban. She also ordered about 200 inmates to be transferred to the state correctional facilities.

No story about horrible prison conditions would be complete without mentioning the Attica prison uprising. It's often regarded as the worst prison riot since the founding of America. This year marks the fiftieth anniversary. On September 9, 1971, there was a riot inside Attica Correctional Facility located between Buffalo and Rochester. This bloody incident resulted in 43 people dead, including 11 prison guards, and 100 wounded.

More than 1,200 inmates participated in the riot and took 20 prison guards hostage. Their demands included allowing them to take a shower every day and handing out more than one roll of toilet paper per month. From today's perspective, they seem reasonable and in accordance with basic human rights. However, then-governor Nelson Rockefeller refused to negotiate. He ordered the prison to be taken back by force, which resulted in bloody suppression.

Fifty years have passed. Now, even the harshest critics would agree that the inmates should enjoy basic human rights. In 2015, the U.N. General Assembly adopted the "Nelson Mandela Rules." They provide the minimum guidelines for the treatment of prison inmates. All member countries must abide by them. These rules were named to commemorate the second anniversary of the death of Nelson Mandela (1918~2013), a South African president who was imprisoned for 27 years for his work against the apartheid government.

Although punishment and rehabilitation fall squarely within the correctional facility's role, it is difficult to find the right balance between these conflicting values. If punishment is emphasized, the inmates' human rights will invariably suffer as the Attica Prison Riot highlights. On the other hand, if rehabilitation is given more weight and correctional facilities provide more accommodations and programs, then the critics complain that it's a waste of valuable tax dollars that can be used to help more deserving recipients.

Against this backdrop, Nassau County's acting district attorney, Joyce Smith, recently announced a new program to offer pre-arraignment diversion to people charged with minor, non-violent crimes. She claimed that the new program would "promote public safety, while helping participants avoid interactions with the criminal justice system, and freeing court resources for more serious offenses." Such reasonable efforts to prevent and reduce the number of prison inmates could be a viable option to promote rehabilitation. (2021.9.29.)

4장 전체 영어 녹음 듣기

Chapter
4

의료·방역
Medicine and Quarantine

공공의 적이 된 제약회사

아편 성분이 들어간 마약성 진통제는 강력한 진통 효과에 수반되는 중독성으로 인해 원래 말기 암 환자 등 불치병 환자들의 극심한 고통을 덜어주기 위해 사용되던 약이었다. 그러나 1995년 제약회사 퍼듀(Purdue Pharma)가 '옥시콘틴'이라는 마약성 진통제를 개발, 출시한 이후 의사들이 대수롭지 않게 마약성 진통제를 처방하기 시작했다.

옥시콘틴은 평균 4시간마다 복용해야 했던 기존 마약성 진통제와는 달리 12시간 진통 효과를 유지할 수 있게 개발된 약이었다. 퍼듀는 옥시콘틴의 마약 성분이 몸 안에서 서서히 침투하기 때문에 환각 증상과 중독성이 거의 없다고 미국 식약청을 설득하여 비교적 가벼운 통증에도 판매할 수 있도록 승인을 받아내는 데 성공했다.

퍼듀는 영업사원들을 동원, 의사들에게 옥시콘틴의 순기능에 대해 공격적인 마케팅을 전개한 결과 이 약 하나만으로 20여 년 동안 350억 달러(약 42조 원)라는 천문학적 영업수익을 거두어들였다. 이 같은 퍼듀의 블록버스터급 성공에 자극을 받은 다른 제약사들도 앞다투어 유사 진통제를 개발, 판매하다 보니 이제 마약성 진통제는 치과에서 사랑니 발치 후에도 처방받을 정도로 흔한 약이 되어 버렸다.

하지만 제약회사의 광고와는 다르게 이 약에 포함된 오피오이드는 헤로인의 몇 배에 달하는 치명적인 중독성을 가지고 있었다. 통계에 의하면 이 같은 중독성으로 1999년에서 2017년 사이 22만 명에 가까운 사람들이 더 자주, 더 강력한 마약성 진통제를 찾다 죽어간 것으로 나타났다.

이처럼 오피오이드 중독 피해자가 급속히 미 전역으로 확산되다 보니 결국 큰 사회문제로 대두하였고, 그에 따라 현재 제약회사나 의사, 판매업자 등을 상대로 한 크고 작은 소송 약 2,000여 건이 미국 전역에서 진행 중이라고 한다.

그중 첫 번째 소송의 결말이 얼마 전 오클라호마 주 클리브랜드 카운티법원에서 가려졌다. '오클라호마 대 퍼듀 제약회사'(Oklahoma v. Purdue Pharma)가 바로 그 사건인데 오클라호마의 검찰총장이 오피오이드 진통제 제약사인 퍼듀, 존슨앤드존슨(Johnson & Johnson), 테바(Teva) 등을 상대로 제기한 소송이다.

퍼듀와 테바는 일찌감치 꽁지를 내리고 각각 2억 7천만 달러와 8천5백만 달러를 배상하기로 합의함으로써 사건이 일단락되었지만 우리에게 타이레놀과 밴드에이드 등으로 익숙한 대형 제약회사 존슨앤드존슨은 합의를 거부하고 험난한 재판의 여정을 선택했다. 존슨앤드존슨이 개발한 오피오이드 진통제는 모르핀보다 100배나 강력한 펜타닐로 만든 패치 타입 '듀라제식'이라는 약이다.

사건을 배당 받은 클리브랜드 카운티법원 '새드 보크먼' 판사는 원고 오클라호마 주의 손을 들어주었는데 무엇보다 판결문의 내용이 꽤 흥미롭다. 오클라호마 법에는 폐수를 정화하지 않고 강물에 그대로 방류한다거나 사업장에서 너무 심한 소음을 일으켜 이웃에게 피해를 주는 경우 사회 공공재 또는 공동체 구성원의 삶의 질에 피해를 입힌다 하여 그 책임을 묻는 공적불법방해법(public nuisance law)이라는 게 있다.

즉 보크먼 판사는 한꺼번에 많은 사회구성원의 건강을 해치는 행위도 이 법에 저촉된다고 법 적용 범위를 폭넓게 해석했다. 따라서 존슨앤드존슨이 외판원들을 통해 의사들에게 오피오이드의 부작용은 감추고 순기능만 과장함으로써 마약성 진통제의 오남용을 야기한 것은 공적불법방해법에 위배된다고 판시하고 피해자들에게 5억 7천만 달러(약 7천억 원)의 손해배상을 하라고 명령했다. 존슨앤드존슨을 공공의 적으로 규정한 셈이다.

이 판결은 향후 다른 주에서 벌어지고 있는 후속 소송에서 유력한 합의의 기준으로 작용하겠지만 존슨앤드존슨 측에서 항소 방침을 밝힌 바 있어 그 귀추가 주목된다. (2019.9.11.)

결과: 새드 보크먼 판사의 결정은 이후 2021.11.9. 오클라호마 주 대법원에 의해 원심파기 되었다. 하지만, 미국 전역에서 아직 오피드오이드 제약회사를 상대로 한 소송이 활발히 진행 중이고 특히 오피오이드 사태를 촉발한 제약회사 퍼듀 파마는 2019년 파산보호를 신청하고 현재 수조 원의 보상금을 협상하고 있는 중이다.

영어 녹음 듣기

Medicine and Quarantine

Big Pharma and Opioid Crisis

Opioid painkillers are highly effective in alleviating pain, but they are also deadly addictive. That is why they were typically reserved for relieving extreme pain experienced by terminally ill patients like those in the last stages of cancer. However, since Purdue Pharma's development and introduction of OxyContin, an opioid painkiller, in 1995, many doctors began to prescribe them without giving it a second thought.

To assuage the initial concerns of the prescribing doctors and the Federal Drug Administration, Purdue Pharma argued that OxyContin was different from other opioid painkillers. It explained that while others had to be taken once every four hours, OxyContin was designed to maintain 12 hours of pain relief by releasing opioids more slowly once inside the body. Because of this slow-release mechanism, Purdue maintained that it is less hallucinogenic and less addictive than its competitors. As a result, the company successfully persuaded the FDA to allow it to market the drug to relieve relatively minor pains.

Then, Purdue launched an aggressive marketing campaign, sending their sales force to doctors and explaining OxyContin's benefits. It was a huge success. This drug alone earned the company an astronomical profit of $35 billion over the next 20 years. Inspired by Purdue's blockbuster success, other pharmaceutical companies followed suit, developing and selling opioid painkillers. Narcotics painkillers became so common that they could be prescribed after a wisdom tooth extraction at the dentist's office.

However, the opioids contained in these pills were many times more addictive than heroin. Between 1999 and 2017, more than 220,000 people died from an overdose as they sought more frequent highs at higher doses.

As a result, there is a widespread opioid crisis in America. There are about 2,000 lawsuits, big and small, against the pharmaceutical companies that manufactured opioid painkillers, and doctors and distributors who prescribed and sold them.

The first of these lawsuits was recently concluded in Oklahoma's Cleveland County Court. In Oklahoma v. Purdue Pharma, Oklahoma's Attorney General filed a lawsuit against opioid painkiller manufacturers, Purdue, Johnson & Johnson, and Teva.

Purdue and Teva settled their cases early and agreed to pay $270 million and $85 million, respectively. However, pharmaceutical giant Johnson & Johnson, the manufacturer of popular household products like Tylenol and Band-Aid, refused to settle and opted instead for the less certain path of a trial. Johnson & Johnson marketed a patch-type opioid painkiller named Duragesic, which contained fentanyl, a drug nearly 100 times more potent than morphine.

Judge Thad Balkman of the Cleveland County Court presided over the case. He ruled in favor of the plaintiff, the State of Oklahoma, and issued a noteworthy decision. Oklahoma has a public nuisance law that recognizes liability in acts that harm the public's quality of life, such as discharging wastewater without treatment or causing neighbors to suffer by making too much noise on one's business site.

By interpreting the law broadly and holding that any act that harms the public's health constitutes a public nuisance, Judge Balkman found that Johnson & Johnson's salespeople violated this law by overemphasizing the drug's upside while downplaying its potential negative consequences. He then directed the company to pay $570 million in damages. Essentially, he was holding the company to be a public enemy.

While this ruling will undoubtedly serve as an important settlement standard in other cases, the legal battle is not over yet, as Johnson & Johnson announced their plans to appeal. (2019.9.11.)

Outcome: Judge Thad Balkman's ruling was vacated by the Oklahoma Supreme Court on November 9, 2021. However, there are many active lawsuits against opioid manufacturers across the country. Purdue Pharma, which triggered the opioid crisis, filed for bankruptcy protection in 2019 and is negotiating a settlement with the victims.

코로나-19 백신을 기다리며

중학교 2학년 때 미국으로 건너와 미시간과 텍사스를 거쳐 지금까지 13년째 뉴요커로 살고 있지만 세계의 심장이라 일컫는 뉴욕의 거리가 이처럼 황량하게 변한 모습은 정말 처음 본다. 팬데믹이 강타한 뉴욕은 마치 유령의 도시와 같다. 의료계에 의하면 코로나 바이러스가 전 세계적으로 전파되었기 때문에 국지적 방역 대책으로는 한계가 있고, 이를 근본적으로 해결하려면 백신 개발만이 지름길이라고 하는데 이번에는 백신에 얽힌 법률문제를 조명해본다.

4월 8일 자 워싱턴포스트지는 코로나-19 백신의 임상시험 첫 단계가 시작되었다고 희망적 뉴스를 보도했다. 백신의 원리는 미약한 균을 미리 건강한 사람 인체에 주입하여 사람 몸이 스스로 바이러스를 이길 수 있도록 항체를 만들어주는 것인데 18세기 후반 영국의 시골 의사 '에드워드 제너'가 처음으로 개발했다. 에드워드는 당시 공포의 대상이었던 천연두가 소를 키우는 사람들에게서는 거의 발병되지 않는다는 데 착안, 우두 균을 사용했기 때문에 암소를 뜻하는 라틴어 vacca에서 vaccine이란 용어가 유래되었다.

이후 저온 살균법으로 유명한 파스퇴르와 같은 과학자와 의사들이 폐결핵, 소아

마비, 디프테리아, 파상풍, 홍역 등의 백신을 지속적으로 개발한 덕분에 인류는 이런 질병의 공포에서 해방될 수 있었다.

흥미로운 점은 한때 미국에서 너무 잦은 소송 문제로 백신 개발과 제조의 명맥이 끊길 뻔한 소동이 있었다는 사실이다.

1905년, 연방대법원은 '제이콥슨 대 매사추세츠'(Jacobson v. Massachusetts) 사건을 통해 공공보건을 위해 개인의 자유는 어느 정도 제한할 수 있다고 선언함으로써 국가가 국민들에게 예방접종을 의무화할 수 있는 법적 근거를 마련해주었다. 하지만 모든 의약품이 그렇듯 백신 역시 부작용이 있어 심할 경우 알레르기 반응 등으로 죽음에까지 이를 수도 있다는 것이다.

특히 1970년대와 80년대에 걸쳐 파상풍(Tetanus)과 디프테리아(Diphtheria), 백일해(Pertussis)를 예방하기 위해 개발된 백신(줄여서 T-D-P)이 접종 대상인 아이들의 뇌에 영구적인 손상을 준다는 논쟁이 일어 T-D-P 제약사들을 상대로 소송이 끊이지 않았다.

문제는 이에 대한 과학적 근거가 입증되지 않았음에도 배심원과 판사들이 툭하면 원고 측 손을 들어주다 보니 결국 손해배상 비용을 감당하지 못한 제약회사들이 백신 생산을 포기하는 상황에까지 이르고 말았다. 그 결과 1985년 T-D-P 미국 제조사는 단 하나만 남게 되었는데 이번에는 백신 공급 부족으로 가격이 폭등하는 또 다른 시장 부작용이 발생하게 된 것이다.

이에 대한 해결책으로 미 의회가 꺼내 든 것이 연방 백신피해 보상제도(National Vaccine Injury Compensation Program, 줄여서 NVICP)였다. 즉 이전에는 피해자들이 제약사의 과실을 증명해야만 했는데 NVICP 시스템 후에는 정부 지정 백신을 맞았다는 사실과 부작용 등을 간단하게 증명하여 제약사 대신 보건복지부 장관을 상대로 문제를 제기하면 조속한 보상을 받을 수 있도록 개선됐다.

이와 함께 제약회사에는 백신의 부작용으로 사망 시 최고 25만 불 등 책임 상한선을 정해 배상 부담을 경감시켜 주었다. 다시 말해 정부가 중간에 개입하여 국민들의 집단면역으로 공공보건을 유지하고 한편으로는 제약회사들을 보호하여 백신의 안정적인 공급도 가능하게 선순환 체계를 구축해준 것이다.

하루빨리 백신이 개발되어 거추장스럽기 짝이 없는 마스크를 훌훌 벗어던져 버리고 뉴욕의 도심이 예전처럼 전 세계에서 찾아온 관광객들로 북적대는 모습을 다시 보고 싶다. (2020.4.22.)

영어 녹음 듣기

Medicine and Quarantine

Waiting for the COVID-19 Vaccine

I have been a New Yorker for 13 years now, having arrived here by way of Michigan and Texas after coming to America in 8th grade. In all my years here, I have never seen the streets of New York City, the world's center, so deserted. This pandemic has hit the city hard and the "city that never sleeps" now looks like a ghost town. The medical community says that local quarantine measures may be limited in their effectiveness against the global fight against coronavirus and the development of a vaccine is the only way to fundamentally solve the problem. Today's column reviews relevant legal issues with vaccines.

The Washington Post published a hopeful news article on April 8th reporting that the first phase of clinical trials for the coronavirus vaccine has begun. Traditional vaccines work by injecting a weakened form of the virus into a healthy person's body to teach the immune system how to fight it. Vaccines were first developed in the late 18th century by Dr. Edward Jenner, a countryside physician from Britain. Dr. Jenner realized that smallpox, a feared disease at the

코로나-19로 텅텅 빈 뉴욕의 거리(2020)
Streets of Manhattan at the height of the
Covid-19 pandemic

time, occurred rarely among cattle farmers because of their exposure to cowpox. He used the cowpox virus to successfully protect people against smallpox. For this reason, the word vaccine comes from the Latin word "vacca," which means cow. Since then, doctors and scientists like Pasteur-widely known for pasteurization-have freed us from tuberculosis, polio, diphtheria, tetanus and measles by developing appropriate vaccines against the viruses that cause them.

Interestingly, despite all the benefits of a vaccine, there was a time in America when its development and production almost came to a screeching halt because of frequent lawsuits.

In 1905, the Supreme Court ruled in Jacobson v. Massachusetts that an individual's freedom may be limited for the sake of public health, providing a legal foundation for mandatory vaccination. However, as with all other medicines, vaccines have side effects. In the most serious cases, they can lead to death by an allergic reaction.

In the 1970s and 80s, reports of permanent brain damage to children from the D-T-P vaccine (short for diphtheria, tetanus, and pertussis) led to endless lawsuits being brought against the vaccine manufacturers. Although there was no scientific basis for the allegation, judges and juries often sided with plaintiffs and awarded huge damages. This caused companies to cease vaccine production.

As a result, in 1985, there was only one D-T-P vaccine manufacturer left in the entire country. Naturally, this led to another side effect – soaring vaccine prices caused by lack of supply.

코로나-19 전의 활기찬 거리 <출처: 구글 어스>
The same streets before the Covid-19 pandemic <source: Google Earth>

To remedy the problem, Congress enacted the National Vaccine Injury Compensation Program (NVICP). Instead of suing the pharmaceutical companies directly, the new program required the victims to sue the Director of the Department of Health and Human Services instead. Under the new program, in order to be compensated for their injuries, victims only needed to show that they received a vaccine shot and point to an injury they suffered on the vaccine injury table.

The program also reduced liability for pharmaceutical companies by capping the maximum amount of damages depending on the injury. For instance, the maximum damage for death was capped at $250,000. This program had the intended effect of ensuring public health by providing sufficient protection to the pharmaceutical companies to maintain a steady supply of vaccines.

I am eagerly awaiting the day when the coronavirus vaccine will be widely available to all of us so that the streets of New York will come back to life once again with tourists from all over the world – as it used to be. (2020.4.22.)

코로나-19로 바뀐 변호사시험 풍경

미국 변호사시험은 '바'(bar) 시험이라고 부르는데 이는 중세 유럽에서 변호사들이 법정 안에 설치된 나무 막대기(bar) 뒤에 서서 변론하던 전통에서 유래된 표현이다. 바 시험은 매년 2월과 7월의 마지막 주 미국 전역에서 이틀에 걸쳐 치러지는데 대부분 UBE(Uniform Bar Examination)를 본다. UBE는 사지선다형 객관식 MBE(Multistate Bar Examination)와 법조 실무 능력을 평가하는 MPT(Multistate Performance Test), 논술형 시험인 MEE(Multistate Essay Examination)로 이루어져 있다.

또 주에 따라 해당 주법의 시험을 따로 치르고, 변호사 윤리 시험인 MPRE(Multistate Professional Responsibility Examination)까지 합격해야 바시험을 통과하게 된다. 영국식 보통법 관습을 따르는 대부분의 주와 달리 프랑스 식민지였던 루이지애나주는 프랑스의 영향을 받아 대륙법을 따르기 때문에 UBE를 보지 않는다.

시험에 합격 후 지금까지 일했던 곳의 고용주 추천서를 비롯 개인추천서, 범죄와 파산, 병무기록, 법적분쟁기록 등을 제출하고 마지막 관문으로 인성위원회와의 인터뷰를 통과하면 비로소 3년 과정 로스쿨의 종착역인 대망의 변호사 선서를 할 수 있게 된다.

연방국가인 미국의 특성상 각 주의 대법원에서 변호사 자격을 인허해주는 체계이다 보니 뉴욕 변호사는 뉴욕주에서만 활동할 수 있고, 다른 주에서 변호사를 하고 싶다면 이런 시험과정을 거쳐 해당 지역 자격증을 다시 따야 한다.

원래 법조계 특성이 현장에서 이미 벌어진 일을 법에 따라 잘잘못을 판단하고 뒷정리를 해주는 성격이다 보니 시대 변화에 한발 늦을 수밖에 없는 실정이라고 보면 코로나-19 관련 소송은 1~2년 뒤쯤 그 봇물이 터질 것으로 보인다. 하지만 코로나 사태 장기화로 당장 많은 지원자가 한 곳에 모여 바 시험 볼 여건이 여의치 않게 되자 법조계 관문이랄 수 있는 바 시험 풍경부터 변화의 바람이 불기 시작했다.

즉, 텍사스와 버지니아주와 같이 7월 바 시험을 예정대로 밀어붙이는 주가 있는가 하면 매사추세츠와 플로리다주는 인터넷으로 대체할 예정이고, 유타주에선 시험 대신 올해 말까지 360시간 이상의 견습경력을 쌓으면 변호사 자격을 주기로, 뉴욕주는 7월 시험을 9월로 미루면서 뉴욕주에 위치한 15개 로스쿨 졸업생에게 시험자격 우선권을 주기로 각각 결정했다.

이런 임시 조치 대신 아예 무시험 통과시켜주기로 통 큰 결정을 한 곳도 있어 찬반 논란이 뜨겁다. 워싱턴주는 7월 응시자 모두 무차별 통과시켜 주기로 했다. 이웃 오리건주는 오리건주립대를 비롯 윌라멧, 루이스 앤 클라크 로스쿨 등 주 내 3개 로스쿨의 2020년 졸업생들과 타주 응시생 중 작년 일정 기준 이상의 합격률을 보였던 로스쿨 출신 졸업생들에게는 시험 없이 변호사가 될 수 있는 '졸업장 특권'(diploma privilege)을 주기로 결정했다.

응시생과 로스쿨 관계자 등 수혜자들은 "그러잖아도 코로나-19 와중에 '조지 플로이드'의 죽음으로 야기된 전국적 항의시위까지 겹쳐 열악한 면학 환경에 처했던 올해 졸업생들에게 예년처럼 바 시험을 고집하는 것은 특히 유색 소수인종에게 불리할 수밖에 없다"고 주장했던 터라 무시험 결정을 전폭 지지한다고 밝혔다.

그러면서 위스콘신주는 이미 1870년부터 로스쿨 졸업생들에게 졸업장 특권을 허락하고 있는데 이들이 바 시험 통과 변호사들에 비해 능력이 떨어진다는 증거가 없다고 부연 설명했다.

이에 반해 포틀랜드 유력 일간지 오리거니언은 사설을 통해 작년 오리건 바 시험 응시자 4명 중 1명이 떨어졌으며 어떤 해에는 응시자의 42%가 통과하지 못한 때도 있었다고 지적하고, 다른 주처럼 온라인 시험이나 일정을 연기하는 대안이 있음에도 졸업장 특권을 주는 것은 행정편의주의로 결국 그 불이익은 클라이언트와 시민들에게 돌아올 것이라 경고했다.

그러면서 무시험 변호사들은 클라이언트들에게 자신은 졸업장 특권으로 변호사가 되었다고 밝혀야 한다고 불편한 심기를 표출했다. (2020.7.15.)

'Korean Day' 퍼레이드에서 뉴욕한인변호사협회 회원들과(맨해튼.2019)
Walking with members of the Korean American Lawyers Association of
Greater New York at the Korean Day parade (Manhattan)

Medicine and Quarantine

How Covid-19 Changed the Bar Exam

In medieval Europe, lawyers used to argue from behind a bar in the middle of the courtroom. Now, a bar exam refers to the test that lawyers must pass to practice law in that jurisdiction. All across America, bar exams are administered over two days in the last week of February and July.

In most states, applicants must take the Uniform Bar Examination (UBE), which consists of Multistate Bar Examination (MBE), Multistate Performance Test (MPT), Multistate Essay Examination (MEE). In addition, they must also pass the ethics exam, Multistate Professional Responsibility Examination (MPRE). Unlike the other jurisdictions that follow the English common law tradition, Louisiana, a former French colony, follows the continental legal tradition and does not administer the UBE.

After passing the bar exam, applicants must submit letters of recommendation from personal contacts and previous employers. In addition, they must submit an affidavit about their criminal and bankruptcy history, military service, and past and current legal disputes. As the final step before taking an oath as a lawyer, they must also go through an interview process with the Character and Fitness Committee. Each state's highest court grants a license to practice law, and New York lawyers can practice only in New York. They must go through this process again if they wish to practice in another jurisdiction.

The legal profession tends to be reactive because most times, lawyers deal with things that have already happened and discuss the right or wrong after the fact. Naturally, COVID-19-related lawsuits will likely flood the courts in a year or two. At the same time, the prolonged COVID situation is already affecting how bar exams are administered by preventing test takers from gathering in one place. Each state is reacting differently. For example, states like Texas and Virginia are pushing through with the July exam without any changes. In other states like Massachusetts and Florida, in-person tests will be replaced by online tests. In Utah, it was announced that applicants would gain bar admission after 360 hours of apprenticeship. New York plans to postpone the July bar exam until September. When the exam is administered, priority to take it will be given to the graduates from 15 New York law schools.

Some states decided to bypass these temporary measures and allow candidates to become lawyers without a test. This decision has sparked an intense debate. For example, the State of Washington has determined to let all applicants for the July exam to pass without actually taking the bar. The neighboring Oregon State has decided that the graduates from law schools with a high passage rate would automatically gain admission. In addition, graduates from three law schools in the State, Oregon State University, Willamette University School of Law, and

Lewis and Clarke Law School, will receive diploma privilege and become a lawyer upon their law school graduation.

The beneficiaries of this new policy, including the bar takers and law school officials, support this decision. They say that insisting on bar exams, as in the previous years, is unfair to the graduates of color who faced extremely challenging academic conditions this year caused by COVID-19 and protests spurred by George Floyd's death. They also point out that the State of Wisconsin has been allowing diploma privilege starting as far back as 1870. Still, there is no evidence that Wisconsin lawyers are inferior to those who passed the bar exam.

On the other hand, Portland's leading daily newspaper, The Oregonian, published an editorial stating that one in four applicants fail the exam in a typical year. In some years, 42% of the test takers failed. It warned that giving diploma privilege for administrative convenience, especially when there are other options like administering the test online or postponing it, would be harmful to clients and citizens alike. Also, it sarcastically remarked that lawyers who gained admission through diploma privilege must disclose to their clients that they did not take the bar. (2020.7.15.)

죽을 수 있는 법적 권리

2018.1.26. 14:00 신체 튼튼한 29세의 네덜란드 여성 '오렐리아 브라우어스'(Aurelia Brouwers)가 정신질환을 명분으로 의사가 건네준 독극물을 스스로 마시고 생을 마감함으로써 전 세계에 충격을 던져주었다. 12세 때부터 경계선 인격장애, 애착 장애, 만성적 자살충동과 우울증 등을 복합적으로 앓고 있었던 오렐리아는 이처럼 안락사를 결심하기 전 "나는 하루하루 숨 쉬는 것 자체가 고문일 정도로 참을 수 없을 만큼 괴롭다"고 밝혔던 것으로 알려졌다.

나라별로 다소 차이는 있지만 임종을 앞둔 환자가 죽음을 선택할 수 있는 법적 권리로는 대체 두 가지가 있다고 볼 수 있다. 하나는 환자의 산소호흡기나 영양공급 호스, 투석과 같은 보조장치를 제거하는 이른바 '존엄사'이고, 나머지는 적극적으로 약물 투입 등을 통해 신체적 고통을 줄이고 인위적으로 생을 마감하는 '안락사'이다.

오렐리아처럼 의료진이 개입하여 생명을 단축시키게 되면 '조력자살'이니 '살인방조'니 하면서 법적으로 문제가 복잡해진다. 이런 문제를 해결하기 위해서는 안락사 관련 입법이 필요한데 그중 제일 앞서가는 나라로 네덜란드를 꼽을 수 있다.

네덜란드는 2002년 제정한 안락사법을 통해 '호전될 가능성이 없으면서 참을 수 없는 고통'과 '합리적 대안의 부재' – 이 두 기준을 충족하는 환자들에게 안락사를 폭넓게 허용하고 있다.

이 법에 의하면 오렐리아와 같은 중증 정신질환자뿐 아니라 불치병에 걸린 12세 미만의 어린이들까지 부모의 동의 하에 안락사가 허용된다. 이렇게 생을 마감한 사람의 수가 2020년 한 해 동안 네덜란드 전체 사망자의 4.3%인 6,938명에 달한다고 한다.

일본은 나고야 고등법원 판례를 통해 임종을 앞둔 환자가 극심한 고통을 호소하고, 본인이 명료한 의식 상태에서 안락사를 승낙했으며, 의사의 시술로 환자의 고통이 완화되고, 시술 방법이 윤리적으로 타당할 때 처벌하지 않는 것으로 안락사 지침을 삼고 있다.

미국은 오리건, 캘리포니아, 콜로라도, 뉴저지, 워싱턴 등 10여 개 주에서 불치병 환자들에 한해 안락사를 허용하고 있다. 워싱턴 주의 경우 18세 이상의 성인이 의사 2명으로부터 6개월 이하의 시한부 인생이라는 의사소견서를 받고, 15일 간격으로 2회에 걸쳐 구두로 안락사 의사를 밝혔으며, 2명의 증인 입회 하에 서면으로 안락사를 요구할 것을 필요로 한다. 하와이 주는 여기에다 최소 20일의 대기기간과 정신 감정까지 요구하고 있다.

사람이 스스로 자기 생명을 포기하겠다고 하는 것은 어쩔 수 없다고 하더라도 의료진이 개입하여 생명을 인위적으로 종결시키는 안락사 문제는 찬반양론이 첨예하게 대립되어 있다.

안락사를 찬성하는 측은 생명연장 기술이 늘어났다곤 하지만 근본적인 치료가 불가능한 상황에서 견딜 수 없는 고통을 감내하라고 하는 것은 환자 자신을 위해서나 이를 지켜보고 간병하는 가족 입장에서 볼 때 차라리 안락사가 생명을 존엄하게 마

오렐리아 브라우어스의 인스타그램 캡처 / Aurelia Brouwers Instagram

무리할 수 있는 해결책이라고 주장한다.

반면, 로마 교황청 등 각 종교단체 중심의 반대 측은 안락사를 인정하게 되면 중증 환자들이 가족이나 주위 이해당사자들로부터 무언 중 그렇게 하도록 강요를 받아 '현대판 고려장'이 될 위험성이 다분하고, 무엇보다 용기를 북돋워 주면서 사람을 치료해야 할 의사들이 오히려 환자의 자살을 도와주는 것은 의사의 윤리 면에서 가당치 않다고 강력하게 거부하고 있다.

보도에 의하면 뉴욕주도 이 같은 세계적 추세를 감안하여 안락사 법안을 상정하였다고 한다. 총 150명 중 1/3에 달하는 40여 명의 하원 의원들과 총 63명 중 16명의 상원 의원들이 지지를 표하고 있는 것으로 알려져 있는데 과연 법안이 통과될지 귀추가 주목된다. (2021.10.14.)

Right to Die

On January 26, 2018, at 14:00 hours, 29-year-old Dutch woman Aurelia Brouwers ended her own life by taking a poison that a doctor supplied. As she was physically healthy, her decision to end her life, after years of suffering from mental illness, shocked the world. Since age 12, she was diagnosed with borderline personality disorder, attachment disorder, and chronic depression. Before her euthanasia, she said, "I suffer unbearably and hopelessly. Every breath I take is torture."

What is available to the patient varies from country to country, but broadly speaking, a patient facing imminent death has two options. The first involves passively ending one's life by withholding life support like the oxygen respirator or a nutritional hose, or stopping dialysis. The second option involves more actively ending one's life by voluntarily taking drugs to speed up the painful and inevitable death.

When medical professionals intervene to end a patient's life, as in Aurelia's case, it can bring about legal complications unless there is an established set of laws that allow euthanasia. Without them, the doctor may face criminal charges for aiding and abetting a murder or committing physician-assisted suicide.

The Netherlands is at the forefront of legalizing euthanasia. In 2002, the "Termination of Life on Request and Assisted Suicide Act" became effective. It allows a person to be euthanized provided that their suffering is "unbearable with no prospect of improvement" and a reasonable alternative is absent. Under the latest iteration of the law, it permits euthanasia not only for patients like Aurelia who have serious mental illness but the children under the age of 12 as well with their parents' consent. In the Netherlands, 6,938 died from euthanasia, or 4.3% of all deaths, in 2020.

In Japan, Nagoya High Court permitted euthanasia under strict conditions. It requires the patient to be incurable with no hope of recovery and death must be imminent. Also, the patient has to give informed, explicit consent and euthanasia must be undertaken to alleviate the patient's pain. Finally, euthanasia must be carried out using ethically acceptable methods.

In the United States, about 10 states including Oregon, California, Colorado, New Jersey, and Washington, allow medical aid in dying for terminally ill patients. In Washington, it's limited to patients over the age of 18 who have a terminal illness with an estimated life expectancy of six months or less that two independent physicians confirm. There is also a requirement of two oral requests with a 15-day waiting period in between and two people must witness a written request for medical aid in dying. Hawaii adds a 20-day waiting period and a psychological evaluation as well.

As tragic as it is, people who are determined to do so will find a way to end their lives. At the same time, it's another matter for the government to allow medical intervention to end a person's life. Such legislation is bound to draw strong arguments from both sides.

The supporters argue that even though life-sustaining medical advances have been made, it's inhumane for the patients and their families to endure treatment when there is no fundamental cure for the patient. They claim that medical aid in dying could help a person to die with dignity.

On the other hand, different religious organizations, including the Roman Catholic Church, counter that allowing euthanasia will subject terminally ill patients to come under pressure from their families or other interested persons to end their lives. Furthermore, ethically speaking, they maintain that medical professionals should focus on treating people and making them better. Therefore, they're not supposed to lend a hand to people ending their lives.

Some bills have been introduced in the state senate and the assembly to allow medical aid in dying in New York. According to one source, about a third of the assembly members, 40 out of 150 members, and 16 out of 63 senators support these bills. It remains to be seen whether they will pass. (2021.10.14.)

백신 멘데이트

학수고대하던 백신만 개발되면 곧 종식될 것처럼 보였던 코로나-19가 '델타'에 이은 '오미크론' 등 새로운 변이의 출현으로 전 세계를 다시 공포 속으로 몰아넣고 있다. 이에 대한 대책의 일환으로 미국 연방정부를 비롯한 일부 주 정부는 백신 맨데이트(mandate)를 발표하고 공무원이나 정부와 거래하는 계약업체 등에 백신 접종을 의무화하고 있다.

특히 '빌 드블라지오' 뉴욕시장은 지난 12월 6일, 미국에서 처음으로 민간영역까지 그 적용 범위를 확대하고 뉴욕 시내에서 영업 중인 184,000여 개의 민간 사업장에 백신을 접종하지 않은 직원은 출근금지와 아울러 백신 의무화 명령을 위반하는 업주에게는 1,000달러의 벌금을 부과키로 했다.

의료계 역시 국민들이 백신을 맞아야 코로나-19에 걸리더라도 중증까지 가지 않고 병마를 이겨낼 수 있을 뿐 아니라 사회적 집단면역도 달성할 수 있다고 보고 정부의 맨데이트 방침에 힘을 보태고 있다. 하지만 아직도 많은 사람이 백신의 부작용에 대한 걱정이나 각종 음모론, 정부의 강제성에 대한 반발심 등으로 백신 접종을 거부하고 있는 실정이다.

그러다 보니 전국적으로 이에 대한 크고 작은 소송이 이어지고 있는 가운데 연방대법원은 2022.1.7. 바이든 행정부의 백신 맨데이트에 대한 적법성을 심리할 예정이다.

개인의 자유를 중시하는 미국에서 백신 의무화 명령에 따른 법정 싸움은 예전부터 있어왔다. 1902년, 천연두의 창궐로 많은 사람이 목숨을 잃자 매사추세츠주는 의무적 예방접종법을 시행해 모든 주민에게 무료로 백신을 맞게 하고, 이를 거부한 사람에게는 5달러(현재 가치로 약 150달러)의 벌금을 물도록 했다. 지금처럼 연방 식품의약국(FDA, Food and Drug Administration)이나 질병통제예방센터(CDC, Center for Disease Control and Prevention) 등도 없어 백신의 안전성도 검증이 되지 않던 시절 얘기이다.

120년 전 당시에도 앤티 백서(anti-vaxxer)들은 현재 미접종자들이 내세우는 똑같은 이유를 대며 백신 접종을 거부했다. 특히 보스턴 인근 도시 케임브리지의 목사 '헤닝 제이콥슨'(Henning Jacobson)은 어렸을 때 그의 고향인 스웨덴에서 강제로 천연두 예방 접종을 받았는데 이로 인해 '평생 백신에 대한 공포'를 느끼게 되었다며 백신을 맞지 않았다. 주 정부가 벌금을 물리자 그는 수정헌법 제14조에 보장된 백신을 맞지 않을 자신의 자유를 침해당했다고 소송을 제기했다.

그러나 연방대법원은 1905년 대법관 7대2로 공공보건을 위해 개인의 자유는 어느 정도 제한할 수 있다고 선언하고 매사추세츠주의 손을 들어주었던 것이다.

이때 다수판결문 작성은 '존 마셜 할런' 판사에게 맡겨졌다. 그는 켄터키 노예농장주의 아들로 태어났지만 노예를 비롯한 인간의 존엄성을 중요하게 생각하는 사람이었다. 할런 판사는 '구성원들의 안전을 보호할 의무가 있는 사회에서, 개인의 권리는 때때로 큰 위험으로부터 일반 대중들의 안전을 지키기 위해 합리적인 규제를 받을 수 있다.

여러 사람이 모여 사는 사회에서 모든 사람의 완전한 자유는 존재할 수 없으며, 필수 예방접종이 국민들의 안전을 위해 합리적으로 요구되는 범위를 벗어나지 않는 한 억압적이지 않다'고 판단했다.

제이콥슨 사건은 이후 1922년, 텍사스주 샌안토니오시의 '주크 대 킹'(Zucht v. King) 사건에서 예방 접종을 하지 않은 학생의 입학을 거부한 샌안토니오시 학구에 승소할 수 있는 발판을 마련해주었다. 아울러 이번 코로나-19 판국에서도 백신 맨데이트를 지지하는 여러 판결문에서 이 판례가 자주 인용되고 있다.

이런 분위기를 감안할 때 바이든 행정부의 이번 백신 멘데이트는 종교적·의료적 예외를 허용하고 있는 데다 안전성 문제도 까다롭기 이를 데 없는 FDA와 CDC의 검사를 거쳤기 때문에 합헌 판결이 지속될 것으로 법조계는 예상하고 있다. (2022.1.5.)

결과: 2022.1.13. 연방대법원은 직업안전보건청(Occupational Safety and Health Administration)이 100인 이상 민간 사업장 종사자에 대한 백신 접종을 의무화한 조치를 6대 3 의견으로 무효화했다. 다만 대법원은 정부 지원금을 받는 의료시설의 종사자들에 대한 백신 접종 의무화는 정당하다고 판단했다.

코로나-19 부스터 샷을 맞는 바이든 대통령 <출처: CNN 캡처>
President Biden getting Covid-19 vaccine booster <source: CNN>

The Vaccine Mandate

Once upon a time, it seemed as though the pandemic would end as soon as the highly anticipated COVID-19 vaccines were developed and distributed. However, with the emergence of new Delta and Omicron variants, the world is cowering in fear yet again. The federal and several state government agencies have announced a vaccine mandate in response. The mandate requires government employees and contractors to be vaccinated.

On December 6, Mayor Bill de Blasio took a step further and announced a vaccine mandate that required roughly 184,000 private businesses in New York City to ban unvaccinated workers from entering the workplace. Employers who do not comply will receive a $1,000 fine. This is the first mandate that applies to private businesses and their employees.

The medical community supports the efforts to get people vaccinated because the data shows that being vaccinated helps reduce the effects of COVID-19. The more vaccinated people also means that we can achieve herd immunity.

However, many people are still adamantly opposed because they believe in a conspiracy theory or are concerned about its side effects. Some have an outright opposition to what they believe is a government overreach.

As a reflection of these sentiments, many lawsuits, big and small, have been filed throughout the country. The U.S. Supreme Court is slated to hear the legality of the Biden Administration's vaccine mandate on January 7, 2022.

Individual freedom is a core American value, and fighting over a vaccine mandate is nothing new. In 1902, many people died when there was a surge in smallpox. In response, Massachusetts adopted a vaccine mandate. Under the new rule, everyone who wanted a vaccine shot could get it free of charge. Those who refused would be fined $5 (about $150 in today's value). Unfortunately, the Federal Food and Drug Administration or the Center for Disease Control and Prevention was not yet in existence, and the vaccine's safety could not be guaranteed.

The anti-vaxxers from 120 years ago refused to get vaccinated for reasons similar to those given today. Henning Jacobson was a pastor living in Cambridge, a city adjacent to Boston. He refused to be vaccinated because he developed a "lifelong horror of the practice" when he received mandatory vaccination in his original home of Sweden. He was fined $5, and he responded by suing the government. He argued that he had a right under the Fourteenth Amendment not to get vaccinated. However, in a 7-2 decision, the Supreme Court held that the state might impose reasonable restrictions on individual freedom to protect public health and secure public safety.

Justice John Marshall Harlan wrote the majority decision. He was born into a prominent slaveholding family in Kentucky. However, he had a strong belief in human dignity including the enslaved people. In the decision, he wrote, "in every well ordered society charged with the duty of conserving the safety of its members[,] the rights of the individual in respect to his liberty may at times, under the pressure of great dangers, be subjected to such restraint, to be enforced by reasonable regulations, as the safety of the general public may demand."

존 마셜 할런(1833-1911)
Justice John Marshall Harlan

He further wrote that "[r]eal liberty for all could not exist under the operation of a principle which recognizes the right of each individual person to use his own [liberty]" and mandate did not "go so far beyond what was reasonably required for the safety of the public."

The Jacobson case served as a legal foundation for the 1922 Supreme Court case Zucht v. King. There, the Court held that the San Antonio school district could constitutionally exclude unvaccinated students from attending the schools in the district. Jacobson has also been cited often in recent decisions that upheld the vaccine mandate.

Given this legal context, the Biden administration's vaccine mandate will likely pass the constitutional muster because the FDA and CDC have approved the vaccines. They also contain provisions for medical and religious exemptions. (2022.1.5.)

Outcome: On January 13, 2022, in a 6-3 decision, the Supreme Court struck down the mandate by the Occupational Safety and Health Administration for businesses with more than 100 employees to require their workers to be vaccinated. However, they allowed the vaccine mandate for health care workers at federally funded facilities to stand.

원격진료의 명암

미국 보건복지부의 작년 12월 통계에 의하면 '텔레메디신'(원격진료) 건수가 코로나19 발병 전인 2019년 한 해 84만 건에서, 팬데믹 후인 2020년에는 5,300만 건으로 1년 만에 무려 63배나 폭증한 것으로 나타났다. 텔레메디신이란 의료진이 환자와 다른 장소에서 원격으로 의료 서비스를 제공하는 것을 일컫는데, 여기에는 화상통화를 비롯하여 환자 모니터링, 의무기록 관리, 원격 디지털 의료장비 사용 등이 포함된다.

인류가 꿈꾸어오던 메디컬 유토피아의 세계-텔레메디신이 그동안 각종 규제로 답보상태에 머물다 생각지 않았던 팬데믹을 계기로 재택 격리와 사회적 거리두기 등이 일상화되면서 성큼 우리 앞에 다가온 것이다.

텔레메디신의 장점은 무엇보다 시간과 장소에 구애받지 않고 의사를 만날 수 있고, 대면 진료보다 비용이 저렴하다는 점이다. 그러나 의료 사고나 의료 과실에 따른 제도적 장치가 뒷받침되지 않아 정착단계까지는 아직 이르지 못하고 있다. 다음의 사례에서 예상 문제점을 진단해본다.

2012. 2. 17. 정오 무렵 뉴욕주 교도소 복역수 '마빈 스나이더'(29세)는 가슴에서

시작된 심한 통증으로 급히 구내 간호실을 찾았다. 주간 간호사는 EKG를 부착하고 심전도 검사를 시도했으나 기계가 작동되지 않아 카운티 병원에 원격진료를 의뢰했다.

교도소의 의무기록을 토대로 환자를 화상으로 진찰한 카운티 병원의 보조 의사는 환자의 신체 상태로 보아 일시적 통증이라고 판단, 타이레놀만 처방하고 스나이더를 감방으로 되돌려 보냈다. 하지만 저녁 10시가 되어도 병세가 호전되지 않아 다시 간호실을 방문한 결과 야간 당직 간호사는 EKG 기계를 재 부팅하는 데 성공하여 그가 심장마비 증세를 보이고 있다는 사실을 알게 되었다.

다행히 병원으로 긴급 후송되어 목숨을 건진 스나이더는 퇴원 후 의료진의 초동 대처 미흡으로 장시간 불필요한 고통과 아울러 더 큰 수술을 받게 되었다고 주장하며 교도소와 병원 의료 관계자들을 상대로 소송을 제기했다. 통상 의료 소송에서의 쟁점은 의료진이 업무상 주의의무를 게을리하지 않고, '의료계의 표준 관행'에 맞게 의료 서비스를 제공했는지 여부다.

이 소송의 결과가 팬데믹으로 텔레메디신이 한창 주목을 받던 2020. 12월에 알려졌다. 뉴욕주 법원에 의하면 간호사는 일단 카운티 병원에 텔레메디신을 요청했으므로 '의료계의 표준 관행'에 맞는 조치를 취했다고 판단하고 스나이더의 청구를 기각했다. 반면 심장병 증세 환자에겐 필수적인 심전도 검사를 거치지 않고 스나이더를 그냥 되돌려 보낸 카운티 병원 의사의 처방은 과실이 있다 하여 재판에 회부했던 것이다. 그 후 더 이상 후속 자료 추적이 되지 않는 것으로 보아 합의로 사건이 종결된 것으로 추측되지만 이 사건을 통해 다음과 같은 문제점을 생각해볼 수 있다.

첫째, 아무래도 의사가 직접 환자를 대면하지 못하다 보니 스나이더처럼 필수 검사를 생략하여 골든타임을 놓칠 수 있다.

둘째, 의료장비가 부족하거나 일부 함량 미달의 동네 의료진이 응급 상황에서 자신의 책임을 회피하기 위해 이를 악용할 소지가 있다.

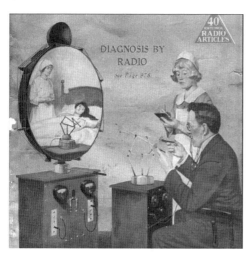

1925년 텔레메디신 상상도
1925 poster about telemedicine

　　마지막으로, 의료사고에 대한 책임을 묻기 위해 법적 기준으로 삼는 '의료계의 표준 관행'이란 게 급속한 의술의 발달, 전문의 여부, 어느 주에서 의료행위가 이루어졌는지 등 각 변수가 너무 많아 이것을 자로 재듯 정량화하기 어렵고, 또 사후 이를 사법적으로 판단하는 데 시간이 너무 걸린다는 점 등이다.

　　따라서 보다 세부적이고, 연방 차원에서의 표준화된 법규가 조속히 뒷받침되지 않는다면 막 탄력 받기 시작한 텔레메디신 열차도 팬데믹 종료와 함께 서서히 동력을 멈출 것으로 우려된다. (2022.3.16.)

Medicine and Quarantine

Pros and Cons of Telemedicine

A new report from the U.S. Department of Health and Human Services (HHS) published last December found that the number of Medicare visits conducted through telehealth has increased 63 times during the COVID-19 pandemic. It went from approximately 840,000 cases in 2019 to 53 million in 2020. According to HHS, telemedicine is defined as "the use of electronic information and telecommunications technologies to support and promote long-distance clinical health care." Technologies include videoconferencing, remote patient monitoring, store-and-forward imaging, and remote medical equipment.

Although telemedicine is the medical utopia that we have all been dreaming of, its growth has been stunted due to various regulations. However, it became an instant reality during the pandemic because of the social distancing and quarantine measures.

The biggest benefit of telemedicine is that it allows the patient and the medical provider to meet whenever and wherever it's convenient for the patient. It's generally cheaper than a face-to-face visit as well. However, there are insufficient guidelines about proper medical care through telemedicine or regulations about malpractice to make it a permanent feature in our lives. Let's review some of the potential problems through the following example.

On February 17, 2012, around noon, Marvin Snyder, an inmate at a New York state correctional facility, experienced sudden chest pain and was taken to the infirmary. The nurse attempted to administer an electrocardiogram (EKG), but could not get it to work. She made a referral to the county hospital to provide telemedicine services.

A physician assistant at the county hospital reviewed the vital signs and medical history sent over from the correctional facility and conducted a telemedicine consultation. The PA concluded that it was a temporary condition and ordered Snyder to be administered Tylenol and sent back to his cell. However, Snyder did not feel any better by 10 p.m. and returned to the infirmary. The night nurse rebooted the EKG machine. Upon performing an EKG, she realized that he had a heart attack.

Fortunately, he was rushed to the hospital and survived the attack. However, following his discharge, he filed a lawsuit against the medical staff at the correctional facility and the county hospital for their failure to timely diagnose and treat a heart attack. Generally, the issue in medical malpractice cases is whether the medical staff was negligent and departed from the accepted standard of medical practice in treating a medical condition.

The court issued a written decision in December 2020 at the height of the pandemic as the number of medical services provided through telemedicine was increasing exponentially. The New York court dismissed the claim against the nurse because it found that she acted within the accepted standard of medical practice by referring the patient to the county hospital for a telemedicine consultation. However, the court held that there were questions about whether the county hospital deviated from the acceptable standard of medical care in rendering telemedicine services by not performing an EKG and allowed the case to go to trial. There are no more records after this decision, so it appears that the case was resolved with an out-of-court settlement. Nevertheless, this decision highlights several potential issues.

Initially, since the medical professional cannot see the patient face-to-face, they may fail to administer medically necessary tests on time, which could lead them to a missed opportunity to save the patient.

Secondly, some medical professionals who are unskilled or lack medical equipment can use telemedicine to avoid liability.

Lastly, the current legal standard to determine if someone committed medical malpractice, a deviation from "accepted standard from medical practice," may not be appropriate for telemedicine because it changes depending on the advances in medical technology, education, and certification of the medical service provider, and where medical service was provided. In addition, without legislation in place, courts will need a long time to determine how it applies to telemedicine.

For these reasons, it may be time for a more specific set of regulations, preferably at the federal level to ensure uniformity across states. Without them, the advances that we have made in telemedicine will lose steam and come to a complete stop after the pandemic. (2022.3.16.)

5장 전체 영어 녹음 듣기

Chapter
5

인종갈등·젠더
Racial and Gender Tension

죽음을 부른 시민체포법

올해 2월 23일 조지아 주의 해안 도시 브런즈윅에서 25세의 흑인 청년 '아머드 알버리'(Ahmaud Arbery)가 조깅을 하던 중 트럭을 타고 뒤쫓아온 검찰 조사관 출신 '그레고리'(64세)와 '트래비스 맥마이클'(34세) 백인 부자의 총에 맞아 즉사하는 사건이 발생했다.

맥마이클 부자는 알버리를 인근에서 발생한 강도 사건의 용의자로 보고 시민체포법에 의거 추격했는데 알버리가 저항했기 때문에 발포할 수밖에 없었다고 경찰 조사에서 진술했다. 경찰도 이들의 행동이 시민체포법 범위 내에서 이루어진 정당행위로 보고 처음에는 문제 삼지 않았다.

그러나 맥마이클 부자의 진술과는 달리 알버리가 맨몸으로 조깅을 하다 아무런 저항도 하기 전에 총을 맞고 죽는 당시의 충격적인 동영상이 인터넷에 공개되면서 '현대판 린칭'이라는 비난 여론이 들끓자 마지못해 검찰은 사건 발생 74일이 지나서야 이들을 살인 혐의로 뒤늦게 체포하고 기소 방침을 밝혔다.

시민체포권은 중세 시절의 영국에서 범죄가 발생하더라도 신속한 출동 방법이 없어 즉각적인 현장 대처가 불가능한 점을 감안, 일반 시민에게도 범인을 체포할 수 있도록 왕이 권한을 부여한 제도에서 유래한다. 이러한 영국의 전통은 미국에도 그대로 이어져 현재 조지아주를 비롯한 대부분의 주에서 법률로 보장하고 있다. 얼마 전까지만 해도 비교적 경비가 허술한 멕시코 접경지대 중심으로 무장 시민단체들이 이 법에 근거, 불법 월경자들을 체포하고 이들을 이민 당국에 넘겨 화제가 되기도 했다.

시민체포 제도는 이런 순기능과 반대로 이번 알버리 사건에서 보듯 아직도 미국 내 흑백 간 인종차별 앙금이 완전히 해소되지 않은 상태에서 총

아머드 알버리 / Ahmaud Arbery

기 소지마저 자유롭다 보니 그 부작용도 만만치 않게 발생한다. 이를 풍자하여 법무부 민권국 출신 '다나 멀하우저' 전 검사는 "우리는 공권력 행사가 민간에 맡겨졌던 서부시대에 살고 있는 것이 아니기 때문에 우리의 법은 19세기를 떠나야 한다"고 워싱턴포스트에 기고하기도 했다.

시민체포권 남용의 대표적인 케이스가 2012년 플로리다주에서 있었던 17세 흑인 고등학생 '트레이본 마틴'(Trayvon Martin) 살인 사건이다. 자율방범대장 '조지 짐머맨'(George Zimmerman)은 동네 순찰을 돌다 후드티셔츠를 입고 걸어가던 낯선 얼굴의 흑인을 주거침입 용의자로 오인하고 추격 끝에 총으로 사살하고 말았다. 트레이본은 당시 맨몸 상태에서 편의점에 들러 군것질거리를 사서 귀가 중이었을 뿐 아무 잘못도 저지르지 않았던 것으로 밝혀졌다.

그럼에도 백인 5명과 히스패닉 1명으로 이루어진 당시의 배심원단은 재판을 통해 짐머맨이 총기 면허를 갖고 있었고 시민체포법에 의거해 트레이본에게 접근하였으며 플로리다 주의 자기방어법에 따라 총으로 자신을 보호할 권리가 있었던 점 등을 들어 짐머맨에게 무죄 평결을 내려주었다. 이 평결은 전국적으로 혐오 범죄 논란

을 불러일으켜 결국 볼티모어와 미주리주 퍼거슨 등지에서 일어난 흑인 폭동의 기폭제 역할을 하였다.

시민에 의한 체포가 성립되는 법적 구성요건은 각 주마다 다르다. 대부분의 주에서 중범죄에 대한 합리적인 의심이 있을 때만 정당화되며 경범죄에 대한 체포는 용납하지 않고 있다. 또 시민체포권을 행사하기 위해 일정 수준의 완력과 무기 사용도 허용되지만 만약 범죄가 실제로 일어나지 않았음에도 알버리 사건처럼 과잉 대처를 한다면 민사적, 형사적 책임에서 자유로울 수 없다는 점에 유의해야 한다. (2020.5.20)

결과: 2022.1.7일, 조지아주 글린 카운티 재판부는 맥마이클 부자에게 무고한 비무장 알버리를 향해 3차례나 격발했다는 점을 이유로 종신형을 선고했다.

영어 녹음 듣기

Death in a Citizen's Arrest

On February 23, 2020, a retired investigator from a local prosecutor's office, Gregory McMichael (64), and his son, Travis (34), fatally shot Ahmaud Arbery, a 25-year-old black man. The McMichaels chased Arbery in a truck while he was jogging in the streets of Brunswick, a coastal city in Georgia. The McMichaels claimed to the police that they were trying to effectuate a citizen's arrest because they suspected Arbery of having committed a burglary in the area. However, as the victim resisted violently, they were forced to fire their shotgun in self-defense. The police obliged and did not make an arrest.

Contrary to the statement by the McMichaels, however, a shocking video footage emerged of the shooting. It showed Arbery being shot even before any signs of physical resistance. As public pressure mounted, prosecutors had the shooters arrested, and belatedly announced a plan to present the case to the grand jury. Seventy-four days had passed since the shooting.

The legal authority to effectuate a citizen's arrest comes from medieval England. In those days, the king did not have the wherewithal to maintain and dispatch the police force in a timely manner. As a solution, he authorized citizens to make an arrest when they observed a crime being committed. This tradition was carried over into the United States, and it is recognized in most states including Georgia. As recently as last year, armed vigilante groups patrolled the U.S.-Mexico border where police presence is relatively weak. These groups detain people who illegally cross the border and report them to the immigration authorities.

However, as highlighted by the Arbery killing, allowing a private citizen to use a gun to make an arrest can exacerbate the situation, especially given racial tensions in America. In an op-ed to The Washington Post, Dana Mulhauser, a former prosecutor with the Justice Department's Civil Rights Bureau, said this about the current situation, "We no longer live in the Wild West, in which law enforcement often had to be left to private citizens. Our laws should leave the nineteenth century and join us here in the twenty-first."

The leading example of how a citizen's arrest may be abused is the 2012 murder of Trayvon Martin, a 17-year-old black high school student, which occurred in Florida. A neighborhood watch coordinator, George Zimmerman, thought that a Black man wearing a hoodie walking around the neighborhood was a suspect in recent burglary attempts. He chased him and, ultimately, fatally shot him. The Black man was Trayvon. He was unarmed and on his way home after buying some snacks at a nearby convenience store. He had done nothing unlawful.

Nevertheless, the trial jury, which was made up of one Hispanic and five white jurors, found Zimmerman not guilty of killing Trayvon. They considered that Zimmerman had a legal gun license and he initiated the encounter with the intent to effectuate a citizen's arrest. Finally, they determined that Zimmerman had a right to protect himself with a gun. This verdict spurred a series of riots by distressed African-Americans across the country, including Baltimore and Ferguson, Missouri.

The legal elements for a citizen's arrest vary from state to state. In most states, a citizen's arrest is justified only when there is reasonable suspicion a felony has been committed. An arrest for misdemeanors is usually not permitted. It should also be noted that even though a reasonable amount of force is allowed to effectuate a citizen's arrest, one may be held accountable civilly and criminally if a crime did not occur or too much force is used, as in Arbery's case. (2020.5.20)

Outcome: On January 7, 2022, the Glynn County court in Georgia sentenced George and Travis McMichael to life in prison for fatally shooting unarmed Arbery.

성 소수자 보호법

지난 6.15. 미국 대법원은 직장에서 성 소수자 차별을 금지하는 판결을 내렸다. 연방 민권법 제7조에 의하면 인종과 종교, 국적, 성별을 이유로 고용 차별을 하지 못하도록 돼있다. 트럼프 행정부는, 이 조문은 남녀의 성차별을 금지하는 것이지 성 소수자는 해당하지 않는 것이라고 주장했으나 대법원은 성적 지향이나 성 정체성에 기반한 차별도 이에 따라 금지되는 것으로 해석한 것이다.

민권법은 1964년 흑인 지도자 '마틴 루터 킹' 목사가 지켜보는 가운데 존슨 대통령이 서명한 미국 현대사의 가장 중요한 법 중 하나이다. 이번 대법원판결로 민권법의 인권보호 범위가 LGBTQ(lesbian, gay, bisexual, transgender, and queer)로 약칭되는 성 소수자들, 즉 보편적인 성 개념을 가지고 있지 않은 동성애자, 양성애자, 성전환자 같은 사람에게도 확대 적용된다.

이번 판결은, 여성 고객을 안심시키기 위해 '나는 100% 게이'라고 밝혔다가 2010년 해고당한 스카이다이빙 강사 '도널드 자다'를 비롯 남자로 일하다 여자로 성전환 수술을 강행한 후 2013년 해고당한 장의사 '에이미 스티븐스', 게이 소프트볼 동호회에 참가해 공무원 품위를 손상시켰다는 이유로 2013년 해고당한 조지아 주 공무원

'제럴드 보스토크' 등 3명이 각각 자신의 고용주를 상대로 제기한 소송의 결과물이다. 안타깝게도 소송 주인공 3명 중 자다는 2014년 사고로, 스티븐스는 올 4월 지병으로 세상을 떠났다.

이번 판결을 두고 미국 성 소수자 단체인 GLAAD는 "성 소수자들이 자신의 정체성 때문에 일자리를 잃을 공포 없이 일할 수 있어야 한다"고 환영 성명을 발표했으며, 민주당의 대선후보인 조 바이든 전 부통령은 "누구나 진정한 자아를 두려움 없이 공개하고 자랑스러워할 수 있어야 한다. 미국에는 중대한 순간"이라고 논평했다.

트럼프 대통령도 "놀라운 판결이다. 대법원이 결정했으니 우리는 따른다"라고 밝혔으나 내심 큰 충격을 받았을 것으로 보인다. 그간 트럼프 행정부는 성 소수자의 건강보험 혜택 축소와 더불어 트랜스젠더의 군복무 금지, 자신의 정체성에 맞는 화장실 사용문제 등 성 소수자 배제정책을 펼쳐왔기 때문이다.

무엇보다 자신이 2017년 대법관으로 지명한 '닐 고서치'(Neil Gorsuch)가 트럼프의 기대와는 전혀 다른 방향으로 이번 판결을 주도한 것으로 나타나 일말의 인간적 배신감을 느꼈을 것으로 짐작된다.

고서치 대법관은 법 원문을 문자 그대로 해석하는 것을 중시하는 '문자주의자'로 유명한 사람이다. 하지만 민권법 자체에 성적 지향이나 성 정체성에 근거한 차별을 금지하는 법문이 없고, 법 제정 당시 의회가 성 소수자들에게도 법을 적용할 의도가 있었다고 볼 증거가 없음에도 불구하고 성 소수자들의 손을 들어주는 다수판결문을 작성했다.

그는 판결문을 통해 고용주에게 능력이 동일한 남녀 두 명의 종업원이 있고 두 종업원 모두 남자를 좋아한다는 사실을 밝혔다고 가정할 때 그중 한 명은 남자라는 이유로 해고를 당하고, 다른 한 명은 여자라서 해고를 당하지 않는다면 이것이야말로 민권법이 명백하게 금지하고 있는 성별에 근거한 차별이 아니겠느냐고 설명했다.

이에 대해 성 소수자들을 반대해온 보수파 측 '사무엘 알리토' 대법관은 "성차별의 구체적인 내용은 의회가 법으로 규정해야 할 일이지 대법원이 해석해 판결할 일은 아니다. 다수판결문은 '문자주의자'의 깃발을 걸고 항해하는 해적선과 같다"라고 신랄하게 비판했다.

특히 보수파로 알려진 로버츠 대법원장도 고서치 편에 가담함으로써 6대 3으로 갈라진 이번 다수 판결은 연방 대법관의 정치적 성향 평가를 바탕으로 주요 판결의 결론을 예측해온 그간의 관행에도 큰 변화가 있을 것으로 법조계는 보고 있다. (2020.7.1.)

'링컨 메모리얼' 앞에 새겨진 마틴 루터 킹 목사의 "I have a dream" 연설을 기리는 기념석에서(워싱턴 D.C.2019)
I Have a Dream marker at the Lincoln Memorial (Washington D.C.)

영어 녹음 듣기

Racial and Gender Tension

Legal Protection for the Sexual Minority

On June 15, the U.S. Supreme Court banned job discrimination based on sexual orientation. Title VII of the Civil Rights Act prohibits employment discrimination based on race, color, religion, sex, and national origin. The Trump administration argued that this law only prohibits gender discrimination between men and women, not based on sexual orientation. The Supreme Court interpreted the phrase "because of sex" in the Act to include sexual orientation and gender identity.

The Civil Rights Act is arguably one of the most important pieces of legislation in modern history. It was signed in 1964 by President Lyndon B. Johnson with Dr. Martin Luther King Jr.'s approval. The recent Supreme Court ruling expands the Act's applicability to sexual minorities, including those in the LGBTQ (lesbian, gay, bisexual, transgender, and queer) community.

Three separate lawsuits culminated in this decision. In the first lawsuit, Plaintiff Donald Zarda was a skydiving instructor fired in 2010 after attempting to reassure a female customer by saying "I'm 100% gay." Another plaintiff was Aimee Stephens. She was fired from her job as a funeral director in 2013 after receiving a gender confirming surgery. The last plaintiff was Gerard Bostock, who was fired for "conduct unbecoming a county employee" after participating in a gay softball league at work. Unfortunately, Zarda died in an accident in 2014, and Stephens died from a medical condition in May 2020.

The Supreme Court decision was welcomed by GLAAD, an advocacy organization for sexual minorities, which stated, "LGBTQ Americans should be able to work without fear of losing jobs because of who they are." Democratic presidential candidate Joe Biden also said, "everyone should be able to live openly, proudly, as their true selves without fear. . . This decision is another step in our march towards equality for all."

President Trump said, "[t]hey've ruled and we live with the decision of the Supreme Court." Internally, though, he must have been disappointed. The Trump administration has been steadily eroding the civil rights of sexual minorities. It reduced their medical benefits, banned transgender people from military service, and revoked transgender bathroom guidance allowing them to use the bathrooms that corresponded with their gender identity.

He may have even felt a sense of betrayal since the decision was written by Justice Neil Gorsuch, whom he nominated in 2017.

Justice Gorsuch is a well-known textualist who values literal interpretation of the law. Interestingly, he wrote the majority decision even though no language in the Civil Rights Act itself prohibits discrimination based on sexual orientation or gender identity. Nor is there any evidence that Congress intended this law to apply to sexual minorities.

In the decision, however, Justice Gorsuch posited a scenario in which an employer has a male and a female employee. If both like a man but only the male employee is fired, he reasoned that the male employee had been discriminated against on the basis of sex, which is illegal under the Civil Rights Act.

Justice Alito, a conservative justice who was once called an "anti-gay culture warrior," wrote a seething dissent. He denounced Justice Gorsuch's decision by writing, "[t]here is only one word for what the Court has done today: legislation. The document that the Court releases is in the form of a judicial opinion interpreting a statute, but that is deceptive. . . The Court's opinion is like a pirate ship. It sails under a textualist flag."

Surprising to many, another conservative justice, Chief Justice Roberts, also voted with Gorsuch, rendering it a 6-3 decision. This decision will also have an impact on how the commentators predict the Supreme Court case's outcome based on the justices' political orientation. (2020.7.1.)

동성 결혼식(워싱턴 D.C.)
Same-sex marriage (Washington D.C.)

'눈물의 길' 새로운 길

2020년 7월 9일, 연방대법원은 '맥거트 대 오클라호마'(*McGirt v. Oklahoma*) 사건 재판에서 인구 50만의 도시 '털사'(Tulsa)를 기준으로 오클라호마 주의 동쪽 절반은 지금으로부터 200여 년 전 이곳으로 강제 이주 당한 다섯 원주민 부족, 즉 체로키, 머스코지, 세미놀, 치카소, 촉토 족의 땅으로 봐야 한다고 판결했다.

이 사건의 발단은 1997년 4세 여아를 성폭행해 오클라호마 주 법원에서 유죄 판결을 받고 복역을 마친 세미놀족 원주민 '짐시 맥거트'(Jimcy McGirt, 71세)가 '현행법상 인디언 보호구역에서 벌어지는 중범죄는 연방법원에서 재판하는 게 맞지 주 법원은 자신을 재판할 권한이 없었다'라고 재심을 청구하며 시작됐다.

맥거트의 이와 같은 법리 주장의 뿌리는 까마득한 19세기 초반으로 거슬러 올라간다. 당시 백인 이주민들은 미국 남동쪽에 터전을 잡고 있던 위 다섯 부족 원주민들의 땅을 야금야금 빼앗고 있었는데 1828년 조지아주 북쪽의 작은 산골 마을 '달로네가'에서 금광이 발견되자 본격적인 야욕을 드러냈다. 대표적으로 조지아 주 당국은 원주민들에게 금 채굴금지를 비롯 토지 매매금지, 백인 상대 불리한 증언 금지 등을 강요하는 차별적 법률을 통과시키고 민병대를 시켜 원주민들을 쫓아냈다.

촉토 같은 부족은 탄압 초기에 일찌감치 연방정부와 조약을 맺고 반 자발적으로 이주했으나 체로키족은 북부에서 온 기독 선교사들의 도움을 얻어 법적 싸움을 전개하며 끈질기게 저항한 케이스에 해당한다.

그 결과 1831년 '체로키족 대 조지아'(*Cherokee Nation v. Georgia*)와 이듬해의 '우스터 대 조지아'(*Worcester v. Georgia*) 사건을 통해 당시 대법원장인 '존 마셜'로부터 '인디언들의 영토는 미국의 준독립 보호령에 속하기 때문에 각 주의 법률은 보호령 안에서는 효력이 없다'는 원고 승 판결을 받는 데 성공했다. 다시 말해 백인들은 원주민 보호구역 안에 있는 인디언들을 괴롭히지 말라는 것이었다.

그러나 변호사에서 군인으로 변신하여 크릭과 세미놀족 토벌작전에서의 전공을 통해 1829년 대통령으로 취임한 '앤드루 잭슨'은 "마셜이 그런 판결을 내렸다고? 그러면 자기가 그렇게 집행해 보라지!"라며 대법원의 결정에 개의치 않았다. 오히려 잭슨은 자신의 주도 하에 미 연방의회가 1830년에 통과시킨 '인디언 이주법'을 내세워 위 다섯 부족 원주민들을 현재의 오클로호마주로 강제 이주시켰던 것이다.

이때 원주민들이 여름의 각종 전염병과 겨울의 혹독한 추위 속에 시달리며 9개 주를 거쳐 걸었던 2,200마일의 루트는 1987년 미 의회에 의해 '눈물의 길 역사의 길'로 지정되었다.

이랬던 아메리칸 원주민 수난의 역사가 맥거트 사건을 계기로 새로운 길을 걷게 된 것이다. 문자주의자 법률가 고서치 대법관은 진보 성향의 다른 대법관 4명과 의견을 함께하며 다수판결문을 작성했다. 그는 "눈물의 길 건너편엔 약속이 있었다"고 운을 뗀 후, 미 의회가 1830년대 초 원주민들을 강제 이주시키며 원주민 대표와 맺은 조약에서 "미시시피강 서쪽에 지정된 보호구역의 땅은 영원토록 원주민들의 것"임을 인정해 주었기 때문에 이 땅의 사법관할권은 아직 원주민들에게 있다고 판결했다.

이를 두고 로버츠 대법원장은 반대의견을 통해 법원의 결정이 오클라호마 형사사법 시스템에 큰 혼란을 가져올 것이라고 경고했다.

 이번 판결은 재심 청구에 따라 형사사법권에 국한된 것이지만 연방정부와 원주민 부족들 간에 맺은 조약이 아직 유효함을 대법원이 인정한 것이기 때문에 이를 근거로 향후 오클라호마주의 유전 수익과 세금, 치안문제 등 많은 분야에 후폭풍이 몰아칠 것으로 전망된다. 가까운 예로 이번 판결의 주인공 짐시 맥거트처럼 주 법원에서 유죄 판결을 받은 원주민 상당수는 당장 다시 재판해달라고 요구할 것이다.

(2020.7.29)

표지판
Road Sign

Racial and **Gender** Tension

New Path That Emerged From 'Trail of Tears'

On July 9, 2020, the U.S. Supreme Court ruled in McGirt v. Oklahoma that the eastern half of the state of Oklahoma including most of Tulsa, the second biggest city in the state with a population of about half a million people, belongs to the five tribes that were forced to relocate there almost 200 years ago. They are the Cherokee, Muscogee, Seminole, Chickasaw, and Choctaw tribal nations.

The case began with Jimcy McGirt, a 71-year-old Seminole man, convicted of sexually abusing a four-year-old girl. He appealed the conviction by arguing that under the Major Crimes Act, only the federal court, and not the state court, had jurisdiction to hear felonies arising out of a Native American reservation.

McGirt's argument was rooted in the nation's history dating back to the nineteenth century. Back then, white settlers were slowly acquiring land across the Southeast portion of the continental United States, which, until that point, was inhabited by the five tribes mentioned above. The settlers became more audacious and the takeover picked up pace when gold was struck in 1827 in

Dahlonega, a small town in northern Georgia. The state of Georgia enacted discriminatory laws banning Native Americans from mining gold, selling or purchasing land, or providing testimony against white settlers. Its militia displaced Native Americans as well.

The Choctaw nation entered into a treaty with the federal government early on in the conflict and left the land somewhat voluntarily. However, with the help of Christian missionaries, the Cherokee nation embarked on a series of legal battles. These efforts had some success. In Cherokee Nation v. Georgia, decided in 1831, and Worcester v. Georgia, decided in 1832, Chief Justice John Marshall ruled in favor of the Cherokee by holding that Georgia's state law had no jurisdiction on Native Americans' sovereign land. In short, white settlers were to leave the Native Americans alone.

Andrew Jackson, a lawyer-turned-general who had a successful military career fighting against the Creeks and the Seminoles, had a different idea. After becoming president in 1829, he reportedly rebuked the Supreme Court's rulings by saying, "John Marshall has made his decision, now let him enforce it." Instead, he led Congress in passing the Indian Removal Act. The five tribal nations had little choice but to be relocated to modern-day Oklahoma under this law. The 2,200-mile route that they had to endure, traversing nine states while suffering from various diseases and the cold weather, was designated as the "Trail of Tears National Historic Trail" by Congress in 1987.

The tragic history was dusted off with the McGirt case, and a new fork in the road emerged. Justice Gorsuch, widely known to be a strict textualist, shocked many legal observers by deciding with four liberal justices on the bench. He also wrote the majority decision. He began the decision by noting, "[o]n the far end of the Trail of Tears was a promise." Under the 1830 treaty as the Native Americans ceded their ancestral land, Congress promised the land "west of the Mississippi" as a "permanent home" for them. Justice Gorsuch held the land is rightfully theirs, and their laws and treaties must govern.

Chief Justice Roberts wrote the dissenting opinion. He warned that the majority's decision would bring about massive confusion and chaos in Oklahoma's criminal justice system.

Although this decision was limited in scope to the question of criminal jurisdiction, it has larger ramifications as it recognized the centuries-old treaty between the federal government and Native American tribes as still being binding. Accordingly, it will affect many Oklahomans' lives such as oil revenue, state taxes, and public safety. For the short term, all Native Americans who, like Jimcy McGirt, were convicted in the state court will ask for a new trial. (2020.7.29)

경찰의 면책권 남용

지난 5.25 미네소타주 미니애폴리스에서 위조화폐 신고를 받고 출동한 경찰관 '데릭 쇼빈'(Derek Chauvin, 44세)이 용의자인 흑인 남성 '조지 플로이드'(George Floyd, 46세)를 체포하는 과정에서 그의 목을 길바닥에 무릎으로 짓눌러 사망케 한 사건이 발생하여 미국 전역을 충격에 빠뜨렸다. 8분 동안 숨을 쉬지 못해 괴로워하며 죽어가던 플로이드의 현장 동영상은 SNS 등을 통해 급속도로 전파되었고, 이에 공분한 시민들은 사건이 일어난 거리에서 '흑인의 생명은 소중하다'라고 적힌 팻말과 함께 '숨을 쉴 수 없다'고 외치며 연일 항의 시위를 펼쳤다.

유감스럽게도 플로이드는 경찰의 과잉진압에 목숨을 잃은 첫 번째 흑인 희생자도, 마지막도 아니라는 점이다. 그의 사망 이후에도 얼마 지나지 않아 술에 취해 자신의 차에서 자고 있던 운전자를 체포하려다 저항하자 총기를 발사해 죽인 '레이샤드 브룩스' 사건이 일어났고, 폭행신고를 받고 출동한 경찰이 용의자가 행동을 멈추지 않고 자동차의 운전석 안으로 들어가려 하자 등에 7발의 총알을 발사한 '제이콥 블레이크' 사건, 남성 정신질환자가 자신은 코로나 확진자라고 외치며 마구 침을 뱉는다는 이유로 얼굴 덮개를 씌워 질식사시킨 '대니엘 프루드' 사건 등이 연이어 발생했다.

왜 이런 황당하고 끔찍한 사건이 빈발하는 것일까? 먼저 심리학자들에 의하면 경찰관들이 가진 인종적 편견이 가장 큰 요인이라고 분석한다. 즉 경찰관들에게 흑인 남성은 위험하다는 잠재의식이 있기 때문에 작은 저항에도 순간적으로 판단력을 잃고 과잉진압으로 이어진다는 주장이다.

그런가 하면 뉴욕타임스와 이코노미스트 등의 유력 매체들은 제도적인 관점에서 '공무원 면책권'을 또 다른 주요 원인으로 보도했다. 공무원 면책권이란 공무집행 중 발생한 일에 대해 국가가 책임을 지는 대신 공무원 개인에게 책임을 묻지 않겠다는 법리로, 흑인 인권운동이 한창이던 1967년 '피어슨 대 레이'(Pierson v. Ray) 사건에서 연방대법원 판례로 처음 확립되었다.

1961년, 인종분리 정책에 맞서 버스를 타고 남부를 돌며 '기도순례'를 하던 흑인과 백인 목사 일행은 미시시피의 주도 잭슨의 버스터미널에서 인종분리 표지를 무시하고 다 같이 백인 전용 대합실에 들어갔다는 이유로 경찰관 레이에게 체포되었다.

이후 이들은 재판을 통해 4개월 징역과 200달러의 벌금형을 선고받았고 당시 뉴욕 주지사 '넬슨 록펠러'의 사위이기도 했던 피어슨 목사는 곧바로 재판장과 경찰이 자신의 헌법적 권리를 침해했다며 민사소송을 제기했다.

대법원은 이때 공무원이 악의 없이 법을 집행하는 과정에서 인권 침해가 발생한 경우에는 면책권이 부여된다고 판결했던 것이다. 국민 누구나 총기를 소지하고 있는 환경에서 소수의 공권력으로 광활한 국토를 감당해야 하며, 변호사 천국으로 불릴 만큼 경찰관에 대한 소송이 잦다는 점 등을 고려할 때 공무집행 중 발생한 일에 대해 공무원 개인이 책임을 져야 한다면 직무 수행을 제대로 할 수 없을 것이라고 본 것이다.

현재 연방대법원은 면책권을 '(공무원은) 상식적인 사람이 알 만큼 명확히 수립된 법적, 헌법적 권리를 침해하지 않는 한 공무 중 행위와 관련해 피소되지 않을 권리'라고 해석하고 있다. 하지만 플로이드의 죽음 이후로 민주당 의원들을 중심으로 경찰이 이 면책권을 믿고 자주 무모한 사고를 일으키는 것으로 판단하고 연방 상원과 하원 합동으로 면책권을 없애는 경찰개혁 법안을 추진하고 있다.

여기에 부응하여 콜로라도 주는 경찰의 면책권을 없앤 첫 번째 주가 되었으며, 뉴욕주 의회는 경찰의 불법 행위로 제기되는 소송에 대비하기 위해 경찰관들로 하여금 개인 책임보험 가입을 의무화하는 법안을 상정했다. (2020.9.23.)

"흑인의 생명은 소중하다" 시위(맨해튼)
'Black Lives Matter' protest (Manhattan)

Racial and **Gender** Tension

Police Abuse of Qualified Immunity

On May 25, George Floyd (46) was killed by Derek Chauvin (44), a police officer, on the streets of Minneapolis, Minnesota. Chauvin kneeled on Floyd's neck until Floyd died. Police had suspected Floyd of using fake currency. The video clip of the incident vividly showed the last 8 minutes of Floyd's life as he gasped for air. It spread quickly on social media. Upset citizens protested in the streets where Floyd suffered and angrily chanted "I can't breathe," and held up "Black Lives Matter" signs for many days in a row.

Unfortunately, Floyd is not the first victim, nor will he likely be the last, whose life was lost due to police use of excessive force. Indeed, only a short time after Floyd's death, the police fatally shot Rayshard Brooks when he resisted arrest. He was intoxicated and sleeping in a car when the police came. Jacob Blake was shot seven times when he did not comply with the police's order to stop and tried to get into the driver's seat of a car. Daniel Prude, suffering from a mental illness, suffocated to death when the police put a covering over his face for spitting and shouting that he had COVID-19.

Why do such tragic incidents occur so frequently? First, according to some psychologists, one of the most significant factors is racial bias. They claim that some police officers subconsciously believe that Black men are dangerous. This belief leads to momentary loss of sensible judgment and overreaction in response to even a small resistance.

Some, like The New York Times and The Economist, claim that another important contributing factor may be the legal protection afforded by qualified immunity. Qualified immunity is a legal doctrine that shields government officials from personal liability when performing an official duty. The U.S. Supreme Court introduced it in 1967 at the height of the Civil Rights Movement in Pierson v. Ray.

In 1961, a group of black and white pastors went on a "prayer pilgrimage" throughout the South. They ignored the "Whites Only" sign inside a bus terminal in Jackson, Mississippi's capital city. Police Officer Ray arrested them. They were found guilty, and sentenced to 4 months in jail and a $200 fine. Reverend Pearson was the son-in-law of New York Governor at the time, Nelson Rockefeller. He immediately filed a civil lawsuit claiming that the judge and the police officer violated his constitutional rights.

The Supreme Court held that public officials must be granted qualified immunity as long as they dutifully carry out the laws without actual malice, even if such conduct results in human rights violations. The Court reasoned that the police officers would not be able to perform their duties if they had to worry about getting sued, especially if they would successfully maintain order in a country where private citizens own and carry arms. In the Court's view, the police officers would go bankrupt paying the lawyers without this protection.

Currently, the Supreme Court defines qualified immunity as immunity from civil lawsuits unless the plaintiff can establish that the official violated "clearly established statutory or constitutional rights of which a reasonable person would have known." Following Floyd's death, however, Democrats are pushing for a bipartisan police reform bill that eliminates qualified immunity because they believe it leads to reckless use of excessive force by the police, who may feel emboldened by the doctrine. In response, Colorado became the first state to disallow police immunity. The New York State legislature has also introduced a bill that mandates police officers to obtain personal liability insurance to prepare for potential lawsuits for police misconduct. (2020.9.23.)

뉴욕시 경찰의 과잉진압으로 사망한 흑인 에릭 가너(Eric Garner) 추모시위 Millions March에서 아들과(뉴욕.2014)
With my son at the Million March organized to remember Eric Garner who was killed by a New York City police officer's use of excessive force (New York)

인종갈등·젠더

미국 여성 투표권의 흑역사

지난 3.8은 유엔이 1977년에 '세계여성의 날'로 지정한 날이었다. 남성 위주였던 과거의 흑역사를 되돌아보고 지구 구성원의 절반인 여성들의 사회적 역할과 공헌 등에 대해 지구촌이 다 같이 생각해보는 기회를 갖자는 게 기념일로 지정한 취지였을 것이다. 'Lady First'의 나라 미국은 여기에서 한술 더 떠 1988년 레이건 대통령 시절부터 아예 매년 3월 한 달을 '여성 역사의 달'이라 하여 기념하고 있다.

'여성 역사의 달'을 맞아 잊혀진 흑역사-미국 여성의 참정권 역정을 따라가 보는 것도 그 의미가 깊다고 생각한다. 오늘날엔 너무나 당연하다고 여기는 여성의 투표권이 현대판 민주주의의 본산이라고 할 수 있는 미국에서조차 이를 공식적으로 인정받은 것은 그리 역사가 오래되지 않았다. 남북전쟁 후 1870년경 노예제를 폐지하고 흑인 남성들에게 투표권을 허용한 수정헌법 제13조~15조가 제정될 당시만 해도 미국 여성들에게는 재산권 행사뿐 아니라 투표권이 여전히 허용되지 않았다.

이에 여성 인권운동 선구자들은 다방면에서 실력을 행사하기 시작했는데 그중에서도 '수잔 앤서니'(Susan B. Anthony)의 활약이 가장 두드러졌다. 남녀평등을 중시하는 퀘이커 교도였던 앤서니는 1872년 실시된 대통령선거 뉴욕주 로체스터의 투표장에서 자신의 동지 여성들과 함께 불법 투표를 한 혐의로 재판에 회부되었다.

법정에 선 그녀는 발언을 제지하는 재판장의 거듭된 명령에도 아랑곳하지 않고 "미국 정부가 받아야 할 심판을 왜 거꾸로 내가 대신 받아야 하는지, 아울러 미국 시민이 자기 대표자를 뽑는 투표를 하는 게 왜 죄가 되는지 나는 도무지 이해할 수 없다"고 당당하게 항의했다.

그녀는 결국 100달러 벌금형의 유죄선고를 받았지만 벌금 납부를 거부하고 투표권 운동에 여생을 바침으로써 미국 여권 운동계의 아이콘으로 길이 남게 되었다. 비록 앤서니는 투표권의 완성을 보지 못하고 세상을 떠났지만 종종 후세에 와서 기념우표나 1달러짜리 기념주화의 모습으로 환생하기도 했다.

앤서니 이후 반세기 동안 여성계의 집요한 공세에 꿈쩍도 하지 않던 여성참정권 문제가 미국의 세계 제1차대전 참전을 계기로 그 실마리를 찾게 된다. 당시 대통령이었던 '우드로우 윌슨'(Woodrow Wilson)은 미국 참전의 대의명분으로 '안전한 민주주의 수호'를 천명했는데 이것이 논쟁을 점화시켰던 것이다.

여권운동가들은 "자국민의 절반인 여성을 민주주의 사각지대에 방치하고 있는 나라에서 남의 나라 민주주의를 지켜주겠다고 해외에까지 나가 청년들 피를 흘리게 하는 게 말이나 되는 소리냐"고 미국 남성들의 정서를 전방위로 자극하고 압박했다. 이것이 주효하여 마침내 종전 직후인 1920년, 소위 '앤서니 헌법'이라고 하는 수정헌법 제19조가 역사적으로 의회를 통과하게 된다.

"미국 시민의 투표권은 성별로 인하여 미합중국이나 주에 의하여 거부 또는 제한되지 아니한다"라는 짤막한 한 문장으로 지난했던 투표권 문제에 종지부를 찍게 된 것이다.

코로나-19 팬데믹의 와중에도 수정헌법 제정 101주년이 되는 올해 3월은 그 의미가 특별하다. 3권분립이 확고하게 자리 잡은 미국 땅에서 행정부에서는 '카말라 해리스'(Kamala Harris)가 여성 최초로 미국 부통령이 되었다. 100년 전에는 상상도 할 수 없는 일이 벌어진 것이다. 입법부에서는 '낸시 펠로시'(Nancy Pelosi)가 미국 권력 서열 3위인 연방 하원의장으로 재선되는가 하면 총 하원 의석 435명 중 역사상 최고 많은 숫자인 118명(27.1%)의 여성이 하원에, 상원 의석 100명 중 24명이 상원의원으로 진출했다.

또 정치에 휘둘리지 않고 연방국가인 미합중국이 나아갈 진로를 제시하는 연방 대법원의 대법관 총 9명 중 3명의 여성이 대법관 자리를 차지했다. 아직 갈 길은 멀지만, 천지개벽할 정도로 여권이 신장된 한 세기 역정을 뒤돌아보는 감회가 새롭다. (2021.3.24.)

Racial and Gender Tension

Dark History of American Women's Suffrage

Designated by the United Nations in 1977, March 8th is celebrated as International Women's Day. Its purpose is to reflect upon history as it has been dominated by males and commemorate women's achievements and accomplishments. America has celebrated the month of March as "Women's History Month" since its designation during the Reagan administration in 1988.

In light of "Women's History Month," today's column traces women's right to vote in America. Nowadays, women's right to vote is taken for granted. But, even in America, the birthplace of modern Democracy, the history of women's vote is not long. Even after the American Civil War when slavery was abolished and Black men were given the right to vote by ratification of the thirteenth, fourteenth and fifteenth amendments around 1870, women were still not allowed to possess any property or cast votes.

Women's rights activists began to organize. Susan B. Anthony was one of the most prominent leaders of the movement. She was raised as a Quaker, whose teachings emphasize equality between men and women. Along with fellow activists, she was arrested for casting an illegal vote in the 1872 presidential election in Rochester, New York.

At her trial, she ignored repeated orders by the judge to stop talking, and asked why she, and not the government, had to stand trial. She further questioned why an American citizen must be tried for casting a vote for a leader in a democratic society. Ultimately, she was found guilty and sentenced to a fine of $100. She refused to pay, and devoted her life to the women's suffrage movement. Although she passed away without seeing the fruits of her labor, she is remembered as an icon and often depicted in commemorative coins and postal stamps.

After Anthony's death, the women's suffrage movement did not gain much traction for half a century. That began to change with America's decision to enter the First World War. Then-President Woodrow Wilson argued that fighting in the War was important to protect democracy.

The suffragists questioned the decision by arguing, "why are we putting our young people in harm's way to protect other countries' democracy when half of the Americans – women – do not have a right to vote?" The strategy worked. The nineteenth amendment granting women the right to vote was ratified in 1920 right after the war. It's sometimes referred to as the "Susan B. Anthony Amendment."

The end to the women's suffrage movement was a short sentence, "The right of citizens of the United States to vote shall not be denied or abridged by the United States or by any State on account of sex."

This year's month of March is special despite the Covid-19 pandemic. It marks the 101st anniversary of the ratification of the nineteenth amendment. More importantly, real change can be seen in all three branches of the government. Kamala Harris became the first female vice president in the executive branch. In the legislative branch, Nancy Pelosi reigns as the Speaker of the House, the third person in the line of succession. Also, 118 members of the 435-member House of Representatives are women (27.1%) and 24 senators in the 100-member Senate are women. It is the highest number of women in American history. In the judiciary, the stalwart of American Democracy, three out of nine justices are women. Without a doubt, there is still a long way to go, but this is the progress that we've made thus far in a century. (2021.3.24.)

수잔 앤서니 기념주화
Susan Anthony commenmorative coin

아시안 수난시대와 증오범죄 유형

지난 3.16. 조지아주 애틀랜타에서 발생한 총격사건으로 6명의 아시안 여성을 포함한 귀중한 인명 8명이 희생되었다. 아시안 여성 희생자 중에는 4명이 한인으로 밝혀져 더욱 우리를 침통하게 만들었다.

조지아 주는 오랜 인종차별의 역사에도 불구하고 증오범죄 처벌조항이 없는 주에 속하다 작년 2.23. 흑인 청년 '아머드 알버리'(Ahmaud Arbery)가 조깅 중에 백인 부자 지간의 총에 즉사하는 사건을 계기로 증오범죄처벌법을 뒤늦게 제정하였다. 이로써 미국 내 아칸소, 사우스캐롤라이나, 와이오밍 3개 주만 제외하곤 증오범죄처벌법이 다 만들어진 셈이다. 주마다 차이는 있지만, 이 법의 핵심은 피해자의 인종, 피부색, 종교, 출신국가, 성별 등의 이유로 범행을 저질렀다면 특별히 가중처벌한다는 것이 골자이다.

이번 살인사건의 피의자인 21세의 백인 청년 '로버트 애론 롱'(Robert Aaron Long)은 '성 중독 때문에 범죄를 저지를 수밖에 없었다'고 경찰조사에서 밝혔고, 그의 문자 메시지나 온라인 게시물 등에서도 별다른 단서를 찾지 못한 것으로 알려져 증오범죄 혐의를 비껴갈 것으로 보인다. 이처럼 법은 구비돼있다 하더라도 동기 입증이 현실적으로 쉽지만은 않다.

최근에 발생한 사건을 중심으로 증오범죄의 유형을 간추려본다.

1. 3.14 뉴욕 맨해튼 대로변에서 한 백인 여성이 일면식도 없던 미국계 한국인 커플을 상대로 '중국으로 꺼져'라고 욕설을 하는 사건이 발생했다. 뉴스를 통해 이 여성은 뉴욕주 출신 전 연방 상원의원의 딸 '마우라 모이니한'으로 알려져 충격을 던져주었다. 우리에게 불쾌한 사건이긴 하지만, 단순한 욕설은 헌법상 표현의 자유에 의해 보호받기 때문에 증오범죄처벌법에 저촉되지 않는다. 그러나 신체적 협박이나 상대방으로 하여금 공포심을 느끼게 할 정도에 이른다면 문제가 달라진다.

2. 3.20 오후 1시 반경, 스키 모자로 얼굴을 가렸지만 백인으로 추정되는 60대 남성이 퀸스행 지하철에 앉아가던 아시안 여성 승객에게 다가와 그녀의 가방과 상의에 오줌을 쏘아댄 희한한 사건이 발생했다. 피해자는 경찰에 그를 고발했는데 범행동기가 입증되지 않아 노출죄 정도의 경범죄 외 증오범죄 혐의를 추가하기 어려워 보인다.

3. 3.24 ABC 7 뉴스에 의하면 캘리포니아주 오렌지 카운티 실버타운에 거주하는 한국계 여성이 남편의 장례식 날 익명의 증오편지를 받았는데 "아시안 한 명이 줄었다. 짐 싸서 당신네 나라로 돌아가라. 밤길 조심해라"와 같은 협박 내용이 담겨 있었다고 한다. 피해자 남편의 장례식 날까지 꿸 정도로 협박의 정도가 구체적이어서 범죄행위로 걸려들 가능성이 높다.

4. 3.19 뉴욕 지하철에서 스리랑카 출신의 68세 노인이 한 흑인 남성에게 무차별 폭행을 당했다. 흑인 용의자가 폭행 도중 '아시안 후레자식'이라고 욕설을 퍼부은 것으로 현장 목격자에 의해 입증되었기 때문에 현재 체포돼 폭행죄에 더해 증오범죄 혐의를 받고 있다.

5. 2.25 맨해튼 차이나타운에서 아랍계 청년이 아무런 이유 없이 중국계 행인의 등을 칼로 찔러 중상을 입힌 사건이 발생했다. 체포된 용의자는 살인미수, 흉기 소지, 폭행 등의 혐의로만 조사를 받다 불과 한 달 전에도 브루클린에서 다른

뉴욕주 최초로 아시안 여성 항소법원 판사로 임명된 Lillian Wan 판사(앞줄 가운데 여성) 및 뉴욕주 아시안 변호사협회 회원들과(맨해튼.2022)
With Hon. Lillian Wan (in pink), the first female Asian-American judge to be appointed to the New York's Appellate Division, and members of the Asian American Bar Association of New York (Manhattan)

코로나-19 팬데믹 관련 뉴욕시 지하철 역 안내문 <이 지하철 역에서는 멸시, 인종 차별, 외국인 혐오가 절대 허용되지 않는다>고 쓰여있다.
Public announcement inside of a New York City subway station during the Covid-19 pandemic

아시안을 폭행했던 사실이 드러나 뒤늦게 증오범죄 혐의가 추가되었다.

캘리포니아 주립대 소속 증오·극단주의 연구센터의 3월 보고서에 따르면 미국에서 증오범죄가 전반적으로 감소 추세를 보이고 있음에도 2019~2020년 사이 유독 아시안에 대한 증오범죄는 149% 급증한 것으로 나타났다.

소수인종 중에서 미국 주류사회에 가장 성공적으로 진입한 것으로 평가받던 아시아인들이 코로나-19의 창궐과 함께 수난을 겪는 시대가 비롯됐다는 뜻이다. 언제쯤 이런 사태가 종식될지 안타깝고, 길거리 나다니기가 불안하기 짝이 없다. (2021.4.7.)

Racial and Gender Tension

Asian Hate and Different Types of Hate Crimes

On March 16, in a shooting in Atlanta, Georgia, eight people died, including six Asian-American women. Among them were four Korean-American women, bringing the tragedy closer to home.

Despite its long history of racism, Georgia was one of the last states without a hate crime law. It was finally enacted after the death of Ahmaud Arbery, an African-American young man who was fatally shot on February 23, 2020, by two white gunmen. Now, except for three states, Arkansas, South Carolina, and Wyoming, there is a hate crime law in all other states in America. The statute varies by state, but at its core, it enhances the sentence if a crime was motivated by the victim's race, ethnicity, religion, country of origin, or sex.

The suspect in the Atlanta shooting, 21-year-old Robert Aaron Long, apparently told the authorities that his crime was motivated by his addiction to sex. Moreover, police could not find any text or online messages that would prove that his crime was motivated by race or ethnicity. At the moment, it looks as though Long will not be charged with a hate crime. As this case highlights, even when the statute exists, it can be challenging to prove a hate crime.

This column examines different types of hate crimes by looking at several recent events:

1. On March 14, a white woman yelled, "go back to China" to a Korean-American couple in the middle of a busy street in Manhattan. The white woman was quickly identified as Maura Moynihan, daughter of a former New York senator. Although it is troubling, mere fighting words are protected under the First Amendment and may not be prosecuted as a hate crime. It would, of course, be a different story if the threat causes the victim to fear for physical safety.

2. On March 20 around 1 p.m., an unidentified man urinated on the bag and jacket of an Asian American woman on a Queens-bound subway train. The perpetrator is suspected to be a white male in his 60s, but his identity remains hidden because he wore a ski mask. Although the victim reported the incident to the police, the true motive behind this bizarre act remains unknown. If caught, he will likely be slapped with a relatively minor misdemeanor crime of public lewdness and harassment and not a hate crime.

3. On March 24, ABC 7 News reported that a Korean-American widow received a threatening letter from an anonymous mailer on the same day she buried her husband. The letter said, "one less Asian to put up with . . . Watch out! Pack your bags and go back to your country where you belong." If caught, the mailer could be charged with a hate crime given the specificity of the threat of physical violence including a reference to the victim's deceased husband.

4. On March 19, a 68-year-old Sri Lankan immigrant was brutally assaulted by an African-American man on the New York City subway. A witness told the police that the assailant shouted a racial insult, "you motherf****** Asian!" The man was arrested for assault and committing a hate crime.

5. On February 25, in Manhattan's Chinatown, a young Arabic man stabbed a pedestrian of Chinese descent, resulting in a severe injury. The perpetrator was investigated for attempted murder, criminal possession of a weapon, and assault. However, it was revealed that he had assaulted another Asian person a month before in Brooklyn. A hate crime charge was brought against him based on the newly discovered evidence.

According to the March report by The Center for the Study of Hate and Extremism at the University of California, hate crimes against Asian-Americans surged by 149% between 2019 and 2020 even though the overall rate of hate crimes declined in the United States.

While Asian-American immigrants have achieved remarkable success in this country, reports such as this show that the COVID-19 pandemic has made us vulnerable. Now, we can hardly walk outside without feeling threatened, a tragedy that must end soon. (2021.4.7.)

트랜스젠더의 올림픽 출전 논란

힘과 체격 등을 바탕으로 기량을 겨루는 운동경기에서 남자였던 선수가 여자로 성전환 수술을 받고 여자 올림픽 경기에 출전하겠다고 한다면 이를 어떻게 받아들여야 하는 걸까?

코로나-19로 1년 연기됐던 동경올림픽이 우여곡절 끝에 대망의 개막식을 앞둔 가운데 뉴질랜드 남자역도 선수였던 '로렐 허버드'(Laurel Hubbard)가 올림픽 역사상 최초의 트랜스젠더(성전환) 선수로 여자역도 경기에 참가하는 문제를 두고 국제적 논란이 뜨거웠다.

올해 43세의 허버드는 남자역도 선수로 활약하다 2012년 성전환 수술 후 2017년부터는 뉴질랜드 여자 국가대표로 활동하고 있다. 여자로 바뀐 후 2017년 미국에서 개최된 세계 역도선수권대회 은메달에 이어, 2019년 사모아 태평양 역도선수권대회에서도 금메달을 목에 걸어 여성 역도부의 신흥 강자로 떠올랐다. 이번 동경올림픽에선 여자 최중량급인 87kg 이상급에 출전할 예정이다.

허버드의 출전 소식에 충격을 받은 각국의 경쟁자들은 '높은 근력을 필요로 하는 역도 경기에서 남성으로서 사춘기를 겪은 허버드의 근육량이나 골밀도가 선천적 여성 선수들에 비해 월등할 수밖에 없는데 이를 고려하지 않고 출전을 허용하게 되면 올림픽 가치 중 하나인 페어플레이를 심각하게 훼손하게 될 것'이라며 IOC(국제올림픽위원회)의 결정에 강력하게 반대하고 있다.

IOC의 성전환 선수 허용 배경에는 트랜스 의학물리학자 '조안나 하퍼'(Joanna Harper)의 역할이 컸다. 자신이 남자 육상선수였다 여자로 성전환한 하퍼의 연구결과에 따르면 성전환 수술로 남성에서 여성으로 바뀌게 되면 신체적으로 남성 호르몬인 테스토스테론이 감소하는 반면 여성 호르몬인 에스트로겐은 증가한다고 한다.

남성 호르몬의 감소는 근육량과 골밀도, 혈액에서 산소를 운반하는 적혈구 감소로 이어지고 여성 호르몬의 증가는 체지방 증가로 이어져 선수의 속력과 근력, 지구력이 약화된다. 따라서 태생적 여자보다 성전환 여자 선수에게 특별한 이점이 존재하지 않는다고 주장했다.

이 연구결과에 근거, IOC는 2004년 '스톡홀름 합의'를 통해 남성에서 여성으로 성전환 수술을 한 선수들에게 올림픽 참여의 길을 열어주었다. 이후 신체 자기결정권을 불필요하게 침해한다는 비판을 받아들여 2015년부터 규정을 바꿔 비록 성전환 수술을 받지 않았더라도 새로운 성별을 공표하고 4년의 기간이 지났으며, 최소 12개월 동안 남성 호르몬인 테스토스테론 혈중농도가 혈액 1리터당 10나노몰 미만으로 유지되는 경우 올림픽 출전을 허용하고 있다.

하지만 성별 호르몬 수치만을 생물학적 남녀 선수 기준으로 삼다 보니 선천적 여성임에도 불구하고 혈중 테스토스테론 농도가 기준치보다 높다는 이유로 여성 경기에 참가할 수 없는 어처구니없는 불상사가 발생했다.

이 기준에 걸려 400m와 1,600m 여자 계주에 각각 참가할 수 없게 된 비운의 주인공은 아프리카 약소국 나미비아의 18세 육상스타 '크리스틴 음보마'와 18세 동갑의 '베아트리체 마실링기'이다. 세계육상연맹은 이 선수들이 생물학적 여자임을 부인하지 않지만 자신들은 혈중 테스토스테론 농도에 따라 여성의 범주를 정의한 새 IOC 규정을 준수할 수밖에 없다고 밝혔다.

그러나 2014년 이와 비슷한 처지를 이미 겪었던 인도의 여성 스프린터 '두티 찬드'(Dutee Chand)는 테스토스테론이 유의미하게 운동선수의 능력을 높인다는 것은 과학적 근거가 부족하다고 스포츠 중재 법원에 소송을 제기하여 2016년 리우올림픽에 출전한 바 있다. 졸지에 새 규정의 희생양이 된 두 어린 선수도 결국 법정에서 재판을 통해 이 문제를 풀어야 할 것으로 보인다. 의술의 발달로 성전환 수술이 점차 일반화되는 추세를 반영하여 IOC는, 명실공히 올림픽이 모든 인류가 즐기는 축제가 될 수 있도록 보다 과학적인 트랜스젠더 기준을 마련하여야 할 것이다. (2021.7.21.)

결과: 2021.8.2, 여자 역도 +87kg급 A그룹 경기에 나선 허버드는 인상 1~3차 시기를 모두 실패하여 실격당했다.

Transgender Athlete at Summer Olympic Games

Is it "fair play" for a transgender woman to compete in an Olympic sports game where an athlete's strength and size matters?

After a year of delays due to COVID-19, the Tokyo Summer Olympics is finally set to hold its long-anticipated opening ceremony soon. An international controversy is brewing over the decision by the International Olympic Committee (IOC) to allow Laurel Hubbard, a New Zealand weightlifter and the first openly transgender woman at the Olympics, to compete in the women's division.

Hubbard, 43, competitively weight-lifted as a man before her transition in 2012, and has been competing on the New Zealand women's team since 2017. After the transition, she won a silver medal at the World Championships held in the United States and a gold medal at the 2019 Pacific Games in Samoa. Hubbard is a rising star in women's weightlifting. At the Tokyo Olympics, she will compete in the women's +87 kg division.

Competitors from different countries have lodged complaints and raised sharp criticism over the IOC's decision. They emphasize the fact that Hubbard spent her adolescent years as a male, and as a consequence, she would have more muscle mass and bone density, allowing her to have an unfair advantage in weightlifting over other athletes who were born as women. Because of this, they argue that it violates one of the tenets of the Olympic games, fair play.

The IOC's decision to allow transgender athletes to compete in the Olympic games was largely based on the advocacy and research by a transgender medical physicist, Joanna Harper. Harper ran competitively as a man, went through hormonal therapy, and transitioned into a woman. Her research suggested that when men undergo hormonal therapy, the production of testosterone is reduced while estrogen, the female sex hormone, increases.

The decrease in testosterone, in turn, results in the reduction of muscle mass, bone density, and red cells that are responsible for carrying oxygen in the blood. At the same time, the rise in estrogen increases body fat, resulting in the reduction of speed, strength, and endurance. Therefore, she argued, transgender women athletes do not have an unfair advantage over natural women.

Based on this study, IOC adopted the "Stockholm Consensus" and opened ways for transgender women to participate in the Olympic games. In responding to the criticism that the rule unnecessarily infringed upon the right to self-determination of the body, it was changed in 2015. Under the new guidelines, a transgender woman may compete in the Olympic games even if she has not undergone a sex reassignment procedure as long as she has maintained a female gender declaration for four years and the testosterone level remains under 10 nanomoles per liter for at least one year.

However, using only the hormone level to measure who can participate in the Olympic games is not without problems. It resulted in precluding biological female athletes from competing because their natural testosterone levels surpassed the threshold.

The unfortunate athletes were 18-year-old track and field stars Christine Mboma and Beatrice Masilingi from Namibia, a small country in Africa. They were prevented from competing in the women's 400-meter and 1600-meter relays because of their naturally high testosterone levels. The World Athletics did not deny that these athletes are women, but announced that it had no choice but to follow the new IOC rules that define a "woman" by her testosterone level.

An Indian female sprinter, Dutee Chand, went through a similar ordeal in 2014. She brought a lawsuit to the Court of Arbitration for Sport claiming that the rule that prevented her from competing based on high natural testosterone levels in women was arbitrary and lacked sufficient scientific basis. The Court agreed and suspended the rule for two years, allowing Chand to compete in the 2016 Rio Olympics. The two young runners who became victims of the new guidelines will also need to litigate their cases in court.

With the growing number of sex reassignment surgeries and hormone therapies worldwide, the IOC must establish a precise scientific definition of a "woman" to make the Olympic games a global festival that everyone can enjoy. (2021.7.21.)

Outcome: On August 2, 2021, Hubbard failed to complete her three snatch lifts in Group A of the women's +87kg weightlifting competition.

인종갈등·젠더

정당방위법

　　　29세의 흑인 남성 '제이콥 블레이크'(Jacob Blake)는 가정불화 출동신고를 받고 현장에 도착한 경찰의 제지에도 불구하고 자신의 여자친구 차량 운전석 문을 열고 들어가려다 경찰로부터 등과 옆구리에 7발의 총을 맞았다. 차량 안에 타고 있던 제이콥의 어린 아들 3명이 이 끔찍한 장면을 보고 있는 가운데 벌어진 일이었다. 하반신 불수가 되었지만 다행히 목숨은 건졌다. 2020.8.23. 위스콘신주 커노샤(Kenosha)의 한 아파트 도로변에서 일어난 사건이다.

　　이 사건 3개월 전에는 경찰에 의한 흑인 남성 '조지 플로이드'의 목눌림 질식사 사건이 발생하여 미국 전역에 BLM(Black Lives Matter, 흑인 목숨도 소중하다)시위가 끊이질 않았다.

　　위스콘신 주지사는 이웃 미네소타주에서 일어난 플로이드의 목눌림 사건이 채 진정되기도 전에 제이콥의 흑인차별 사건이 또 발생하자 커노샤에 통행금지령을 발동하였다. 그러나 과격 시위대는 통행금지령에도 아랑곳하지 않고 거리로 나와 벽돌과 화염병 등으로 경찰에 저항하며 트럭과 가게 등에 불을 질렀다. 경찰을 도와 이 혼란을 수습하기 위해 시민 자경단이 조직되었는데 이때 17세의 청소년 '카일 리튼하우스'(Kyle Rittenhouse)도 자동소총으로 무장하고 자경단에 가담하였다.

리튼하우스는 시위대 진압과정에서 백인 3명에게 총격을 가해 2명은 사망, 1명에게는 부상을 입힌 혐의를 받고 일리노이주 자택에서 체포되어 1급살인죄로 기소되었다. 리튼하우스는 재판에서 시위 대원 '조세프 로젠바움'이 자신에게 비닐봉지를 던지며 총을 빼앗으려 했고, '앤서니 후버'는 스케이트보드를 휘두르며 접근하였으며, '그로스크레츠'는 권총을 든 채 다가와 신변에 위협을 느끼고 각각 총격으로 대응할 수밖에 없었다고 밝혔다. 한마디로 정당방위였다는 것이다.

'정당방위'란 '자기 또는 타인의 법익에 대한 현재의 부당한 침해를 방위하기 위한 행위'를 일컫는 것인데 이에 대해서는 처벌하지 않는 게 형법의 기본 법리이다. 하지만 각 주마다 정당방위의 구성요건이 다르므로 주의가 필요하다.

예컨대 뉴욕주의 정당방위법은 대체로 다음과 같다. 우선, 힘을 사용해 자신을 지키기 전에 안전하다면 위험 상황에서 도망칠 것을 요구한다. 사람의 안전이나 목숨을 지키기 위해선 총이나 칼 등 치명적인 무기의 힘을 이용할 수 있지만, 단지 재산을 지키기 위한 것이라면 허용되지 않는다.

그러나 집에 도둑이 들었을 때는 곧바로 무기를 사용할 수 있도록 예외를 인정해 주는데 이를 법률용어로 '성의 원칙'(castle doctrine)이라고 한다. '집은 자신만의 성으로 그곳은 절대적으로 지켜져야만 한다'고 믿기 때문에 생긴 전통으로 17세기 영국으로부터 전해졌다.

또 선제 공격자는 정당방위가 인정되지 않지만 상대방이 더 센 무기로 반격을 해 온다면 선제 공격자도 무기를 사용할 수 있다. 다시 말해 A가 B에게 주먹을 날렸는데, B는 칼로 반격해 온다면 A 역시 칼이나 총으로 방어할 수 있다는 뜻이다.

플로리다나 조지아 주에서는 뉴욕과 달리 후퇴의 의무가 없기 때문에 공공장소에서도 치명적인 위협을 받았다면 도망가지 않고 총이나 칼과 같은 살상무기로 공격이 허용된다. 2012년 플로리다에서 비무장 17세의 흑인 고등학생 '트레이본 마틴'을 사살한 자율방범대장 '조지 짐머맨'이 무죄평결을 받은 것도 이 같은 법리에 따른 것이라 볼 수 있다.

　이번 재판처럼 정당방위가 쟁점이 된 경우에는 검사가 책임지고 배심원에게 정당방위가 성립되지 않는다는 것을 입증해야 한다. 그래서 '토마스 빈저' 검사가 "은행강도가 은행을 털고 도망가는 도중에 군중들이 그를 추격해온다고 해서 아무한테나 총을 쏘고 정당방위를 주장할 수 있느냐?"고 반문하면서 부당성을 호소했던 것인데 배심원단은 리튼하우스의 모든 혐의를 정당방위로 인정하고 최근 11월19일 무죄를 평결했던 것이다. (2021.12.8.)

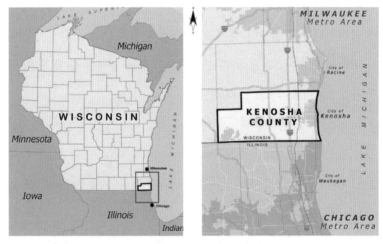

커노샤 지도 <출처: 커노샤 카운티 웹사이트>
Map of Kenosha <source: Kenosha County website>

Racial and Gender Tension

Justification of Self-Defense

Officers shot Jacob Blake, a 29-year-old Black man, in the
back and the side seven times as Blake opened his girlfriend's car door. Police
had responded to a 911 call for domestic violence and told Blake to stop, believing
that he was trying to get a knife. The police shooting happened in front of Blake's
three young boys. Although he survived the shooting, he's paralyzed from the
waist down. This incident took place on the streets outside of an apartment
building in Kenosha, Wisconsin, on August 23, 2020.

Three months before the incident, another Black man, George Floyd, was
choked to death by the police. His death sparked the Black Lives Matter protests
throughout the United States.

Fearing civil unrest from the police shooting of Blake, Wisconsin's governor
issued a curfew order in Kenosha. Floyd's death, which happened in the
neighboring state of Minnesota, was still fresh in people's minds. Despite the
curfew, angry protesters poured out onto the streets. They threw bricks and

Molotov cocktails, pushed police officers, and set trucks and buildings on fire. A civilian vigilante group was organized, ostensibly to help the police control the chaotic situation. Seventeen-year-old Kyle Rittenhouse armed himself with a semi-automatic weapon and joined the vigilante group.

At the protests, Rittenhouse shot three people, all white, killing two and injuring one. He was arrested on charges of homicide at his Illinois home. At his trial, Rittenhouse testified that a protester, who was later identified to be Joseph Rosenbaum, chased him swinging a plastic bag and tried to take away his gun. Rittenhouse also testified that he feared for his physical safety when another victim, Anthony Huber, swung a skateboard at him. Grosskreutz, the third victim, approached him while being armed with a handgun. He argued that he shot them in self-defense.

Self-defense is a justification that allows a person to avoid criminal punishment if he used necessary and reasonable force to defend himself from an attack or imminent physical threat. The requirements vary by state, so it is important to know the difference.

For example, under New York Law, a person may be justified in using self-defense if certain conditions are met. First, there is a duty to retreat. The person must leave the scene if it is safe to do so before resorting to force. Also, a person may use deadly physical force like a firearm or a knife if it's to protect a person's life or physical safety; but it's not allowed if it's merely for the defense of property.

To make it more complicated, there is an exception to this rule for when a burglar comes into the house. This is called the castle doctrine. It originated in seventeenth century England because they believed that "a man's home is his castle, et domus sua cuique est tutissimum refugium [and each man's home is his safest refuge]." Finally, the initial aggressor normally may not claim self-defense. However, if the victim reacts by using deadly force, even the initial aggressor can use deadly force to defend himself. In other words, if A threw a punch at B, and B responded by swinging a knife, then A may defend by using a knife or a firearm.

Unlike New York, there is no duty to retreat in Florida and Georgia. Thus, even in public spaces, any one may use a gun or a knife to defend himself if he feels threatened. This may have contributed to the jury's decision to find the neighborhood watch volunteer, George Zimmerman, not guilty after trial in 2012 even though he fatally shot an unarmed 17-year-old Trayvon Martin.

Where self-defense is an issue at trial, the burden is on the prosecutor to disprove it beyond a reasonable doubt. At Rittenhouse's trial, prosecutor Thomas Binger tried to disprove his claim of self-defense by questioning the jury, "[w]hen a bank robber robs a bank and runs away and the crowd comes after him, can he just shoot anybody and claim self-defense?" Despite this argument, the jury accepted Rittenhouse's claim that he acted in self-defense and found him not guilty on all charges on November 19, 2021. (2021.12.8.)

Chapter
6

교육
Education

학교성적 좋은 게 잘못인가요?

아이들의 새 학기가 시작되었다. 올 상반기 뉴욕시 교육계 키워드 중 하나는 '드블라지오' 뉴욕시장이 추진한 뉴욕시 특목고 입학시험(SHSAT)의 폐지 시도였다고 할 것이다.

시험을 거쳐 뉴욕시 특목고에 경쟁 입학한 60% 이상의 아시안 학생 편중 현상을 완화, 인종의 다양성을 꾀한다는 명분 하에 시도한 것이었지만 아시안 커뮤니티와 공청회 한 번 거치지 않고 추진한 결과 오히려 아시아 아메리칸 차별이라는 반감만 불러일으키고 뉴욕주 의회를 통과하지 못해 자동 폐기되고 말았다.

드블라지오 시장은 이어 아시안 학생들이 많이 등록되어 있는 '영재교육 프로그램'의 폐지도 고려하고 있는 것으로 알려져 이래저래 차별 논란은 계속될 전망이다.

뉴욕시 외에서도 아시아계 학생들에 대한 차별 문제로 여러 건의 소송이 진행 중인데 그중 대표적 사례가 현재 보스턴에서 진행 중인 '공정한 입학을 위한 학생들 대 하버드대'(*Students for Fair Admissions v. Harvard*) 사건이다.

올여름쯤으로 예상되었던 1심 재판 결과는 아직 나오지 않고 있지만 어떤 판결이 나오든 양쪽 다 항소 방침을 밝히고 있어 귀추가 주목된다.

이 스토리는 1990년 휴스턴에 살던 유대계 증권맨 '에드워드 블럼'(Edward Blum)으로 거슬러 올라간다. 자신이 살던 지역구에 공화당 연방하원 후보로 출마한 블럼은 선거 활동 중 지역구의 경계가 인종에 근거하여 민주당에 유리하도록 획정되었다는 사실을 깨달았다. 그는 선거 패배 후 텍사스주를 상대로 소송을 걸었고 결국 연방대법원까지 올라가 지역구의 경계가 헌법상 용납될 수 없을 정도로 기형적 분할이었다는 걸 입증해 승소했다.

블럼은 승소 후 여러 보수 시민단체 회장으로 활약하면서 인종에 근거한 선거구 분할, 소수계 우대 대학 입학정책인 '어퍼미티브 액션'(affirmative action) 등 인종 계층화 반대소송을 왕성하게 전개하였다. 2008년엔 백인 여학생 '애비게일 피셔'를 내세워 텍사스 주립대가 어퍼미티브 액션을 통해 백인 학생들을 역차별했다는 소송을 진행했다가 대법원에서 고배를 마시기도 했다.

이런 시행착오를 거쳐 대법원 소송 엔지니어로 변신한 블럼 회장의 최신 작품이 위의 하버드 사건이다. 그는 텍사스 주립대 재판을 통해 터득한 몇 가지 소송전략을 하버드 사건에 구사했는데 바로 백인 대신 아시아계 학생들을 소송 전면에 내세운 점이다.

블럼은 하버드의 제도연구소가 2013년 하버드대의 입학처장인 '윌리엄 피츠시몬스'에게 제출한 리포트를 입수, 증거물로 제시했는데 그 내용이 우리의 관심을 끈다.

이 리포트에 의하면 만약 학업성취도만을 유일한 하버드 입학기준으로 삼을 경우 아시안 학생의 입학률이 신입생의 43%를 차지하지만 하버드 동문 자녀에 대한 가산점 및 운동선수 가산점 등까지 고려한다면 그 수치가 31%로 하락하고, 과외활동 및 개인 인성 점수를 고려하면 26%, 마지막으로 인구 적 요인까지 더하면 18%로 떨어지게 된다는 것이다.

실제 2013년의 아시아계 하버드 신입 학생 비율이 19%였는데 이 리포트의 예측과 얼추 맞아떨어진다고 보면 백인 학생들과 비교해 아시안 학생들이 차별받고 있다는 것이 증명된 셈이다.

아울러 이 수치는 입학 사정 시 학생의 인종을 고려하지 않는 것으로 알려진 UC 버클리, UCLA, 칼텍 등 서부 명문대에서 40%를 상회한다는 아시아계 학생 통계와도 별 차이가 없어 증거력을 더해준다.

재판 중 제시된 또 다른 하버드의 내부자료에 따르면 11학년에 재학 중인 학생들에게 보내졌던 하버드대 지원 초청장의 컷오프도 백인 학생은 PSAT에서 1,310점, 아시아계 여학생은 1,350점, 아시아계 남학생에게는 1,380점으로 기준을 달리 적용했던 것으로 알려졌다.

공평한 실력주의를 바탕으로 삼는 아메리칸드림과 인종백화점 이민 국가 미국의 다양성 사이에서 미국 교육계의 시름이 깊어지고 있다. (2019.9.25.)

결과: '공정한 입학을 위한 학생들' 대 하버드대 사건은 1차 재판과 항소심에서 하버드대가 승소하였다. 2022년 1월, 연방대법원은 이 사건에 대한 심리를 진행하기로 결정함으로써 아직도 사건이 종결되진 않았다.

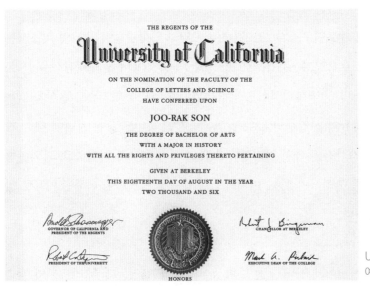

UC버클리 졸업장
예(저자의 동생)

Punishing the Overachievers

A new school year has begun. One of the most controversial issues in education from the first half of the year was New York City Mayor de Blasio's attempt to eliminate the Specialized High Schools Admissions Test (SHSAT), the entrance exam for specialized high schools in New York City.

De Blasio argued that eliminating the test would promote diversity and reduce racial disparity in specialized schools. Specialized schools consist of more than 60% Asian-American students. It was sharply criticized because his attempt was widely perceived as discriminatory against Asians-Americans. The bill was proposed without a single hearing from the Asian-American community. The State legislature did not adopt the proposal.

However, the controversy is far from over as Mayor de Blasio is reportedly contemplating elimination of New York City's Gifted and Talented program, another education program with a high percentage of Asian-American student enrollment.

Outside of New York, there are several court cases that involve discriminatory treatment of Asian students. Perhaps the best known among them is the case currently pending in Boston, Students for Fair Admissions v. Harvard.

A verdict was expected last summer, but the judge has yet to render her decision. Both parties are already vowing to appeal the unknown verdict.

The history of the case can be traced to 1990 with a Jewish stockbroker named Edward Blum. Blum ran for a congressional seat as a Republican in his hometown, Houston, Texas. He quickly realized that his district was gerrymandered in favor of the Democratic incumbent. After his electoral defeat, he filed a lawsuit against the state of Texas. Ultimately, he prevailed in the U.S. Supreme Court by proving that his district was a product of constitutionally impermissible racial gerrymandering.

After his Supreme Court victory, Blum served as a chairman of several conservative activist groups and began a dynamic career as a professional litigant focusing on racial issues such as gerrymandering and affirmative action. Affirmative action refers to the college admissions policy which gives preferential treatment to minority students. For example, in 2008, he brought a lawsuit on behalf of a Caucasian college applicant, Abigail Fisher, against the University of Texas, at Austin. In that case, he argued that Fisher was rejected because Caucasian applicants were racially discriminated against during the admissions process. The Supreme Court disagreed.

Through trial and error, Blum became an engineer of the Supreme Court docket like no other. SFFA v. Harvard is his latest contribution. Interestingly, he employed several strategies that he learned from the Fisher case. One of these strategies is to use Asian students, not Caucasian students, as the face of litigation.

Blum also presented a 2013 report from Harvard's Office of Institutional Research, prepared by William Fitzsimmons, the dean of Harvard's admissions office. His findings were noteworthy.

According to the report, if Harvard were to consider only the academic ratings of its applicants, Asian-Americans would make up 43 percent of the incoming class. If legacy and athletic preferences were thrown into the mix, the proportion would decrease to about 31 percent of the incoming class. Taking extracurricular and personal ratings into account pushed the number down to 26 percent of the incoming class. Finally, the report found, adding demographic factors depressed the number to about 18 percent of the incoming class.

In 2013, the percentage of admitted Asian-American students at Harvard was around 19 percent, nearly on the mark with the report's estimation. Thus, the report provided evidence that the admissions process discriminated against Asian students based on demographic factors compared to their Caucasian counterparts, Blum argued.

Further, he maintained that the report's findings were even more credible because at top-tier West Coast universities such as UC Berkeley, UCLA and CalTech where race is not an admissions factor, Asian students made up over 40 percent of new students – once again, closely matching the report's numbers.

According to another Harvard internal document presented at trial, the cutoff PSAT score to receive an invitation to apply in eleventh grade was 1310 for Caucasian students, but 1350 and 1380, respectively, for female and male Asian-

American students.

The American education system continues its struggle to keep a delicate balance between the ideals of promoting access to a fair and merit-based American dream and ensuring diversity in its schools. (2019.9.25.)

Outcome: In Students for Fair Admissions v. Harvard, Harvard prevailed in the trial and appellate courts. However, the case is not yet over as the Supreme Court said in January 2022 that it would hear this case.

하버드대 설립자 존 하버드 동상 앞에서(보스턴.1997)
Statue of John Harvard, the founder of Harvard University (Boston)

드리머들의 꿈을 응원합니다

올해 초 뉴욕타임스에 보도된 박진규 군의 칼럼을 읽으며 마음이 심란했던 기억이 난다. 뉴욕 퀸스 플러싱 출신인 박 군은 7세 때 부모님 손에 이끌려 미국으로 건너와 비자가 만료된 불법체류자였지만 오바마 행정부의 DACA(Deferred Action for Childhood Arrivals; 불법체류청년 추방유예제도) 덕분에 하버드에 입학할 수 있었다.

그는 하버드 졸업 후 영예롭게도 DACA 수혜자 신분으론 처음으로 매년 미국 전체에서 32명만이 선발되는 로즈 장학생으로 뽑혔다고 소개되어 우리 교민들에게 큰 자긍심과 감동을 선사하였다. 로즈 장학제도는 영국의 명문 옥스퍼드대에서 향후 2년간 생활비까지 받으며 공부할 기회가 제공되는 특전이다.

그러나 안타깝게도 박 군은 영국 생활을 끝내고 다시 미국으로 귀환하지 못하게 될지도 모른다. 왜냐하면 현재 뜨거운 감자가 되어 대법원에서 심리 중인 DACA가 폐지 쪽으로 기울 경우 미국으로 돌아올 때 입국 거부를 당할 수도 있기 때문이다.

DACA는 2012년 당시 오바마 행정부에서 대폭 심사를 완화하는 방향으로 이민법 개혁을 추진하다 미 의회의 승인을 받지 못하자 대통령 행정명령으로 출발한 프로그램이다.

다시 말해 박 군처럼 어려서 관광비자 등으로 와 불체자가 된 청년들에게 의회가 이민법을 개정할 때까지 합법적으로 미국에 머물 수 있도록 해주기 위해 만들어진 프로그램이다. 행정명령이다 보니 수혜자들은 2년마다 갱신을 해야 하며 시민권을 받을 수 있는 통로도 마련되지 않은 그야말로 임시방편의 미봉책이었다.

처음 만들어질 당시만 해도 곧 사회적 합의가 이루어져 이민법 개정이 이루어질 것처럼 많은 기대를 하였지만 이민자들에게 적대적인 트럼프 행정부가 들어서면서 그 시한부 명줄의 끝이 점점 가까워진 것으로 보인다.

2017년 트럼프 행정부가 이 프로그램의 폐지를 선언하자 DACA의 수혜자들과 이민자 옹호 단체들, 심지어 캘리포니아 주립대까지 연대하여 뉴욕과 캘리포니아의 연방법원 등에 소송을 제기했다. 뉴욕과 캘리포니아의 법원에선 각각 이민자 단체들의 손을 들어주며 예비 금지명령과 더불어 항소심이 완료될 때까지 프로그램의 종료 기간을 2년 정도 늘려주었다.

그 사건의 대법원 심리가 지난 11월 12일에 시작되었는데 법정 밖에서부터 찬반 논란이 뜨거웠다. 심리 당일 아침 트럼프 대통령은 트위터에 "DACA 수혜자는 더 이상 어리지 않으며 '천사'와는 거리가 멀고 포악하다"고 주장하며 대법원에서 DACA를 위헌판결로 폐지시켜 줄 것을 요청했다. 반면 많은 이민자 옹호 그룹들은 그들 나름대로 이런 시도가 얼마나 비인권적인 조치인지 대법원 밖에서 집단시위로 폐지 반대를 호소하였다.

대법원 심리에서 트럼프 행정부의 법무차관은 행정부의 권한으로 만들어진 DACA는 만들어질 때와 마찬가지로 언제든 행정부의 권한으로 폐지할 수 있다고 주장했다. 그는 또 텍사스와 다른 9개의 보수적인 주의 검찰총장들과 함께 DACA가 지속되면 불체자들에 대한 의료보험과 교육혜택 등으로 미국 재정이 더 악화될 수밖에 없다고 강변했다.

이에 대해 DACA 측 변호인단은 트럼프 대통령이 임기 초반 DACA를 존속시킬 것이라고 약속해놓고 지금 와서 아무런 대안 없이 폐지하는 것은 너무나 비인간적이며 무책임하다고 대응했다.

법조계에서는 현재 트럼프 대통령이 지명한 2명의 대법관을 포함해 보수성향 대법관이 다수여서 내년 전반기쯤 5 대 4 결정으로 DACA가 폐지될 것으로 예측하고 있다. 다만 폐지되더라도 트럼프 대통령이 트위터를 통해 민주당과 협상을 할 것이라고 언급한 바 있어 한 가닥 희망의 불씨는 살아있는 것으로 보인다.

통계에 의하면 미국 전체 80여만 명의 DACA 해당자 중 국경을 접하고 있는 멕시코가 62만 명으로 단연 으뜸이고 우리 한국은 약 7,200명으로 페루, 브라질에 이어 아홉 번째로 많다. 박 군 같은 우리 교민 드리머들이 아메리칸드림을 계속 꿈꿀 수 있기를 응원해 본다. (2019.12.12.)

결과: 2020.6.18. 연방대법원은 5대4로 트럼프 행정부가 DACA를 폐지할 수 없다고 판결했다. 보수 성향의 로버츠 대법원장이 정부가 절차적인 요건을 충족하지 못했다며 DACA를 유지하는 찬성표를 던져 이례적인 판결이 나온 것이다. 2021.1.20. 새롭게 대통령이 된 조 바이든은 행정명령을 통해 DACA를 유지하도록 했다.

영어 녹음 듣기

Education

I'm Rooting for Your Dreams, Dreamers

I remember being upset earlier this year after reading Park Jin-Kyu's op-ed in The New York Times. Park, a native of Flushing, New York, came to America with his parents at seven. Although he overstayed the expiration of his visa and did not have a valid status, he was able to gain entry into Harvard as a recipient of Obama's Deferred Action for Childhood Arrivals (DACA) relief.

Following his graduation from Harvard, he became the first DACA recipient to be awarded the prestigious Rhodes Scholarship, which only selects 32 students from America each year. This news brought great pride and joy to the Korean-American community. Rhodes Scholars receive an opportunity to study for two years at Oxford, a world-renowned university in England, with a full scholarship and a stipend. Unfortunately, however, Park may not be able to return to America after his studies because DACA may be gone by then. It depends on the upcoming Supreme Court's ruling.

DACA began in 2012 as an executive order when President Obama failed to obtain congressional support for a comprehensive immigration law overhaul.

It was designed as a "stopgap measure" to allow young people who, like Park, came to the country as minors and did not have a valid immigration status to legally stay in the country until something could be done to give them status. It was no more than a temporary fix as an executive order and required the recipients to renew every two years. It also did not provide a clear path to citizenship.

At the time of its introduction, hopes were high that a consensus could be built within a short time to change the immigration laws. However, as President Trump - no friend to the immigrants - took over the White House, those hopes were quickly lost.

When President Trump announced he would shut down the program in 2017, a coalition of DACA recipients, immigrant groups and the University of California system filed suits in New York and California district courts to stop it. These courts ruled in favor of the immigrant coalition and granted a preliminary injunction, temporarily extending the program's life by two years until the appeals process could be completed.

The Supreme Court heard these cases on November 12. A heated exchange took place outside the courthouse. On the morning of the hearing, President Trump opened fire by tweeting, "Many of the People in DACA, no longer very young, are far from 'angels.' Some are very tough, hardened criminals" and pressured the Court to find DACA unconstitutional. On the other side was a coalition of immigrant advocacy groups protesting outside the Supreme Court building. They implored the Court to see how President Trump's attempt to shut down the program was unjust and inhumane.

At the Supreme Court hearing, the Trump Administration's Solicitor General argued that just as DACA was created by an executive order, it may be terminated by another executive order anytime the president wished. Along with attorney generals from Texas and nine other conservative states, he also claimed that keeping DACA alive would put a financial strain on the government to provide medical and education services to DACA recipients.

In response, DACA lawyers argued that because President Trump promised to keep DACA alive earlier in his presidential term and there was no alternative, his decision to rescind DACA constituted an abuse of discretion and was irresponsible.

Since there are five conservative justices on the Court, including two Trump appointees, legal commentators predict that DACA will be abolished in a 5-4 decision. Even if the Court decides against it, however, there is a glimmer of hope based on President Trump's tweet that he would negotiate with the Democrats.

There are an estimated number of 800,000 DACA recipients. Mexicans, whose country shares a common border with the United States, tops the list with 620,000. There are about 7,200 Korean DACA recipients, making it the ninth-largest group after Peruvians and Brazilians. I am rooting for Korean-American Dreamers like Park to continue pursuing their American dreams. (2019.12.12.)

Outcome: On June 18, 2020, the Supreme Court ruled in a 5-4 decision that the Trump administration could not terminate DACA. Conservative-leaning Chief Justice Roberts sided with the liberal justices to hold that the government acted in an arbitrary and capricious manner in ending DACA. Nevertheless, the new president Joe Biden issued an executive order to keep DACA on January 20, 2021.

'3월의 광란'과 아마추어리즘

미국대학 남자농구 토너먼트가 3월 17일 첫 경기를 시작으로 4월 6일 결승전까지 20일간에 걸친 대장정의 막을 올린다. 여기에는 미국 전역에서 지역 리그를 거쳐 올라온 남자농구 명가 68개 대학이 총출동한다.

이 대회는 수십 년간 연례행사로 이어져 오는 가운데 조성된 각 지역 간 라이벌 의식에다 단판 승부의 짜릿한 시합방식, 젊은 패기의 대학생들이 부딪치는 과정에서 속출하는 예측불허의 승부 결과, 이를 둘러싸고 장외에서 이루어지는 스포츠 베팅 업계의 어마어마한 판돈 등이 어우러져 흔히 '3월의 광란'(March Madness)이라고 불린다.

미국 경제 전문지 포브스는 이 경기를 통해 한 해 벌어들이는 전국 TV 광고 수입이 약 13억 2,000만 달러(약 1조 6,040억 원) 정도라고 추정했는데 이는 프로농구(NBA) 플레이오프의 9억 7,000만 달러나 프로야구(MLB) 플레이오프의 4억 6,800만 달러의 TV 광고 수입을 훨씬 상회하는 금액이다.

이 천문학적인 돈은 토너먼트 주최자인 NCAA(National Collegiate Athletic Association; 전미대학체육협회)와 이에 소속된 대학들이 고스란히 다 가져갔고 정작 코트 위에서 온몸을 던져 땀 흘린 선수들에겐 아마추어리즘이란 미명 하에 땡전 한 푼도 나눠주지 않았다.

즉 NCAA는 이미 스포츠 장학금을 받고 있는 선수들은 학비 내지 않고 학위를 받는 것으로 만족해야지 돈에 눈독을 들이는 것은 학생 신분뿐 아니라 스포츠 정신에도 어긋난다고 명분을 채색했던 것이다.

이런 잣대 하에 NCAA는 선수들이 장학금 외 광고 수익이나 선수로서의 유명세 등을 이용해 돈 버는 것을 엄격히 금지해왔다. 한 예로 2017년 '도널드 데 라 헤이'는 자신이 센트럴 플로리다 대학에서 풋볼 선수로 겪은 경험담들을 유튜브에 소개하고 그 구독료로 꽤 많은 돈을 벌다 선수로서의 유명세를 이용했다는 이유로 대학 풋볼 팀에서 축출되고 장학금까지 박탈당하는 수모를 겪기도 했다.

하지만 NCAA에 의해 철옹성처럼 둘러쳐 있던 아마추어리즘이란 명분은 작년을 기점으로 서서히 퇴색되고 있는 추세다. 이 같은 분위기 형성의 배경에는 1995년 당시 대학농구 챔피언 팀인 UCLA의 스타팅 파워 포워드 '오배넌'의 힘이 컸다.

오배넌은 우연히 한 대학농구 게임에 자신을 묘사하는 캐릭터가 나온 것을 보고 NCAA가 자신의 초상권을 판매했다는 것을 알게 되었다. 그는 2009년 선수들이 직접 게임업체 등과 라이센싱 계약하는 것을 차단하기 위해 NCAA와 대학들이 선수들의 이미지 사용료를 담합했다는 것을 밝혀내고 NCAA를 상대로 독점규제법 위반 혐의로 집단소송을 제기했다.

이 사건은 오랜 기간에 걸친 재판 끝에 2014년 캘리포니아 지방법원의 '클라우디아 윌켄' 판사가 비디오게임이나 TV 광고 등으로 생기는 수익은 해당 선수들에게도 배당되어야 한다는 판결을 내리고 이를 제9 순회법원에서 추인함으로써 원고 승으로 일단락되었다. 사법부는 선수들이 땀을 흘린 대가와 아마추어리즘과는 별개이므로 NCAA 측에서 선수들의 초상권 사용에 대해 응분의 보상을 치러야 한다고 본 것이다.

이 판결에 힘입어 작년 캘리포니아의 '개빈 뉴섬'(Gavin Newsom) 주지사는 미국 최초로 대학 선수에게 성명권, 초상권 이용과 아울러 스폰서 권리가 보장될 수 있도록 제정된 법률에 서명함으로써 대학선수도 프로선수처럼 에이전트를 두고 수입을 올릴 수 있는 길을 마련해주었다.

오배넌 사건의 판결과 새로운 캘리포니아주 입법은 아마추어리즘을 전면에 내세워 막대한 수익을 독식했던 NCAA로부터 결국 작년 말 대학 선수들의 성명권과 초상권에 대한 대가 지불 방법을 모색해보겠다는 항서를 받아내는 데 크게 일조했다. 그래서 작년과 달리 올해 '3월의 광란'은 심기일전한 선수들을 중심으로 특수를 노리는 맥주회사와 스포츠 베팅 업체들의 상술 등이 가미되어 더욱 뜨거운 축제가 될 것으로 보인다. (2020.3.11.)

Education

'March Madness' and Amateurism

The college men's basketball tournament will kick off on March 17. Sixty-eight teams that have advanced through different conferences from all across the country will compete against each other for the next 20 days. It will culminate with a championship game on April 6.

This decades-old tradition is aptly named "March Madness" for its regional rivalries, electrifying plays by young college athletes, single-elimination rounds that allow "Cinderella" teams to advance, and huge betting pots.

The business magazine Forbes estimates that the annual revenue from TV commercials during March Madness is around $1.32 billion (about 1.604 trillion Korean Won), well above the $970 million from the professional basketball playoffs or the $468 million during the Major League Baseball playoffs.

Most of this astronomical amount of money has gone to the tournament organizer, National Collegiate Athletic Association (NCAA) and its affiliated universities. Unfortunately, the players who put their blood, sweat and tears into the game, walked away with nothing – all in the name of amateurism. The NCAA declared that student-athletes who wanted to compete in intercollegiate sports had to be amateurs and their participation must be motivated by education.

The NCAA imposed strict rules barring students from profiting from an outside source like sponsorships by using their fame or appearing in commercials. For example, Donald De La Haye was a kicker for Central Florida University's football team. He made money by posting video recordings that described his experiences as a college football player. When the NCAA found out, he was kicked off the team and stripped of his scholarship because he had used fame gained from playing in an NCAA sport to make money.

However, starting last year, the veil of amateurism perpetuated by the NCAA is slowly fading into the background. A man behind this change is Ed O'Bannon, a former starting power forward for UCLA's 1995 national championship team. One day, O'Bannon saw a college basketball video game player that resembled him. He realized that the NCAA had sold his image to the game producer. So, in 2009, he became the lead plaintiff in an antitrust class-action lawsuit against the NCAA. The class action alleged that the NCAA and its affiliates improperly restrained student-athletes from being compensated for using and selling their names, images and likeness through licensing agreements with game developers.

After lengthy court proceedings, Judge Claudia Wilken of the Northern District of California ruled in favor of the plaintiffs. Judge Wilken held that profits generated by selling the college athletes' names, images and likeness to video game companies or TV commercials must be shared with the players. The

Ninth Circuit Court of Appeals affirmed Judge Wilken's decision and cemented the plaintiffs' victory. The court saw the sale of the players' names, images and likeness as a separate issue from amateurism, and as such, the NCAA must provide adequate compensation.

Following this ruling, California Governor Gavin Newsom signed a law that would allow student-athletes to make money by selling their name, image, and likeness and sign endorsement deals like professional athletes. It also allows them to hire agents. This law is the first of its kind in the country.

The O'Bannon decision and California law led to a concession by the NCAA. The organization, which had been earning an enormous amount of money under amateurism, announced that it would modify the rules to allow college athletes to profit from selling their names, images, and likeness. For these reasons, this year's March Madness is poised to be the craziest ever, with beer and sports betting companies trying to drive up the demand by their creative commercials, and the players who are looking to make a name, not only for their schools, but for themselves as well. (2020.3.11.)

Law School Life

　　　　　　이번 칼럼에선 미국 변호사가 되기 위해 필수 코스로 거쳐야 하는 로스쿨에 대해 알아본다. 통상 미국의 로스쿨이라 함은 대학원에서 3년간 공부하는 JD(Juris doctor) 과정을 일컫는다.

　　먼저 로스쿨에 입학하려면 4년간 대학에서의 학부성적과 동아리 활동실적 등에다 로스쿨 입학고사인 LSAT(Law School Admission Test)에서 좋은 점수를 받아야 한다. 여기서 합격한 1학년생들은 50명 정도씩 여러 섹션으로 나뉘는데 같은 섹션 학생들은 1년 내내 똑같은 수업을 들을 친구이자 동시에 선의의 경쟁자들도 된다. 1학년의 정규과목은 헌법, 민사소송법, 형사법, 재산법, 계약법, 불법행위법, 법률문서 작성 등으로 이뤄진다.

　　학생들에겐 로스쿨의 좋고 나쁨을 떠나 3년 과정 중 공통적으로 1학년 때가 가장 힘들고, 심적으로도 부담스러운 시간이다. 왜냐하면 대부분의 경우 2학년이 시작되면서 로펌과 취업 인터뷰를 통해 진로가 정해지는데 이때 전적으로 1학년 성적을 참고하므로 상대평가에서 좋은 성적을 얻으려면 죽기 살기로 친구들과의 경쟁에서 이겨야 하기 때문이다.

로스쿨 강의는 법률지식 주입보다 법률가로서 법리적으로 문제를 해결하고 생각하는 방법을 가르치는 데 주안점을 두기 때문에 주로 '소크라테스식 문답법'으로 진행된다. 예컨대 민사소송법 시간이라면, "조지아 주민이, 뉴저지 상점에서, 뉴욕주 회사가 만든 TV를 구매했는데, 사용 도중 TV가 폭발하여 부상을 입었다면 어느 주 법원에서 소송을 걸어야 하는지 말해보라"는 식이다.

갑작스러운 지명을 받고 준비해 간 판례를 인용하면서 의견을 개진해보지만, 문제는 한 번 답으로 끝나는 게 아니고 교수님의 질문이 집요하게 이어진다는 점이다. 급우들 앞에서 무안을 당하지 않으려면 수업을 빡세게 준비하는 수밖에 없다.

성적 평가는 리포트나, 퀴즈시험, 중간고사 같은 것 없이 기말고사 한방으로 끝을 낸다. 그래서 시험 날엔 모두들 비장한 눈빛으로 등교한다. 참고서나 암기노트 보는 것을 허용하지만 일일이 답을 찾다 보면 시간이 부족하기 때문에 중요 판례들은 자기 것으로 만들어놓아야 한다.

또 어렵사리 판례를 달달 외웠다 하더라도 "18세 미만의 청소년은 어른으로 형사처벌할 수 없는데, 어른도 아이도 아닌 피터팬이 범죄를 저질렀다면 어떻게 처벌해야 하나?"와 같은 황당한 형사법 시험이 나올 때도 있어 한시도 긴장의 끈을 놓을 수 없다.

이렇게 정신없이 쫓기듯 1년을 보내고 2학년 가을 신학기가 시작될 즈음이면 로스쿨 최대 이벤트인 취업 인터뷰가 이뤄진다. 로펌 인사담당들이 학교로 찾아와 2학년 마친 후 자기들 식구로 데리고 갈 인재들을 채용하기 위해서이다.

이 행사를 신호탄으로 비로소 캠퍼스에 사람 사는 온기가 느껴지기 시작한다. 공부 잘하는 친구들은 벌써 반쯤 취업이 결정된 터라 악착같이 공부에만 매달리지 않고, 이들 선두 그룹의 승부욕이 식어진 만큼 나머지 학생들도 상대적으로 압박감이 덜하기 때문이다. 2학년부터는 평소 듣고 싶었던 수업을 선택할 수 있고 인턴십이나 동아리 활동에도 눈 돌릴 시간이 생긴다. 특히 미국 검사가 되고자 하는 학생에겐 좋은 성적 못지않게 검찰청 인턴 경험을 쌓는 게 중요하다. 국선변호사가 되려 해도 인턴과정 없이 바로 국선변호사로 직행하는 것은 하늘의 별 따기보다 어렵다고 보면 된다.

요즘엔 로스쿨마다 재학 시절에 많은 실무 경험을 쌓게 해주기 위해 '세금법 클리닉'을 비롯하여 이민법, 지적재산권 클리닉 등 다양한 프로그램을 운영하고 있다. 이런 수업을 통해 나머지 2년간 졸업학점을 채우면 미국 변호사시험인 이른바 바(Bar) 시험을 거쳐 대망의 새내기 변호사가 탄생하는 것이다. (2022.2.16.)

로스쿨 시절 인권법 클리닉 일원으로 수(Sioux)부족 여성들과 인권법 관련 인터뷰 (사우스 다코타.2009)
Conducting an interview with women from the Sioux tribe as a member of Fordham Law School's human rights clinic (South Dakota)

영어 녹음 듣기

Education

Law School Life

Law school education is a necessary step in becoming a lawyer in America. In today's column, we will look at what goes on inside a law school. The typical journey to a legal career is a three-year legal program to earn a Juris Doctor (J.D.).

To gain admission into a law school, students must have an excellent GPA, LSAT score, and a solid resume with extracurricular activities. Once admitted, new students are divided into several sections. Each section consists of about 50 students. All of the students in the section take the same class for the first year. They are not only friends, but competitors as well. The first-year curriculum consists of constitutional law, civil procedure, criminal law, property, contracts, tort, and legal writing.

The first year is probably the most challenging out of three years in law school for most students. It's the most stressful and physically draining because when students apply to law firms at the beginning of their second year, they will look at the first-year grades. To stand out among the classmates, students need to get good grades.

Law school instruction is not focused on teaching knowledge, but on how to think and approach a problem like a lawyer. Most professors use the Socratic method in which they will continuously pose questions to their students. Instead of regurgitating an answer from the textbook, students will be asked to come up with their own solutions to questions like, "which state is a proper forum for a plaintiff if he is domiciled in Georgia, but bought a TV in New Jersey if it exploded and it was manufactured by a New York company?" Whatever the answer is, the students are expected to provide reasons based on the cases they read. If they want to avoid being embarrassed in front of their classmates, they must study hard.

Grades are determined by one final examination without reports, quizzes, or mid-terms. Naturally, on final exam days, students seem tired and determined at the same time. Although it's an open book test and students may use their notes, textbooks and supplemental books during the exam, there's not enough time to look up all the answers. It's best to memorize the most consequential decisions.

Even when they memorize the law, they may get surprised with questions like, "individuals under 18-years-old cannot be prosecuted as an adult in State A. Can Peter Pan, who is neither a child nor an adult, be prosecuted as an adult?"

The first year of law school flies by. Then, at the beginning of the second year, the most significant law school event takes place: the on-campus interview. Interviewers from law firms visit law schools and try to recruit the best talent to their firms.

Once the on-campus interviews are completed, the atmosphere becomes much less stressful. By then, most of the students near the top of the class have been offered a position and are more relaxed about grades. This trickles down to the rest of the students. Students can choose elective classes, and have more time for internships or other extracurricular activities. For example, students who want to become a prosecutor must get an internship at the prosecutor's office. The same goes for the students who want to become a public defender. Without these internships, it is challenging to get a job as one.

These days, law schools have clinics to give students more hands-on experience. There are tax law clinics, immigration law clinics, intellectual property clinics, and many more. Once students fulfill the graduation requirements by completing these courses and gaining valuable experiences, they earn the right to take the bar exam. Once they pass the exam, they become freshly minted lawyers. (2022.2.16.)

멘토링 프로그램에서 로스쿨 학생들과 함께(뉴욕.2019)
With law students at a mentoring program (New York)

7장 전체 영어녹음 듣기

Chapter
7

정치·언론
Politics and Media

미국의 탄핵제도

최근 트럼프 대통령이 우크라이나에 대한 원조를 빌미로 자신의 정적이자 민주당의 유력 대선 후보인 '조 바이든'(Joe Biden) 전 부통령을 궁지에 빠뜨리려 했다는 정부 내부고발자의 제보에 따라 미 하원은 공식적 탄핵소추 조사에 착수했다.

연방 헌법 2조 4항은 "대통령을 비롯한 미국의 모든 공무원은 반역죄, 뇌물죄 등 각종 중·경범죄에 따른 소추 및 유죄 선고에 따라 탄핵될 수 있다"고 명시하고 있는데 탄핵을 하려면 연방하원에서 우선 법사위원장이 수사를 거쳐 탄핵결의안을 발의해야 한다. 하원의원 과반수가 결의안에 찬성하면 상원으로 공이 넘어가는데 상원에서는 표결로 유무죄만을 판단하여 탄핵을 최종 결정한다. 다시 말해 일반재판으로 치자면 하원은 대배심이 되어 수사 및 기소하고 상원은 소배심이 되어 심리, 재판하는 셈이다.

대통령에 대한 상원에서의 탄핵재판은 연방대법원장이 재판장이 되어 주재하고 연방하원 의원 중 몇 명을 매니저라는 이름으로 선출하여 검사의 역할을 맡긴다. 상원의원 100명 전원은 배심원이 되어 결의안 심리 후 표결로 3분의 2 이상이 찬성하면 즉각 탄핵이 되고, 남은 임기는 부통령이 승계한다.

지금까지 240여 년의 미국 건국 역사상 '앤드루 존슨'(Andrew Johnson)과 우리에게도 이름이 친숙한 '빌 클린턴'(Bill Clinton) 두 명의 대통령이 탄핵소추되었지만 실제로 대통령 탄핵이 성공한 적은 아직 한 번도 없다.

존슨은 남부출신 민주당 정치인이었지만 공화당의 링컨이 남북전쟁을 성공리에 끝내고 압도적인 표차로 재선되었을 때 남북화합 차원에서 부통령으로 발탁한 사람이었는데 링컨이 재선 직후 40일 만에 암살되는 바람에 대통령직을 승계하였다.

1868년 당시 전쟁장관 해임 문제를 둘러싸고 다수파 공화당 의원들과 충돌이 잦아 결국 탄핵소추되었으나 재판 도중 반대파 의원들과 협상을 통해 당시 상원 재적 54명 중 의결정족수 3분의 2(36표)에 한 표 부족한 35대19로 기각되어 남은 임기를 수행할 수 있었다. 그는 후에 알래스카를 러시아로부터 720만 불에 매입하는 업적을 남기게 된다.

클린턴은 재정적자 해소와 미국경제를 되살린 호평으로 1996년 당당히 재선된 후 20대 초반의 백악관 인턴'모니카 르윈스키'(Monica Lewinsky)등과의 지퍼게이트 스캔들로 소추되어 공화당이 다수인 하원에서 고발되었으나 역시 상원에서 부결되었다. 당시 상원 공화당 의원들도 부결표를 다수 던진 것으로 확인되었는데 표결 이유를 밝히지 않고 판결문 작성도 하지 않기 때문에 왜 공화당 의원들도 부결에 동참했는지 알 방법이 없다.

워터게이트 사건에 연루된 닉슨 대통령은 탄핵된 것으로 오해하기 쉽지만 1974년 탄핵소추 과정 중에 탄핵결의안이 가결될 가능성이 높아지자 하원에서 가결되기 직전에 '제럴드 포드'(Gerald Ford)부통령에게 자리를 물려주고 자진 사퇴했기 때문에 탄핵된 것이 아니다.

대통령에 비해 다른 고위직 중 연방판사들은 실제 다수 탄핵된 사례가 있다고 보면 미국의 탄핵제도는 엄격한 법리에 따른 사법절차라기보다 입법부가 행정부와 사법부를 견제하는 삼권분립의 한 민주 장치 정도로 이해하면 타당할 듯하다.

그런 의미에서 만약 트럼프 대통령의 탄핵재판이 진행된다면 민주당 소속 매니저들은 어떻게 트럼프 대통령을 궁지에 빠뜨릴 것이며, 상원을 장악하고 있는 공화당 소속 상원의원들은 어떤 식으로 재판 절차를 어렵게 만들어 그것을 잘 방어해내는지 또 민주와 공화 양당이 탄핵이라는 정치적 이슈를 자기 당에 얼마나 유리하게 활용해서 내년 대선 승리를 이끌어 내는지 하는 것 등이 관전 포인트가 될 것이다. (2019.10.23.)

결과: 2019.12.18. 미 하원은 트럼프 대통령을 직권 남용과 의회 방해 혐의로 탄핵 소추하였으나 2020.2.5. 상원이 직권 남용 혐의에 대해 48대52, 의회 방해 혐의에 대해 47대53으로 기각함으로써 탄핵은 무위에 그쳤다.

앤드루 존슨 대통령 생가와 무덤(테네시 그린빌.2020)
Home and the final resting place of the 17th President, Andrew Johnson (Greenville, Tennessee)

Politics and Media

Impeachment Process

The House of Representatives recently launched an official impeachment probe following a whistleblower complaint that President Trump attempted to withhold congressionally approved aid to Ukraine to gain a personal advantage against leading Democratic presidential candidate, former Vice President Joe Biden.

Article 2 Clause 4 of the U.S. Constitution provides, "The President, Vice President and all Civil Officers of the United States, shall be removed from Office on Impeachment for, and Conviction of, Treason, Bribery, or other high Crimes and Misdemeanors." The formal impeachment process begins with the chairperson of the Judiciary Committee introducing the Articles of Impeachment to the House after an investigation has concluded. If the majority in the House passes the resolution, it goes over to the Senate. The Senate makes a final decision on the president's removal. In simpler terms, the House works as a grand jury, investigating and indicting the president. The Senate resembles the work of a petit jury, rendering a verdict based on the evidence.

The Chief Justice of the Supreme Court presides over the Senate's impeachment trial. Several members of the House are called "managers" and assume the role of a prosecutor. The 100 senators serve as jurors. If two-thirds of the senators approve, the president is removed. The vice president succeeds the president.

In the 240 years of the nation's history, only two presidents have been impeached, Andrew Johnson and Bill Clinton, whose story we are familiar with based on its recency. However, neither one has been removed.

Andrew Johnson was a southern Democrat who was tapped by President Lincoln, a Republican, to balance the ticket in his re-election bid. Lincoln won the reelection in a landslide during the Civil War for his leadership. However, he was assassinated only forty days into his second term, leaving Johnson to take over the rest of the term. As a Democrat, Johnson had frequent clashes with Republican legislators, who had the majority in Congress. The tumultuous relationship culminated in his impeachment in 1868 for firing the Secretary of War. While the impeachment trial was taking place, he was able to negotiate with some Republican senators and narrowly avoided removal. The Senate's final vote was 35-19 to remove him, just one vote shy of 36 votes (two-thirds of 54 eligible voters). Johnson's legacy is in purchasing Alaska from Russia for $7.2 million.

Clinton was re-elected in 1996 for his success in reviving the American economy. However, following the Zippergate scandal involving a twenty-something White House intern Monica Lewinsky, he was impeached by the

House Republicans. The Senate ultimately voted down his removal. Interestingly, even some Republican senators voted down the removal. Their reasons for doing so remain largely a mystery because neither an explanation nor a legal decision is required.

It is a popular myth that President Nixon was impeached for his role in the Watergate scandal. In truth, he resigned voluntarily in 1974 and handed his post to Vice President Gerald Ford as the likelihood of the House's passing of the Articles of Impeachment became near certain.

Unlike the removal of presidents, there have been several examples of federal judges who have been removed from the bench. When examining these cases, what becomes apparent is that the impeachment process should be understood less as a strict legal proceeding, but more as a political mechanism that allows

백악관 (Washington D.C.)
The White House

the legislature to check the other two branches of the government. In that sense, if President Trump were to be impeached, it would be interesting to see how the Democratic managers will prove their case, how the Republican majority in the Senate will maneuver to make the trial rules more difficult for the managers, and how each party will use the trial to their advantage in the upcoming presidential election. (2019.10.23.)

Outcome: On December 18, 2019, the House of Representatives adopted two Articles of Impeachment against President Trump for abuse of power and obstruction of Congress. On February 5, 2020, the Senate voted against the impeachment by 48-52 for abuse of power, and 47-53 for obstruction of Congress.

누구를 위한 사면인가?

우크라이나 원조 문제 등 권력 남용 혐의로 탄핵 재판을 받았던 트럼프 대통령은 상원 표결에서 자신의 탄핵안이 부결되기 무섭게 풍부한 자금력이나 지명도 등으로 정치적 영향력이 큰 거물급 범죄자 11명을 사면 및 감형함으로써 대통령의 사면권 남용 논쟁에 불을 지폈다.

지난 2월 18일 트럼프 대통령으로부터 사면이나 감형을 받은 사람 중에는 매관매직을 시도한 전 일리노이 주지사 '라드 브라고예비치'를 비롯 탈세로 징역형을 살았던 전 뉴욕시 경찰총장 '버나드 케릭', 부패행위로 유죄 선고를 받았던 미식축구팀 전 구단주 '에드워드 디바르톨로'와 같은 유명인사들이 다수 포함되어 있다. 언론과 야권에선 이번 사면이 통상 법무부에서 실시하는 기본적인 심사조차 하지 않고 오로지 트럼프의 정치적 목적과 사적 인연만을 고려해 결정된 것으로 보인다고 비판했다.

한 예로 '루디 줄리아니'(Rudy Giuliani)가 뉴욕시장으로 재임하던 시절 그의 비호 아래 뉴욕시 경찰총장을 지낸 버나드 케릭은 헌신적인 자세로 2001년 9.11 테러를 훌륭하게 수습하여 전국구 스타로 떠올랐던 인물이다. 이후 부시 대통령에 의해 국토안보부 장관 후보에 지명되어 꽃길을 걷는 듯했지만 인사청문회를 앞두고 탈세와 뇌물수수 혐의 등이 언론에 폭로됨으로써 지명철회뿐 아니라 재판에 넘겨져 기구하게도 4년의 실형까지 살게 되었다. 뉴욕타임스는 케릭의 이번 사면이 트럼프의 개인 변호사로 변신해 활약하고 있는 줄리아니의 작품으로 보인다고 꼬집었다.

범죄를 용서하고 형벌을 면제해주는 사면제도는 중세 전제국가 시대에 전권을 행사하던 군주 은전권의 유물이라고 할 수 있다. 따라서 삼권분립이 확립된 현대 민주 국가에서는 사법부의 결정에 대한 행정부의 간섭으로 여겨 채택하지 않는 게 원칙임에도 미국은 헌법 2조 2항을 통해 이 막강한 권한을 대통령에게 허용해주었던 것이다.

사실 영국 왕실의 사면권 남용을 직접 목도한 건국 당시 미국의 지도자들은 처음엔 대통령에게 사면권을 주지 않는 것으로 가닥을 잡았던 것으로 전해진다.

하지만 강력한 연방 정부를 희구했던 '알렉산더 해밀턴'(Alexander Hamilton)은 주와 주간의 내전이나 독재 정부에 항거하기 위한 민중봉기 같은 국가 위기상황에 봉착했을 때 사후 수습책으로 통치 권력의 적절한 사면이 미국연방 전체의 안정과 통합에 기여할 수 있을 것으로 내다봤다. 이를 구현하려면 다수로 구성된 다양한 목소리의 의회보다 '균형감각과 통찰력을 두루 갖춘 대통령 한 사람이 독단적으로 결정하는 게 더욱 합리적'이라고 판단하여 헌법에 대통령의 사면권이 들어가게 된 것이다.

이후 대통령들은 해밀턴의 입법 취지에 부응이라도 하듯 미국의 화합과 안정을 위해 적극적으로 사면권을 행사했다. 예컨대 초대 조지 워싱턴 대통령은 정부의 위스키 과세 결정에 반발해 폭동을 일으킨 농민들에게 사면을 베풀었고, 남북전쟁을 북부의 승리로 이끌어 압도적 지지로 재선된 링컨 대통령이 재임 초 암살당하자 대통령직을 승계한 앤드루 존슨은 남부연합군 장병들에게 죄를 묻지 않고 사면권을 행사했던 것이다.

지미 카터 대통령 역시 자신의 취임식 바로 다음 날 베트남 전쟁 징병 거부로 기소 및 수배된 20만여 명의 젊은이들을 무조건 사면함으로써 전쟁의 상흔을 치유하는 데 크게 기여했다.

무엇보다 흥미로운 건 미국 연방제의 특성상 연방정부와 주 정부가 각자 독립적인 형벌 체계를 갖다 보니 대통령의 사면 범위는 연방법 위반자에게만 적용되고 각 주법 위반자는 주지사만이 사면할 수 있다는 점이다. 지금까지의 관례상 정치인이나 경제인 같은 화이트칼라 범죄자들은 연방 검찰과 주 검찰의 수사 공조를 거쳐 연방법원 또는 주 법원 한 곳에서만 처벌을 받았는데 연방법원에서 재판을 받은 죄인들이 트럼프로부터 사면을 받았음에도 다시 주 법원 재판에 넘겨질 것인지 여부가 주목된다.

왜냐하면 트럼프의 사면 남발에 대한 대책으로 그들을 주법으로 다시 재판할 수 있도록 법을 보완하는 주들이 생기고 있기 때문이다. (2020.3.26.)

영어 녹음 듣기

For Whom Should Pardons Be Granted?

Soon after his acquittal in the Senate on charges of abuse of power for withholding congressionally approved aid to Ukraine and obstructing congress, President Trump made headlines again for granting pardons to 11 wealthy and influential criminals. A public debate is raging over whether he abused power in granting these pardons.

Among those who received a pardon or had their sentences commuted were Rod Blagojevich, a former Illinois governor who went to prison for soliciting bribes for a political appointment, Bernard Kerik, who had been convicted for tax evasion, and Edward DeBartolo, an ex-football team executive who was convicted on corruption charges. The president's decision was heavily criticized by news pundits and the Democratic Party who claimed that it appeared to be based on nothing more than the president's political agenda and personal ties. They further accused the president of granting pardons without employing the standard review process by the justice department.

For example, Bernard Kerik was the chief of the New York City Police Department under Mayor Rudy Giuliani. He became a household name for his devoted service and effective handling of the 9/11 aftermath. His political ascent seemed unstoppable when President Bush later nominated him as the new director of the Department of Homeland Security. However, it came crashing down when the media brought out tax evasion and bribery allegations before his confirmation hearing. This led to the withdrawal of his nomination and a four-year prison term. The New York Times pointed out that the president's pardon of Kerik appeared to be the handiwork of Giuliani who has since become Trump's lawyer.

The power to pardon is a relic of the plenary power exercised by the Middle Age monarchs. Under the firmly established principle of separation of powers in a modern democracy, however, allowing an official from the executive branch to absolve someone's wrongdoing or commute sentences that the court has imposed seems like unjustifiable interference. However, the founders of America gave this enormous power to the president by codifying it in Article 2, Clause 2 of the Constitution.

At first, the founding fathers, who had witnessed first-hand the British crown's abuse of its clemency powers, did not wish to give the same authority to the president. However, Alexander Hamilton, a proponent of a strong federal government, thought that the appropriate use of a presidential pardon could contribute to the stability and unity of the republic, especially in the middle of national crises like a civil war or a popular uprising against dictatorship.

Instead of giving this power to Congress, he further argued that "a single man of prudence and good sense is better fitted, in delicate conjunctures, to balance the motives which may plead for and against the remission of the punishment, than any numerous body whatever." His argument prevailed, and a presidential pardon was written into the Constitution.

As Hamilton imagined, presidents have exercised their pardon powers to restore unity and stability. For instance, the first president, George Washington, granted a pardon to the farmers involved in the Whiskey Rebellion. After Lincoln's assassination early in his second term, Andrew Johnson granted pardon to Confederate soldiers rather than accusing them of treason.

Similarly, on the very next day after his inauguration, President Jimmy Carter granted pardon to over 200,000 young men who had been indicted for draft dodging to heal the nation from the scars of the Vietnam War.

Interestingly, in the American federal system of government, the scope of presidential pardon is limited only to the offenders of federal law. Concomitantly, only governors may grant pardons to state law offenders. Historically, white-collar criminals such as politicians and businessmen have been prosecuted in either federal or state court depending on the outcome of the investigation, and not typically both. However, with Trump's "abuse of power," several states have enacted laws to prosecute the pardoned criminals in state court. It remains to be seen whether they will be prosecuted again, though. (2020.3.26.)

코로나-19로 본 '국가비상사태법'

코로나-19로 전 세계가 패닉 상태에 빠졌다. 이 호흡기 질환은 우선 백신과 치료법이 개발되지 않은 데다 빠른 전염성과 높은 치사율, 급증하는 환자에 비해 전문 의료 인력과 시설마저 부족하여 지구촌을 전대미문의 공포로 몰아넣고 있다.

코로나19가 중국을 시작으로 올림픽 개최 예정지인 일본, 한국, 이란, 이탈리아, 미국까지 걷잡을 수 없이 확산되자 세계보건기구는 지난 3월 12일 '팬데믹(세계적 유행병)'을 선언하였고 트럼프 대통령은 이를 기다리고나 있었다는 듯이 바로 다음 날 미국에 '국가비상사태'를 선포하였다.

이 선포를 근거로 연방 재난관리청은 각 주에 약 400억 불의 재난기금을 지원할 수 있게 됐으며 보건복지부는 의료진의 면허 범위 확대를 비롯 원격진료, 병실 상한 해제 등 각종 법적 규제를 풀어주는 일이 가능해졌다.

전쟁이나 천재지변 발생 시 선포되는 미국 대통령의 '국가비상사태'는 1976년 제정된 국가비상사태법과 1988년 제정된 스태포드 재해구조 및 긴급사태법에 근거를 두고 있다. 물론 이 법의 제정 이전에도 미국 대통령들은 국가적 위기 때마다 사태를 수습하기 위해 비상사태를 선포하곤 했다. 한 예로 남북전쟁 초 남부군 핵심지역인 버지니아주 인접 워싱턴 D.C 역시 다수의 노예제도 찬성파로 혼란이 극심해지자 링컨 대통령은 비상사태를 선포하고 이들을 기소도 하지 않고 바로 체포, 구금했던 것이다.

이후 세계 1, 2차 양 대전과 한국전, 베트남전 등을 치르면서 비상 선포에 따른 대통령의 권한이 무소불위로 막강해지자 이를 견제하기 위해 의회가 강구한 것이 바로 '국가비상사태법'이다. 미 상원에 따르면 이 법 제정 전 이런저런 구실로 국가비상사태를 발동할 수 있는 연방법 조항이 470개나 되었다고 하니 대통령이 마음만 먹으면 언제든 발동이 가능한 셈이었다.

그러나 대통령의 권한을 견제하기 위해 만든 국가비상사태법은 입법 취지와 달리 실패작으로 평가받고 있다. 왜냐하면 이 법의 가장 핵심은 의회 투표로 대통령의 비상사태 선포를 무효화시키는 조항이었는데 나중에 대법원이 '미국이민국 대 차다'(Immigration and Naturalization Service v. Chadha) 사건을 통해 위헌 판결을 내림으로써 이 조항 자체가 무의미해졌기 때문이다.

이 대법원판결 이후 의회가 비상사태 결정을 뒤집으려면 먼저 상·하 양원을 거쳐 무효화 법안을 제정해야 하고 대통령이 이에 거부권을 행사할 경우 다시 양원에서 각각 2/3 동의가 필요하기 때문에 사실상 불가능에 가깝게 된 것이다.

1976년 법 제정 이후 미국 대통령들은 총 61번이나 국가비상사태를 선포했는데 클린턴 대통령이 17번으로 이 법을 가장 애용한 것으로 알려졌다. 흥미로운 점은 이란과 북한에 대한 경제 제재 등도 바로 이 국가비상사태법에 근거를 두고 있기 때문에 2020년 4월 현재 세계의 경찰국가 미국은 하루도 바람 잘 날 없이 여전히 크고 작은 30여 건의 국가비상사태가 진행 중이라는 점이다.

한편 1988년 제정된 스태포드법은 천재지변 시 연방 재난관리청이 28개에 이르는 정부기관과 NGO 등을 통해 재난지역에 자금과 물자를 지원할 수 있도록 해주는 법이다. 연방정부 지원책을 적절하게 처분하고 배분하는 것은 각 주와 지방 정부의 재량이다. 이 법도 국가비상사태법과 마찬가지로 대통령의 남용을 방지하기 위해 비상사태 선포 전 재난 해당 주지사가 먼저 연방정부에 도움을 요청하도록 명시하고 있다.

이번 트럼프 대통령의 국가비상사태 선포는 두 가지 법 모두에 기반한 것으로 알려졌다. 효과적인 대처로 하루빨리 코로나-19 난세와 아울러 국가비상사태가 종식되길 바라는 마음이 간절하다. (2020.4.10.)

Examining the National Emergencies Act
Through the COVID-19 Crisis

The whole world is in panic mode with the COVID-19 outbreak. This respiratory illness has no vaccine or treatment. It is highly contagious, and it has a high mortality rate. To make matters worse, there is a shortage of medical staff and necessary medical equipment, the need for which grows exponentially by the day with the surge in the number of patients. The entire world is experiencing this threat at an unprecedented scale.

After China failed to contain it, COVID-19 spread quickly to countries like Japan, the site of the 2020 Summer Olympics, Korea, Iran, and Italy. The World Health Organization (WHO) declared it a global pandemic on March 12, 2020. The next day, President Trump immediately followed up by declaring a national emergency in the United States. The president's declaration allowed the Federal Emergency Management Agency (FEMA) to provide approximately $40 billion in emergency disaster funds to the states. Also, the Department of Health and Human Services could increase medical capacity by easing restrictions on licensing requirements for medical professionals and provision of telemedicine and removing caps on hospital beds.

The president's power to declare a state of emergency in a war or natural disaster is based on the National Emergencies Act of 1976 and the Stafford Disaster Relief Act of 1988. Indeed, presidents could, and have, declared a state of emergency even before enacting these laws. For instance, during the Civil War, President Lincoln declared a state of emergency and arrested pro-slavery sympathizers when they caused disruptions in Washington D.C. It was a proactive measure since the city's geographic proximity to Virginia, the heart of the Confederacy, made it particularly vulnerable.

Since then, the president's authority to declare a state of emergency steadily grew as the nation went through a series of wars including the two world wars, the Korean War and the Vietnam War. As a result, Congress enacted the National Emergencies Act to check the president's powers. A survey by the Senate before enacting this law found that there existed 470 federal provisions that allowed the president to declare a state of emergency. In short, a president could declare a state of emergency whenever he wanted.

However, the National Emergencies Act is considered by many to be a failure. The legislation's crux was a provision that allowed Congress to invalidate the president's state of emergency declaration. However, in Immigration and Naturalization Service v. Chadha, the Supreme Court ruled it to be unconstitutional, taking the teeth out of the statute.

After this ruling by the Supreme Court, terminating a national emergency requires a joint resolution by Congress. If the president has a veto, Congress needs a two-thirds vote in both houses to override it. It's a near impossibility in most cases.

Since the National Emergencies Law was enacted in 1976, 61 national emergencies have been declared. President Clinton is reported to have used it the most, having declared 17 national emergencies. Interestingly, economic sanctions against countries like Iran and North Korea are also based on this law. Accordingly, as of April of 2020, there are about 30 active national emergency declarations, proving the point that America is the world's police.

The Stafford Act of 1988 allows FEMA to provide funds and supplies to disaster areas by coordinating 28 government agencies and non-government organizations. Like the National Emergencies Act, this law also requires the governors of disaster-stricken states to request federal aid before the president can declare a state of emergency. Once approved, state and local governments have the discretion to determine how to distribute federal assistance.

President Trump's March 13 declaration is based on both laws. Such effective measures are required to end the COVID-19 crisis as quickly as possible. (2020.4.10.)

문답으로 풀어보는 미국 대통령 선거⑴

11월 3일로 예정된 미국의 대선이 이제 두 달 남짓 앞으로 다가왔다. 이번에는 미국 대통령 선거 절차와 방법, 그 역사 등에 대해 2회에 걸쳐 문답식으로 풀어본다.

대선 절차는 크게 코커스와 예비선거(프라이머리)에서 이뤄지는 후보자 경선 → 전당대회 → 선거인단 선거 → 당선의 단계로 이루어진다. 코커스는 체육관이나 학교 강당 같은 곳에서 공개적인 토론을 통해 후보자를 정하는 반면, 예비선거는 투표소에 가서 비밀 투표로 진행한다.

각 주는 이와 같은 경선을 통해 공화, 민주 양당의 특정 후보자를 지지하기로 한 대의원을 먼저 뽑게 된다. 뉴햄프셔 주에서 경선을 먼저 시작하기 때문에 이때부터 선거 분위기에 돌입하지만 거의 절반 가량의 주가 경선을 치르는 화요일에 후보자의 윤곽이 드러나는데 이날을 특별히 슈퍼화요일이라 일컫는다.

여기서 뽑힌 대의원들은 당내 경선에 나온 여러 대통령 후보 중 한 명을 선출한다. 거꾸로 말하자면 대통령 후보로 선출되려면 당내 경선에서 대의원을 많이 확보하는 게 중요하다는 뜻이다.

전당대회는 4년에 한 번 열리는데 이 자리에서 몇 달에 걸쳐 대의원들이 뽑은 대통령 후보를 추대한다. 이미 대의원을 많이 확보한 사람이 후보로 정해졌기 때문에 분위기를 고조시키기 위한 일종의 자축 행사라고 볼 수 있다. 이 전당대회를 민주당은 얼마 전 8월 17일부터 3일간에 걸쳐 마쳤고, 공화당은 8월 24일부터 오늘까지 (8.26) 진행 중이므로 지금은 선거절차 중 나머지 두 단계만 남겨놓고 있는 상태이다.

문) 대통령후보 자격은 어떻게 되는가?

답) 대통령 취임일 기준으로 만 35세 이상, 미국에 14년 이상 거주해야 하고, 부통령도 그 기준이 같다.

문) 미국은 대통령 중심제를 채택하면서도 왜 선거인들이 간접선거로 대통령을 뽑는가?

답) 첫째 이유는 땅이 넓기 때문이다. 예를 들어 알래스카가 오후 8시면 뉴욕은 자정이 된다. 국민들이 직접선거를 동시에 하자면 투표시간에 문제가 생기게 된다. 간접선거를 하게 된 또 다른 이유는 연방제로서의 미국의 정체성 때문이라고 할 수 있다.

달리 말하면 각개 주의 독립적인 주권을 존중해서, 한 주가 인구 소멸 등 문제로 다른 주에 의해 압도당하지 않게 하기 위한 배려이다. 만약 대통령을 선거인단 대신 전체 국민이 1표씩 행사하여 직선제로 뽑아 버린다면, 인구가 적은 주의 주권은 인구가 많은 주의 주권보다 저평가될 것이나, 중간에 선거인단을 통하게 되면 어느 정도 이 문제를 인위적으로 조정할 수 있게 된다.

그런 의미에서 선거인단은 개별적인 시민의 의지가 아닌 소속된 주의 전반적인 의지를 대표하는 것으로, 미국 국민들이 투표하는 것은 대통령이 아니고 내가 속한 주가 어느 후보를 지지할지를 투표하는 것이라고 보면 된다.

이는 자신이 A후보를 70%만큼 지지하고 B후보를 30% 지지한다고 해서 A에게 0.7표, B에게 0.3표를 줄 수 없고 무조건 후보 한 명에게 1표를 줘야 하듯이 '하나의 주'는 '한 명의 대통령'을 지지하는 것이 원칙이다. 직선제로 가게 되면 작은 주들의 정치적 의사는 완전히 묻히게 될 것이지만 간선제 시스템은 작은 주들이 어떤 경우에도 시스템에 참가할 수 있도록 권리를 보장한다.

문) 선거일은 매 4년마다 11월 첫 월요일이 낀 주의 화요일에 실시하도록 돼있는데 왜 이렇게 복잡하게 정해놓은 건가?

답) 미 대통령 선거일은 1845년 의회에서 제정되어 지금까지 내려오고 있다. 이 법 제정 당시 미국은 농업에 기반을 둔 기독교 국가였는데 이것이 중요한 고려 요소였다. 그래서 가을 추수를 끝낸 후 날씨가 추워지기 전에 11월 초로 시기를 정했고, 화요일로 정한 것은 각 요일마다 사정이 있었기 때문이다.

예를 들면 일요일은 교회, 수요일은 장날이라 선거일로 정할 수 없었고 마차로 투표장까지 가는데 꼬박 하루가 걸리는 지역에 사는 유권자들이 많았기 때문에 교회 다음 날인 월요일이나 장날 다음날인 목요일 역시 될 수 없었다. 그리고 11월 1일이 화요일인 경우 전 달의 회계 처리 등으로 바쁠 것을 우려해 첫 월요일이 낀 주의 화요일에 선거를 실시하도록 했다. 11월의 첫 월요일이 낀 주면 그 화요일이 1일에 걸릴 염려가 없기 때문이다. (다음 회에 계속) (2020.8.26.)

Politics and Media

Presidential Election Q & A: Part 1

The presidential election is scheduled to take place on November 3, only two months away. Over the following two columns, we will review the presidential election process and its history in a Q&A format.

The election process begins with primary elections and caucuses. Then, it proceeds with a nominating convention, voting for the electors, and election of the president. A caucus usually takes place in a school gym or auditorium. In a caucus, members of the same party gather and publicly discuss which candidate they will support. On the other hand, voters vote secretly at a voting booth in a primary. Each state picks delegates for both the Democratic and Republican parties through this process. These delegates pledge to vote for a designated candidate. Typically, the primary election season begins in New Hampshire and about half of the states hold their primaries on Super Tuesday. We begin to get a good grasp of who the ultimate winner will be after the votes from Super Tuesday have been tallied.

The delegates cast their votes for a candidate within their party. In other words, to be nominated by the party, the candidates need to secure as many delegates' votes as possible. The nominating convention takes place every four years. The delegates cast votes for their candidate at the convention. Since everyone knows beforehand which candidate will be nominated by the party, it's more of a celebration for the members and the eventual candidate. The Democratic Party recently concluded its three-day national convention on August 20. The Republican Party's national convention started on August 24 and continues to today, August 26. Now, we're only two steps away from electing a president.

Q) Who can be a presidential candidate?

A) The president must be at least 35 years old and must have been a resident of the United States for 14 years on the date of inauguration. The requirements are the same for the vice president.

Q) Why does the United States have an indirect election even though it elects a president?

A) First, America is huge. When it is 8 p.m. in Alaska, it is midnight in New York. There is a problem with establishing a voting period if everyone has to vote directly. Another reason for the indirect voting process is America's identity as a federalist country. In other words, it respects the sovereignty of each state and wants to ensure that no state is dominated by another state because of things like population decrease. If everyone were to vote directly for a candidate, then the sovereignty of less populous states would be diluted by the more populous states. With the electoral college in the middle, it can be artificially adjusted.

In that sense, the electoral college represents the state's overall will, not its individual citizens. In essence, Americans are not voting for a presidential candidate they like, but for the candidate their state will support. In most states, just as it would be absurd for a person to give 0.7 votes to candidate A and 0.3 votes to candidate B, one state votes as a whole for one candidate. With the direct election, the political will of the people living in smaller states is likely to get buried. The indirect election guarantees their right to participate in the political process.

Q) Why is the election held on the first Tuesday following the first Monday in November?

A) Congress designated the election day in 1845. When the law was written, America was a largely agrarian Christian country. Early November was picked to avoid fall harvest. Tuesday was chosen because other days did not work for various reasons. For example, Sunday was reserved for church. Wednesday was market day. Also, many people lived in rural parts of the country where they often had to travel for at least a day to vote. Thus, neither Monday nor Thursday worked because it was the day after church and market day. The lawmakers were also concerned that if November 1 fell on a Tuesday, many people would be busy making entries into their accounting books from the previous month. So, they figured that if the election were held on the first Tuesday following the first Monday in November, it would never fall on November 1. (To be continued) (2020.8.26.)

문답으로 풀어보는 미국 대통령 선거⑵

지난 칼럼(8.26)에서 대통령후보의 자격, 선거일 택일 배경, 간선제 이유 등에 대해 알아보았고, 이어 나머지 궁금증에 대해 풀어본다.

문) 선거인은 모두 몇 명을 선출하는가?

답) 미국은 50개 주에 상원의원 각 2명씩 100명이 있고, 하원의원은 인구에 비례하여 전국에서 435명이 있는데 이들을 모두 합한 숫자만큼인 535명과 어느 주에도 속하지 않는 워싱턴 D.C.에서 3명의 선거인을 더해 총 538명을 뽑는다.

이 숫자는 1964년 이후 변동 없이 유지되고 있다. 그러므로 538명의 과반인 269명에서 1명이라도 많은 270명 이상의 선거인만 확보하면 백악관의 주인이 된다.

문) 선거인은 어떻게 선출하며 선거인단은 어디서 모이는가?

답) 선거인은 연방헌법에 따라 각 주의회가 정하는 바에 따라 결정이 되는데 상원이나 하원의원, 또는 연방정부 공무원은 선출될 자격이 없다. 선거인은 각 주 또는 지구당 중앙위원회가 충실한 정당 지지자를 임명하거나 선거를 통해 뽑게 되며 선거인단에 뽑히게 되면 각 주의 수도에 모여 투표를 하게 된다.

문) '승자독식제도'란 무엇인가?

답) 쉽게 얘기하자면 민주당, 공화당 또는 그 어느 당이든 1표라도 많으면 그 주의 선거인을 모두 싹쓸이 차지하는 제도이다. 예를 들어 캘리포니아주의 경우 선거인 수는 55명인데 투표결과 A당 득표율 46% X 55명 = 25.3→25명, B당 53% X 55명= 29.15→29명, 기타 당→1명이라고 하면 한 표라도 더 많이 받은 B당이 캘리포니아 선거인 55명을 몽땅 차지하고 다른 당은 단 1명도 안 되는 것이 바로 승자독식제도이다.

메인(4명)과 네브래스카(5명) 주는 득표율대로 분배를 하고 나머지 주들은 이 제도를 채택하고 있다. 이런 제도의 맹점 때문에 전국 득표율에서는 앞서고도 선거인단 수에서 밀려 승부가 뒤바뀐 게 미국 역사상 5번이나 있었고 그 대표적 사례가 2016년 대선으로, 힐러리 후보는 트럼프보다 전국적으로 300만 표 이상을 더 득표하고도 선거인단 수에 밀려 고배를 마셨다.

문) 이런 황당한 제도는 왜 생기게 된 것인가?

답) 지난 칼럼에서 적시한 것처럼 미국 연방제의 정체성 문제 외에도 반란표 방지 목적도 있다. 만약 각 주마다 정당별 득표 비율대로 선거인들이 대통령선거에 투표한다면 55명의 선거인들은 A당 25명, B당 29명으로 섞이게 되어 A당의 선거인으로 뽑힌 사람이 투표한 유권자의 기대를 저버리고 개인적으로 B당 후보에게 투표하는 경우가 생길 수 있다. 그렇게 되면 어떤 주에서 보낸 A당 선거인은 10명인데 A후보 지지 표가 6표밖에 안 나오는 경우가 생길 수 있고, 한 주에서 뿐 아니라 여러 주에서 이런 '배신행위'가 생기지 않는다는 보장이 없다. 그래서 한 주의 선거인이 모두 같은 당 당원이면 그들이 모두 한 정당 후보를 지지한다고 약속했기 때문에 투표결과 '반란표'가 나오기 어렵게 되기 때문이다.

문) 그럼에도 '반란표'가 나오면 어떻게 되는가?

답) 충실한 정당 지지자들이 선거인이 되는 현실상 배신 투표를 하는 행위는 역사적으로 매우 드물다. 하지만 아웃사이더들의 돌풍이 뜨거웠던 지난 2016년 대선 때는 무려 10명의 선거인이 선거 결과에 반하는 배신투표를 했거나 시도하려다 저지됐다.

미국 헌법상 어느 후보도 과반수를 넘지 못할 경우에 하원이 대통령을 결정하게 된다는 점에 착안해 트럼프의 대통령 선출을 막기 위해 여러 주의 선거인들이 공모한 전대미문의 일이었는데 막상 뚜껑을 열어보니 뜻밖에도 힐러리 쪽에서 5표, 트럼프 쪽에서 2명의 반란표가 나왔으나 전체 선거결과에는 영향을 미치지 않았다.

이후 워싱턴 주정부가 약속을 지키지 않은 3명의 선거인들에게 1천 달러의 벌금을 부과하자 선거인들이 자신들은 자유롭게 투표할 권리가 있다며 법정싸움을 전개했으나 지난 7월 연방대법원이 각 주에서 선거인단 투표 시 주별 선거 승리자를 지지하도록 의무화할 수 있다고 결론을 내려 일단락되었다. (2020.9.9.)

Politics and Media

Presidential Election Q & A: Part 2

In the last column (Aug. 26), we reviewed the presidential candidate's qualifications, the history behind the election day, and why America has an indirect election. We will look at some other questions about the presidential election process.

Q) How many electors are there?

A) There are 538 electors. It is the same number as 100 senators (two senators for each of the 50 states), 435 representatives (apportioned by population), and three for Washington D.C., which does not belong to any state. This number has remained the same since 1964. Thus, to occupy the White House, a candidate must earn at least 270 votes, one more vote than half of 538, or 269 votes.

Q) How are electors selected and where do they meet?

A) The Constitution mandates the electors to be chosen by the method specified by the individual state's legislature. The Constitution also states that electors cannot be a member of Congress or hold federal office. Typically, electors will be chosen by the state party's central committee to reward its loyal members or by a vote taken at state party conventions. Once selected, electors vote in a meeting held in the state capital.

Q) What is "winner-take-all"?

A) Quite simply, it is a system that gives all of the electoral votes to the winning candidate, regardless of whether it is a Democrat or a Republican. For example, California has 55 electors. Under the proportional assignment system, if Party A takes 46% of the vote, it would result in 25 electors (46% x 55 electors = 25.3). If Party B takes 53%, it would result in 29 electors (53% x 55 electors = 29.15). Assuming Party C takes the remaining votes, it would yield one elector. However, since Party B's candidate has more votes than the others, she would take all 55 votes from California under the winner-take-all system. The candidates from the other parties do not get any electoral vote. All of the states have adopted this rule except Maine, which has four electors, and Nebraska, which has five electors. These two states apportion electors according to popular vote. Because of the winner-take-all system, five candidates in American history have received a more popular vote but lost in the electoral college. The most recent one was during the 2016 election. Hillary Clinton received three million more votes than Trump, but lost in the electoral college.

Q) Why do we have this rule?

A) As discussed in the last column, this rule is based on how states function in the federalist government. It also serves to prevent the problem of faithless electors. For instance, in the previous example, if California sent a mixed group of electors chosen proportionally to the popular votes received by each candidate, it would send 25 electors who pledged to vote for Party A, and 29 who pledged to vote for Party B. However, there can be collusion among the electors to break their pledge in that scenario. This means that if a state sent ten pledged electors for Party A, there's no guarantee that they will all vote for the candidate from Party A. If this happens on a broader scale, the electoral college can effectively usurp the will of the voters. On the other hand, under the winner-take-all system, the likelihood of a faithless elector decreases since everyone in the state delegation belongs to the same party.

Q) What happens when there's a faithless elector?

A) Historically speaking, faithless electors are very rare because only the loyal members of the party are chosen to be electors. During the 2016 election in which Washington outsiders had an outsized influence, ten electors voted or attempted to vote for a different candidate than they were pledged. Several electors noted that if no candidate receives the majority of votes, then the president is elected by the House of Representatives under the Constitution. Thus, in an unprecedented move, they attempted to collude to stop Trump from being elected. However, when the results came out, it turned out that Hillary had five faithless votes while Trump only had two. It was not enough to overturn the election result. Afterwards, the state of Washington imposed a fine of $1,000 on three electors who did not keep their pledge. The electors fought back by arguing that they had a right to vote as they wished. The U.S. Supreme Court decided in July of last year that state legislatures were allowed to make laws to mandate electors to vote according to their pledge. (2020.9.9.)

가짜 뉴스와 언론의 명암

정보통신기술의 획기적인 발달에 힘입어 이젠 개인도 유튜브나 페이스북, 트위터 등을 통해 온라인으로 손쉽게 뉴스를 만들어 전파할 수 있는 세상이 되었다. 그러다 보니 검증되지 않은 출처 불명의 각종 뉴스가 한 사람씩 거칠 때마다 왜곡되거나 증폭되어 작년 한 해만 해도 미국과 중국 정부의 코로나-19 관련 각종 음모론, 북한 김정은 피격설, 미국 대선 부정 주장 등 셀 수 없이 많은 메가톤급의 가짜 뉴스가 유포됐다.

이런 가짜 뉴스의 홍수 가운데 최근 미국의 유력 언론사가 가짜 뉴스 송사에 휘말려 눈길을 끈다. 바로 폭스뉴스가 그 주인공인데 전자개표기 제조회사인 '스마트매틱'(Smartmatic)으로부터 무려 27억 달러, 한국 돈으로 3조 원대의 천문학적 명예훼손 소송을 당한 것이다.

작년 미국 대선 직후, 트럼프의 개인 변호사 '루디 줄리아니'와 법률 고문 '시드니 파월'(Sidney Powell) 변호사는 폭스뉴스를 비롯 뉴스맥스 등의 여러 대담 프로그램에 각각 출연해 전자개표기 회사들이 소프트웨어 조작을 통해 트럼프 지지표를 바이든 지지표로 바꿔치기했다며 선거무효를 주장했다.

이들의 주장은 여러 주에서 진행된 선거위원회의 검표를 통해 곧 거짓임이 판명났지만 한철 선거로 주로 먹고사는 회사인 스마트매틱의 브랜드 가치는 이미 걷잡을 수 없이 추락한 다음이었다. 기업 신뢰도 상실로 큰 영업손실을 입게 된 스마트매틱은 줄리아니와 파월뿐 아니라 그들에게 가짜 뉴스의 '발언대'를 제공한 언론사와 뉴스 진행자들까지 명예훼손 혐의로 싸잡아 소송을 제기했던 것이다.

또 다른 피해업체인 '도미니언' 전자개표기 제작사(Dominion Voting Systems)도 줄리아니와 파월 변호사를 상대로 13억 달러(1조4천억원)의 소송을 1차 제기한 데 그치지 않고 이들의 거짓 주장을 여과없이 방출한 방송사들에까지 장차 전선을 확대하겠다고 벼르고 있는 참이다.

미국법 상 가짜 뉴스는 고의로 허위사실을 만들어 타인의 명예를 훼손한 가해자뿐 아니라 이를 확인하지 않고 보도한 언론사에도 책임을 묻는다. 이때 중요한 것은 명예를 훼손당한 피해자가 일반인인지 아니면 공인 자격인지에 따라 귀책 사유가 달리 적용되는데 일반인이라면 허위사실의 말이나 글 등으로 입은 피해 사실만 입증하면 된다.

그러나 공인이 피해를 입었다면 이에 더해 가짜뉴스 가해자가 악의를 가지고 그런 일을 했다는 이유를 추가로 입증할 수 있어야 책임추궁이 가능하다. 즉 일반인보다 쉽게 대중에 노출될 수밖에 없는 공인은 늘 이런저런 이유로 공격 당할 개연성이 높기 때문에 가해자에 대한 책임추궁 요건을 더 까다롭게 정해놓은 것이다.

따라서 소송을 당한 언론사의 방어 입장에서는 원고 측의 공격을 어렵게 하기 위해 전자개표기 제작사는 공적인 선거업무를 다루기 때문에 당연히 공인의 위치에 있다고 몰아가기 마련이다. 덧붙여 자신들은 전혀 편파보도의 악의가 없었음에도 이렇게 소송을 남발하여 언론사를 괴롭히는 것은 수정헌법 1조에 명시돼 있는 언론과 표현의 자유에 정면으로 배치되는 것으로 언론에 재갈을 물리는 탄압이라고 법원에 호소했다.

이에 대해 '스마트매틱'과 '도미니언' 측은 폭스뉴스가 언론기관으로서의 단순한 발언대 제공 수준을 넘어 시청률을 높이기 위한 돈벌이 수단으로 대선 의혹을 증폭시켜 거짓 방송을 줄기차게 내보낸 것은 그 의도가 다분히 악의적이었음을 쟁점화하고 있다.

바야흐로 가짜 뉴스의 팬데믹 시대를 맞아 동전의 양면처럼, 여론 조성을 위해 발언대를 제공해야 할 의무와 더불어 거짓 정보의 확산을 저지해야 할 문지기의 의무도 동시에 가지고 있는 언론사의 역할에 대해 법원은 어떻게 정리해줄지 결과가 궁금하다. (2021.2.24.)

Politics and Media

Fake News and the Role of Media

Owing to the rapid advancements in information and communications technology, anyone can easily create news and dispense them through various online platforms like YouTube, Facebook, and Twitter. However, without an independent, neutral fact-checker, false and inaccurate information has been widespread on the internet. Last year alone, we've heard various conspiracy theories related to the American and Chinese governments' handling of the COVID-19 situation, the assassination of North Korean dictator Kim Jong-un, and allegations of election fraud, to name just a few big ones.

Amidst the tsunami of fake news, a prominent American media company made the headlines by being sued for its alleged role in spreading false information. Fox News was sued by an electronic voting technology company named Smartmatic for an astronomical sum of $2.7 billion, or about three trillion Korean won, in damages.

Shortly after last year's presidential election, Trump's lawyer Rudy Giuliani

Fake News and the Role of Media 363

and legal advisor Sidney Powell appeared in several interviews on Fox News and Newsmax. They claimed that the election result could not be validated because the electronic voting systems makers, such as Smartmatic, used software to switch Trump votes into Biden votes.

Their arguments were investigated by the states' election authorities and soon proved to be false. However, severe damage has already been inflicted on Smartmatic's brand name. Claiming loss of goodwill and ability to conduct business now and in the future, Smartmatic sued not only Giuliani and Powell for defamation, but the media companies and news hosts as well, on the grounds that they have enabled patently false claims to be made.

Another company, Dominion Voting Systems, claiming to be a victim of such defamation, also filed a lawsuit against Giuliani and Powell for $1.3 billion. The company is expected to expand the lawsuit's scope to include the news media companies that have aired these interviews without checking them first.

Under American law, a lawsuit for defamation may be brought if a false statement of fact about someone has caused their reputation to be harmed. A lawsuit may be brought against the media companies as well if it can be shown that they knowingly or recklessly published false information. Another critical aspect in a defamation case is whether the plaintiff is a public or private figure. If the plaintiff is a private party, she just needs to show the financial harm that she suffered due to the false statement of fact made by the defendant. In contrast, public figures must prove an additional element, actual malice, to succeed. The courts justify this distinction because public figures have voluntarily placed themselves in positions that invite public scrutiny and commentary.

As a defendant, then, it is only reasonable for the media companies to argue that the electronic voting systems manufacturers do business in the public realm and, accordingly, are public figures. In addition, they pleaded to the court that plaintiffs were attempting to suppress the freedom of the press enshrined in the First Amendment by filing frivolous lawsuits even when there was no bias or actual malice.

In response, Smartmatic and Dominion emphasized that Fox News went above and beyond merely providing a platform for diverse views, but intentionally amplified false statements about the election to increase their ratings and revenues. This, they argued, was done out of actual malice.

These days, media companies are caught in the middle of two essential duties. They must provide citizens with the space to express their views, but, as gatekeepers, they must also stop the spread of false information. The outcome of this lawsuit may give them some clarity on how to navigate between these two responsibilities. (2021.2.24.)

변호사 링컨

역대 미국 대통령 인기도 조사에 의하면 시대 변함없이 단연 인기 1위의 대통령은 에이브러햄 링컨(1809~1865)이다. 남북전쟁을 승리로 이끌어 노예제도를 종식시킨 불멸의 업적 외에도 "국민의, 국민에 의한, 국민을 위한 정부는 지구 상에서 영원히 사라지지 않을 것"이라고 민주주의의 기본문법을 완성한 그의 게티즈버그 명연설은 그야말로 인류가 멸망할 때까지 두고두고 회자될 것이다.

워낙 큰 업적들에 가려 잘 알려지진 않았지만 링컨은 1836년 27세에 변호사가 된 이후, 제16대 대통령으로 취임하던 1861년까지 무려 25년간 변호사 생활을 했다. 이는 지금까지 총 45명의 미국 대통령 중 27명이나 되는 변호사 출신 대통령 중에서도 독보적인 기록이다.

일리노이 주의 수도 스프링필드에 있던 당시 링컨 변호사 사무실의 주 업무는 약속어음 사건 해결이었다. 교통수단이 변변치 않아 현금이 제때 돌지 않다 보니 대부분의 경제활동이 약속어음으로 이뤄지던 시대였다. 기록에 따르면 링컨은 개업 6년차 되던 1842년에는 한 해 219건의 사건 중 그 80%인 175건의 어음사건을 처리했으며, 이렇게 처리한 어음사건이 25년간 총 2,000여 건에 달한 것으로 나타나 있다.

물론 링컨의 변호 업무가 따분한 어음사건에만 국한된 것은 아니었다. 예를 들면 1년에 3개월 정도는 순회판사를 따라다니며 일리노이주 14개 카운티에서 상법·형사법 사건 등도 수임했던 것으로 보인다. 링컨이 활약하던 19세기 중반 미국은 각 지역마다 법원 청사나 전담판사를 둘 여력이 되지 않아 한 명의 판사가 봄과 가을에 각 카운티를 돌며 재판업무를 수행했다.

다양한 사건 중에서도 살인사건 재판은 지역 주민들에게 최고의 관심거리였는데 링컨은 총 25건의 살인사건을 변호했다. 그중 11건은 유죄, 14건은 무죄판결을 이끌어 낸 것으로 집계됐다. 링컨의 가장 유명한 무죄사건 재판 하나를 소개한다.

1857년의 8월 어느 무더운 저녁, 동네 선술집에서 '제임스 메츠커'는 '윌리엄 암스트롱'과 언쟁 끝에 한바탕 싸움질을 하고, 귀갓길에 '제임스 노리스'와 또 싸움이 붙어 결국 죽고 말았다.

부검결과 메츠커의 사인은 두개골 앞과 뒤의 함몰로 확인되었다. 재판은 두 번째로 싸웠던 노리스부터 먼저 진행되었는데 노리스가 메츠커를 뒤에서 흉기로 내려친 것으로 밝혀져 살인죄 판결이 내려졌다. 그러나 노리스가 메츠커를 뒤에서 가격했다는 증거만 있었기 때문에 두개골 앞부분 함몰에 대한 책임소재를 가리기 위해 첫 번째 싸움자 윌리엄도 같이 기소되었다. 이에 다급해진 윌리엄의 모친 해나는 사별한 남편 잭의 절친이었던 링컨을 찾아와 아들의 변론을 부탁했다.

이어진 재판에서 윌리엄은, "메츠커가 채찍을 가져와 자기를 협박하길래 정당방위 차원에서 주먹으로 메츠커의 얼굴을 한 번 때렸을 뿐이고, 메츠커의 죽음은 전적으로 노리스와의 두 번째 싸움이 원인"이라고 주장했다. 하지만, 사건의 유일한 목격자 '찰스 앨런'은 "윌리엄이 밧줄에다 쇠뭉치를 매단 흉기 슬렁샷(slungshot)으로 메츠커의 얼굴을 내려치는 것을 두 눈으로 똑똑히 보았다"라고 증언했다.

링컨은 증인 반대신문에서 사건 당일 날씨와 현장의 조명 상황에 대해 질문했는데 찰스는 "보름달이 머리 위에 떠있어 윌리엄의 일거수일투족을 똑똑히 볼 수 있었다"고 진술했다.

링컨은 당일 날씨를 거듭 알아본 후 청원경찰에게 날씨를 기록한 달력을 가지고 와줄 것을 주문했다. 배심원석 앞에서 펼쳐진 달력에 그날은 보름달이 아닌 달빛이 없는 초승달이었다고 기록되어 있었다. 찰스의 증언이 허위로 밝혀지면서 윌리엄은 살인누명에서 벗어나는 순간이었다.

아들의 재판이 끝난 후, 가난한 과부 해나가 감사의 눈물을 흘리며 링컨에게 수임료에 대해 묻자, 링컨은 "해나, 나는 당신으로부터 페니 하나도 절대로 받을 수 없소"라며 고사했다고 전해진다. (2021.11.10.)

링컨 기념관(워싱턴 D.C.)
Lincoln Memorial(Washington D.C.)

Lincoln the Lawyer

Abraham Lincoln (1809-1865) is often praised as the greatest American president. Not only did he lead the divided country through the Civil War and abolish slavery, but he also provided a firm foundation for modern democracy by proclaiming, "the government of the people, by the people, for the people, shall not perish from the earth." This phrase will be remembered and recited for generations to come.

His presidential achievements frequently overshadow Lincoln's years as a practicing attorney. However, from becoming a lawyer at the age of 27 in 1836 until he retired to take up residence at the White House in 1861, Lincoln practiced law for 25 years. Out of 45 American presidents, 27 have been lawyers; and among them, Lincoln stands out as having practiced law the longest.

Lincoln's law office was in Springfield, the capital of Illinois. The bread and butter of his practice were litigating disputes over promissory notes. Back then, Springfield was still a relatively small frontier town. Cash was scarce because of poor transportation. Naturally, most of the economic activities were carried out through promissory notes. Records show that in Lincoln's sixth year as an attorney, 1842, 175 out of 219 cases he handled, or about 80%, had something to do with a promissory note dispute. During his 25-year career, Lincoln handled about 2,000 such disputes.

Of course, Lincoln's law practice was not just confined to dry litigation about promissory notes. For three months out of the year, he would ride with a circuit judge and visit 14 different counties in Illinois. In nineteenth Century America, when Lincoln was practicing, counties lacked resources to keep and maintain courthouses and judges. So, a single judge would visit these counties in the spring and fall, and handle various disputes for the townspeople. Lincoln would also pick up business in whatever form they came, from contract disputes to criminal cases. Among them, murder cases were the talk of the town. Records show that Lincoln handled a total of 25 homicide cases. Eleven resulted in a conviction and 14 ended in an acquittal. "The almanac trial" is perhaps Lincoln's most famous acquittal.

On a hot summer August night in 1857, James Metzker got into a fight with William Armstrong at a "whiskey camp," and later that night, another one with James Norris on his way back home. Metzker died a few days later from the injuries that he sustained from these fights.

An autopsy revealed that the cause of his death was blunt force trauma to the front and back of the skull. The Norris' trial went first and resulted in a conviction. The jury determined that Norris struck Metzker from behind with a wooden object. However, there was still the question of what caused the frontal damage as it was revealed that Norris had only struck Metzker from behind. As such, William Armstrong was also indicted. Desperate, William's mother, Hanna, came to Lincoln, a longtime friend of her deceased husband, Jack.

At trial, Armstrong testified that Metzker was threatening him with a whip, and he punched Metzker in the face once in self-defense. He claimed the second fight with Norris caused Metzker's death. However, the only eyewitness to the incident, Charles Allen, testified that he saw Armstrong hit Metzker's face with a slungshot, a cord with metal objects affixed to the end.

Lincoln asked about the weather and lighting conditions during the incident on cross examination. Allen testified that there was a full moon and he could see everything. Lincoln confirmed this answer and asked for the almanac. When the almanac was presented before the jury, it showed no full moon, but a quarter-moon with dim lights. The jury couldn't believe Allen's testimony, and Armstrong was acquitted.

Following this trial, with tears in her eyes, Hanna, a poor widow, asked Lincoln how much she owed him. Lincoln said, "Why, Hanna, I cannot accept a penny from you."(2021.11.10.)

헌법과 수정헌법의 차이

신문이나 TV 등을 보다 보면 미국만 유독 헌법 대신 '수정헌법'이란 색다른 용어를 사용하여 사람을 혼란스럽게 만드는데 이의 차이점에 대해 간략하게 살펴본다.

미국 헌법은 '건국의 아버지'라 불리는 13개 주 55명의 대표가 필라델피아에 모여 1787년 5월부터 9월까지 약 16주에 걸친 마라톤 제헌회의 끝에 탄생한 결과물이었다. 총 7개 조항에 걸쳐 삼권분립 원칙에 근거한 연방정부 구성 방법과, 주 정부와 연방정부의 관계 등에 대해 정의하였다.

제1조는 상원과 하원을 설립하고, 양원의 입법 과정과 권한, 의원 선출 방법과 자격에 관해 규정하고 있다. 2조는 대통령과 부통령의 선출 방법과 자격, 권한 및 탄핵 방법을 규정하고 있고, 미 대선 때마다 단골 메뉴로 등장하는 선거인단 제도도 이 2조에서 유래한다.

3조는 사법부 규정으로 연방대법원과 하급법원 설치에 관한 것이다. 원래 헌법에는 의회가 제정한 법률이 헌법에 위반되는지 여부를 누가 심판할 것인지 그 주체가 명시되지 않았다. 그러나 당시 대법원장 존 마셜이 판결문을 통해, '연방대법원에서 이를 심사하여 판단하는 것'으로 기지를 발휘했다고 지난 칼럼 '위헌법률심판권의 시원'(2021.11.24)에서 다룬 바 있다.

4조는 주와 연방정부의 관계, 또 각주 간의 관계에 대해 정의하고 있다. 특히 '완전한 믿음과 신용' 항목은 현재 미국의 모습을 만드는 데 크게 일조했다. 헌법 제정 전에는 주마다 법이 달라 주 경계선을 넘는 순간부터 불편한 게 많았으나 4조 덕에 모두 동등한 권리를 가진 '미국인' 대우를 받게 되었다. 예컨대 2004년 매사추세츠주는 미국에서 처음으로 동성 결혼을 허용하였는데 여기서 결혼한 커플들이 동성혼이 허용되지 않는 다른 주에 가더라도 부부관계로 인정되는 것 등이다.

5조는 헌법 개정에 대한 절차, 6조는 헌법과 헌법에 따라 만들어진 연방 법률과 조약이 미국 내 최고의 규범이라는 것이고, 마지막으로 제7조는 헌법의 비준 요건을 규정했다.

헌법 비준 당시, 갓 독립전쟁을 끝낸 미국 국민들은 연방정부가 헌법을 빌미로 영국 왕정처럼 폭압적인 정부가 될지도 모른다는 걱정이 많았다. 헌법 비준이 이런 반대 기류로 난항을 겪자 그 해결책으로 연방정부의 권한을 제한하는 수정헌법 제1조에서 10조가 만들어졌다.

이 10개 조항을 특별히 '권리 장전'이라 칭하는데 1791년에 발효되었다. 권리장전에는 우리가 잘 아는 종교와 언론의 자유, 총기 소지, 미란다 원칙, 사유 재산권 등 국민의 기본권을 보장하고 있다.

시대 변천에 따라 개헌 필요가 있을 때는 헌법 자체를 전면 개정하는 대부분의 나라와 달리 미국은 기존 헌법은 손대지 않고 새로운 조항만을 추가하는 방식을 취하기 때문에 수정헌법이라 불린다. 헌법 개정은 상, 하원에서 각 2/3 이상의 동의로 발의되고, 3/4(50개 주 중 38개) 이상의 주가 비준함으로써 비로소 수정헌법이 추가된다.

이 같은 과정을 거쳐 건국 이후 지금까지 총 27개 조항이 추가되었다. 재미있는 사항으로 18조의 금주법은 이후 수정헌법 21조로 폐기된 불명예를 안고 있다. 또 가장 최근에 추가된 것으로, 연방의원의 급여 인상을 제한한 수정헌법 제27조는 건국 당시 '제임스 매디슨'(후에 제4대 대통령이 됨)에 의해 제청되었다가 비준 정족수 미달로 휴면 상태였던 것을 1982년 텍사스 주립대생 '그레고리 왓슨'(Gregory Watson, 19세)이 학교과제 도중 발견, 통과 운동을 전개함으로써 202년 만에 비준되었다.

온갖 인종들이 뒤섞여 살고, 각 주들이 연방을 이뤄 돌아가는 거대한 국가의 최고 규범치곤 미국 헌법이 이처럼 간단하다는 게 신기하게 여겨질 따름이다. (2022.3.30.)

제헌회의가 열렸던 인디펜던스 홀(필라델피아)
Independence Hall where the U.S. Constitution was debated(Philadelphia)

Politics and Media

What's Up with the Constitutional Amendments?

We often hear about the constitutional amendments in the news. Many Koreans find it confusing because they do not know the difference between the Constitution and the Constitutional Amendments. Today's column reviews the difference.

The "Founding Fathers," who were the 55 representatives from 13 states, came together in Philadelphia, and wrote the Constitution after a 16-week-long constitutional convention that started in May and ended in September 1787. The Constitution comprises seven articles that lay out the basic structure and separation of powers among three branches of the federal government. It also defines the relationship between the federal and state governments.

Article 1 creates the Senate and the House of Representatives. It provides how to pass legislation in both houses, their constitutional authority, and how to select the members and their qualifications. Article 2 governs how to elect the president and the vice president, their eligibility, authority and how to impeach them. The electoral college, which always comes to the center of controversy during election season, is established through Article 2.

Article 3 establishes the federal judiciary. It creates the Supreme Court and authorizes other courts that Congress may set up from time to time. The Constitution doesn't specify which branch can determine the constitutionality of the statutes passed by Congress. However, as discussed in the previous column, The Origin Story of Judicial Review, published on November 24, 2021, Chief Justice John Marshall acquired the authority for judicial review through a Supreme Court decision.

Article 4 defines the relationship between the state and federal government and the relationship among the states. The "full faith and credit" clause contained in this article played an essential role in fostering a sense of one nation. Before the Constitution, each state had different laws, making it difficult for people to cross the state lines. However, under this clause, everyone is an "American" who carries their rights everywhere in the United States of America. For example, Massachusetts became the first state to legalize same-sex marriage in 2004. However, the marital status for the same-sex couples who got married in Massachusetts did not change even when they went to states that did not allow such marriages.

Article 5 directs the process for amending the Constitution. Article 6 states that the Constitution, the laws and treaties are the "supreme law of the land." Finally, Article 7 provides how to ratify the Constitution.

When the Constitution was ratified, many Americans, who had just won the

메이플라워호 모형 (보스턴)
Mayflower Replica ship(Boston)

Independence War against the British Crown, were concerned that the federal government would become just as oppressive. As ratification was delayed because of these fears, 10 amendments were proposed to limit the federal government's power. They are called the "Bill of Rights" and became effective in 1791. Among the Bill of Rights are familiar and basic rights for the citizens, such as the freedom of religion and press, right to keep and bear arms, due process rights contained in the Miranda warning, and the right to private property.

Unlike many other countries that amend the entire constitution when there's a need, America instead adds an amendment. To start the amendment process, a resolution must pass with a 2/3 vote in both the Senate and the House of Representatives. Then, the resolution must be ratified by 3/4 of the states (38 out of 50 states).

Since the country's founding, only 27 amendments have passed such a rigorous process. The eighteenth Amendment was the only amendment to be repealed, being repealed by the twenty-first Amendment. The most recent addition was the twenty-seventh Amendment, which limits the salary increase for federal legislators. It was proposed along with the Bill of Rights by James Madison, who later became the fourth president. However, it was inactive as it failed to get the requisite votes to be ratified. In 1982, Gregory Watson, a 19-year-old undergraduate student at the University of Texas, discovered it and began a movement to ratify it. It was finally ratified 202 years after its proposal.

The Constitution is remarkably simple for a great country in which 50 states and the people from all over the world have come together "to form a more perfect Union." It's only four pages long. (2022.3.30.)

8장 전체 영어 녹음 듣기

Chapter
8

한국 재판 소식
Korean Legal Cases

은밀한 '박사방'과 함정수사

미끼 광고로 여성들을 유인하여 성 착취 음란물을 제작하고 이를 온라인에 유포한 'n번방'에 이어 '박사방' 사건 등으로 한국이 시끌벅적하다. 이들 성범죄 주동자들은 단속을 피하기 위해 해외 암호화 메신저인 텔레그램을 범행에 이용하였으며 수시로 방을 바꿔가며 가상화폐로 유료회원을 모집한 것으로 알려졌다. 피해 여성 중에는 미성년자들도 다수 포함돼있어 더욱 충격을 주고 있다.

가공할 만한 것은 이런 류의 음란물 유통방 유료 가입자가 무려 26만 명에 이를 정도로 인터넷 성범죄가 한국 사회에 만연해있지만 워낙 음성적으로 거래되는 데다 메신저 보안기술의 발달로 단속이 쉽지 않다는 점이다.

이의 해결책으로 미국처럼 함정수사를 허용해야 한다는 주장이 여성단체 중심으로 강력하게 대두되고 있다. 현행 한국법상 신분을 숨기고 범죄정보를 수집하는 잠입수사는 합법이지만 함정수사는 불법으로 재판에서 증거로 인정되지 않는다.

함정수사는 비밀 공간에서 은밀하게 이루어지는 디지털 성범죄를 비롯 마약, 도박, 밀수사범 등을 검거하는 데 효과적이기 때문에 미국에선 종종 사용하는 수사 방식이다.

가까운 예로 4월 24일 자 폭스뉴스에 따르면 버지니아주 페어팩스 카운티 경찰은 코로나-19로 휴교 중인 기간에 온라인 사이트에서 어린이로 가장하여 '코비드 단속 작전'을 펼친 결과 함정수사에 나선 경찰관들에게 노골적으로 접근해 성관계를 요구한 성범죄자 30명을 약속장소에서 체포했다고 밝히고 이들의 신상을 공개했다.

하지만 함정수사가 장점만 있는 것은 아니다. 한때 뉴욕 시경은 절도 범죄를 줄이기 위해 사람이 붐비는 공원 같은 곳에 일부러 자전거나 유모차 등에 돈지갑을 걸어두고 이를 손댄 사람들을 검거하는 이른바 '행운의 가방 작전'(Operation Lucky Bag)을 전개한 적이 있었는데 주인에게 돌려줄 의도로 지갑을 주운 사람 3명까지 무분별 검거하는 바람에 이들에게 총 5만 불의 배상금을 지급하고 작전을 완화한 사례가 있다.

또 2018년 시카고 경찰은 시카고의 한적한 흑인 동네에 명품 운동화를 가득 실은 트럭을 방치한 뒤 운동화를 훔친 사람들을 체포하였는데 경찰이 애먼 흑인 동네를 타깃으로 삼았다며 거센 비난을 받기도 했다.

이처럼 억울하게 함정수사에 걸려든 사람들을 위해 법원은 소위 '함정의 항변'(entrapment defense)으로 이들을 심판하게 된다. 함정의 항변은 피고인이 범의가 없었음에도 불구, 수사기관의 함정에 걸려 범죄를 저지르게 되었다는 것을 증명할 때 무죄가 되는 법리로 '셔먼 대 미국'(Sherman v. United States) 사건에서 판례가 확립되었다.

뉴욕의 마약중독자 '조세프 셔먼'(Joseph Sherman)은 헤로인 중독을 치료하기 위해 마약 금단증상 완화 약물인 메타돈을 복용하고 있었는데 병원에서 만난 다른 중독자 '칼치니안'과 서로 친해지게 되었다. 어느 날 칼치니안은 더 이상 메타돈으로는 버틸 수 없겠다며 셔먼에게 마약을 구해달라고 여러 차례 부탁했고 셔먼은 마지못해 이 청을 들어주고야 말았다. 하지만 칼치니안은 이미 다른 범죄로 기소된 상태에서 검찰과의 유리한 플리바게닝을 얻어내기 위해 마약상 정보를 제공하고 있는 상황이었는데 여기에 셔먼이 이용된 것이었다.

당시 연방대법원장 워렌 판사는 셔먼이 성실하게 약물치료 중이었고, 가택수색에서 마약이 발견되지 않았으며 마약을 전달만 했지 이윤을 남기지 않았다는 점 등을 이유로 원심을 뒤집고 무죄 판결을 내려주었다.

앞선 사건 등에서 보듯 성범죄를 소탕하는 것도 중요하지만 이를 단속하기 위한 함정수사는 여러 부작용이 따를 수밖에 없기 때문에 신중한 접근 방법이 요구된다. (2020.5.6)

결과: 한국 역시 법이 개정되어 2021년 9월부터 아동·청소년 디지털 성범죄를 수사할 때 신분을 위장하는 잠입 수사가 허용되었다. 경찰은 2022년 3월까지 90건의 위장 수사에 착수해 총 96명을 검거하고 이 중 6명을 구속했다고 밝혔다.

Korean Legal Cases

Secret "Doctor's Room" and Sting Operations

With each passing day, more shocking news comes out of Korea about how young women were lured by sexual predators and blackmailed into being subjects of sexually exploitative video recordings. These videos were distributed in secret online chat rooms, with names like "Nth room" or "Doctor's Room." To avoid getting caught, perpetrators allegedly used Telegram, an instant messaging app known for its encryption architecture. They also changed chatrooms frequently and received their payment in cryptocurrency. Adding to the outrage, many victims were minors.

Law enforcement estimates that 260,000 users have paid subscriptions to these illegal messenger chat rooms. While it's widespread in Korea, perpetrators are difficult to catch given the messenger encryption technology and clandestine operation. To combat these crimes, women's rights groups are advocating for law enforcement to adopt American-style sting operations. Under current Korean law, police officers may infiltrate criminal enterprises, but they are forbidden from engaging in deceptive operations to lure would-be criminals. Since it's illegal, prosecutors may not use evidence obtained from sting operations in a trial.

Sting operations are frequently used in America. They effectively ferret out crimes in discrete places, such as online sex crimes, drug, gambling and trafficking operations. Recently, Fox News reported that Fairfax County police in Virginia carried out "Operation COVID Crackdown" on April 24. It resulted in the arrest of 30 individuals who allegedly used online platforms to solicit sex from undercover police officers pretending to be underage children. Police took these would-be sexual predators into custody when they showed up at agreed-upon locations. Their identities were publicly announced.

There are disadvantages to sting operations as well. For example, to reduce theft, the New York City Police Department once conducted "Operation Lucky Bag" Police intentionally left a wallet or a purse on a bicycle or a stroller in crowded places like public parks. They then arrested the people who attempted to steal the item. However, police mistakenly detained three people who retrieved the wallet to return it to the rightful owner. The city ended up giving away $50,000 in damages. In 2018, the Chicago Police Department received nationwide criticism for unfair policing when they left a truck full of Nike sneakers in a black neighborhood and arrested people who stole them.

Individuals arrested in a sting operation can rely on an "entrapment defense" to prove their lack of guilt. Under this legal doctrine, if the defendant can successfully show that he had no intention of committing a crime but was induced by the law enforcement to do so, then he's deemed not guilty of the crime and can walk away scot-free. This 1958 legal case of Sherman v. United

States established this defense.

Joseph Sherman was a heroin addict from New York who was in methadone treatment. He would frequently run into another addict named Kalchinian at the clinic. Kalchinian often asked Sherman to get him some heroin as methadone treatment was not working for him. After several demands by Kalchinian, Sherman reluctantly acquiesced. As it turned out, Kalchinian was already under a criminal indictment for an unrelated case. He provided drug dealer information to the prosecution to obtain a favorable plea offer. So, he gave Sherman up as a drug dealer.

Earl Warren, the Chief Justice of the Supreme Court presiding over the case, wrote the majority opinion. He vacated Sherman's guilty verdict. The judge highlighted that Sherman would not have committed a crime had it not been for Kalchinian's entrapment. He noted that Sherman was faithfully undergoing methadone treatment, no drugs were found in the subsequent police search of his house, and he only delivered the drugs and did not make any profit.

As Sherman's case shows, sting operations may have unwitting victims. Although it is crucial to detect and punish sex crimes, it is important to approach sting operations with caution to avoid arresting those who would not commit a crime otherwise. (2020.5.6)

Outcome: Effective September 2021, Korea changed the law to allow the police to use sting operations to investigate online sex crimes involving minors and teens. Using this new investigative technique, the police reported that they have participated in 90 sting operations as of March 2022, and arrested 96 people. Six of them are currently physically detained and awaiting trial.

범죄인 인도조약

　　세계 최대 아동 음란물 사이트 중 하나인 '웰컴 투 비디오'의 운영자 손○○에 대한 미국의 범죄인 인도 요청 심사·재판이 얼마 전 한국의 고등법원에서 열렸다. 손 씨는 2015~18년까지 특정 브라우저로만 접속할 수 있는 다크웹을 통해 총 22만여 건의 영유아 성 착취 영상물을 유통시킨 혐의로 1년 6월의 징역형을 선고받고 한국에서의 형기를 마쳤다. 손 씨는 이 같은 범행으로 32개국의 유료 가입자 3,400여 명으로부터 가상화폐인 비트코인으로 수십억 원의 수입을 올린 것으로 알려졌다.

　　손 씨는 한국에 서버를 두고 범행을 저질렀기 때문에 한국법에 따라 죗값을 치렀으나 문제는 국경이 없는 사이버 범죄의 특성상 미국과 영국 등지 가입자들과의 양형에 대한 형평성 문제가 제기됐다. 이들 해외 가입자들은 해당 사이트에서 동영상을 다운받았다는 이유만으로 자국에서 5년 이상의 중형을 받고 아직 복역 중인 사람들이 많은 데 반해 주범의 형량이 오히려 그보다 가벼웠기 때문이다. 2년 전 한국 경찰과 함께 손 씨의 검거에 참여했던 미국 사법당국은 한국의 솜방망이 처벌을 보고 손 씨에 대한 범죄인 인도를 요청했고 그 심문이 지난 5월 19일 고등법원에서 열린 것이다.

  세계의 경찰을 자처하는 미국은 범죄행위로 인한 자국민의 피해를 용납하지 않고 끝까지 본국으로 송환시켜 미국법으로 응징하는 경향이 강하다. 대표적인 예로 미국 검찰은 1987년에 금세기 최대의 마약상으로 악명을 떨쳐 미 FBI가 선정한 '세계 10대 지명수배자' 명단에 2번 연속 이름을 올렸던 멕시코인 '엘차포'를 기소한 후 끝내 2017년 멕시코로부터 그를 넘겨받아 연방 재판에 회부한 바 있다.

  엘차포는 멕시코 수감 시절 교도관을 매수, 빨래 바구니에 몸을 숨겨 탈옥한 적이 있는가 하면 다시 체포된 후 2015년에는 1.5km 교도소 밖 건물까지 땅굴을 파 탈옥에 성공한 전설적 인물이다. 지금은 미국법원으로부터 종신형을 선고받고 최고의 보안 수준을 자랑하는 뉴욕 맨해튼 남부 연방교도소에서 복역 중이다.

  엘차포처럼 손 씨 사건도 그 연장선 상에 있는 것으로 보인다. 그러나 아무리 범죄혐의가 인정되어 미국 재판에 넘겨지는 것이 당연하다고 하더라도 의사소통이 되지 않아 재판과 수형생활에서 여러모로 불리할 것이 뻔한 타국 땅에 자국민을 넘겨주는 것은 인도적 문제뿐 아니라 자국민을 우선 보호해야 하는 국가의 기본책무에 반하기 때문에 입장 정리가 쉽지 않다.

  범죄인 인도조약은 몇 가지 원칙을 따르는데 쌍방 가벌성, 범죄특정의 원칙, 이중처벌금지 등이 바로 그것이다. 쌍방 가벌성은 인도 대상 범죄가 인도를 요청한 청구국가와 피 청구국 양측에서 모두 범죄에 해당할 때 넘겨줄 수 있다는 것이고, 범죄특정의 원칙은 범죄인을 인도받아 재판할 때 인도 청구 시 나열한 범죄에 대해서만 처벌할 수 있다는 법리이다. 이중 처벌금지는 말 그대로 동일 범죄에 대해 거듭 처벌하는 것을 금지한다는 원칙이다.

  손 씨의 아버지는 아들이 이 원칙에 따라 차라리 한국에서 재판을 받는 게 유리하다고 보고 자기 아들을 범죄수익 은닉 혐의로 한국 검찰에 고발해놓은 상태이다. 같

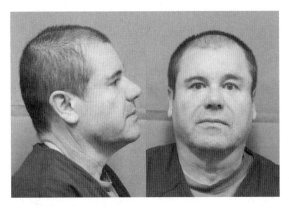

호아킨 '엘차포' 구즈만(2017)
Joaquin "El Chapo" Guzman

은 죄명으로 미국에서 재판을 받을 경우 형량이 한국보다 4배나 많아지기 때문이다.

한국과 미국은 중범죄자의 신병 인도를 골자로 하는 범죄인 인도조약을 1998년 체결한 바 있다. 이에 따라 미국은 1997년 서울 이태원에서 살인을 저지른 후 미국으로 도주한 주한미군 '아더 패터슨(Arthur Patterson)'을 18년 만인 2015년에 한국으로 송환한 사례가 있다. 자국민을 우선 보호해야 하는 국가적 책무와 사안의 경중 차이는 있지만 이태원 살인범의 송환사례, 아버지가 세간의 비난을 무릅쓰고 아들을 위해 먼저 고발 조치한 법적 절차 등 여러 문제가 뒤엉켜 한국 사법당국이 어떤 결정을 내릴지 자못 향배가 궁금하다. (2020.6.3)

결과: 2020.7.6. 서울고법 형사20부는 "손 씨를 미국으로 인도하면 한국은 수사에 지장이 생길 가능성이 있고, 또 필요하면 미국과 공조 수사도 적극 할 수 있다"는 이유 등을 들어 손 씨를 송환하기 어렵다고 판단했다. 한편 손 씨는 2022.2.4. 범죄수익은닉규제법 위반, 도박 혐의로 불구속 기소됐다.

International Extradition Treaty

The Korea High Court in Seoul recently conducted a hearing on the request brought by the United States to extradite a Korean national named Son◯◯. Son ran one of the world's biggest child pornography hosting websites, Welcome to Video. He recently finished an 18-month jail sentence for distributing 220,000 infant and child pornography videos between 2015 and 2018 through the Dark Web, a part of the internet that can only be accessed using a specific browser. Son reportedly earned billions of Korean Won in profit while 3,400 subscribers from 32 countries paid him in Bitcoins, a cryptocurrency.

Son was punished in Korea as the website's server was there. However, given the nature of cybercrimes, which has no national boundaries, a question arose over the adequacy of Son's punishment. The website's British and American subscribers received more than five years of imprisonment for downloading the videos from the website. In comparison, Son, as the website host, received a relatively light sentence. Considering this discrepancy, American authorities, who had participated in his apprehension two years ago along with their Korean counterparts, requested Son's extradition. The Korea High Court heard this request on May 19.

When a criminal wrongdoing harms an American citizen, America will punish criminals according to its laws regardless of their nationality. To that end, it will often seek to extradite foreign nationals suspected of the crime. A prime example of this is El Chapo, who the American prosecutors indicted in 1987. Considered by many to be the world's most powerful drug trafficker, he was a Mexican drug lord who made the FBI's "10 Most Wanted" list in two consecutive years. He was extradited in 2017 and put to trial in an American federal court.

El Chapo is notorious for his ability to escape from prison. While he was in a federal prison in Mexico, he bribed prison guards and got away by hiding in a laundry cart. After his re-arrest, he escaped again in 2015 by making a tunnel that was 1.5 km long. He was convicted in America, and is currently serving a life sentence in a maximum-security prison.

As with El Chapo, Americans want Son Jung-woo to be punished in America. At the same time, even if the Americans have the right to extradite an offender who commits a crime against its citizens, it's a delicate matter for the Korean government to aid. The Korean government would have to detain and extradite their citizen while being aware that they may suffer many disadvantages at trial including language and cultural barriers. As such, doing so would be in direct contravention of the national government's duty to protect its citizens, and because of this, there is no easy answer.

Extradition treaties generally follow several rules such as double criminality and specialty, and the prohibition against double jeopardy. The principle of double criminality means that the crime committed must be a crime in both countries. The principle of specialty permits extradited offenders to be tried only for the charges listed on the extradition request. Finally, the prohibition against double jeopardy means that the offender may not be tried again for the same crime.

Based on these principles, Son Jung-woo's father made a formal complaint against his son for money laundering in Korea. If Son is tried and convicted for this crime in Korea, he would not need to be extradited to face similar charges in America where his prison sentence could be four times as long for the same crime.

South Korea and the United States signed an extradition treaty in 1998, which allows the extradition of people charged with felonies. Under this treaty, the United States allowed Arthur Patterson to be extradited in 2015 for his suspected role in committing a murder in Itaewon, Seoul, as an American soldier stationed in Korea 18 years ago. Given these moving parts – the government's duty to protect its citizens, the history of extradition involving the Itaewon murderer and the criminal complaint filed by Son Jung-woo's father – it will be interesting to see how the Korean High Court ultimately decides in this case. (2020.6.3)

Outcome: On July 6, 2020, Seoul High Court's Criminal Division refused to extradite Son because "the investigation in Korea will suffer if Son is handed over to the United States . . . and as a sovereign nation, Korea can exercise our right to prosecute as it sees fit, and coordinate with the United States." On February 4, 2022, Son was arrested for illegal gambling and violating the prohibition against concealing criminal proceeds.

외출제한과 재택근무 등 코로나-19로 부부가 집에서 같이 지내는 시간이 많아지자 그만큼 부부싸움도 잦아졌다는 우스갯소리가 들리곤 한다. 한국 대법원은 6.16. 부부의 주거공간 문제에 얽힌 2건의 주거침입 사건을 공개재판으로 진행하여 뜨거운 관심을 불러 모았다.

첫 번째 사건은 아내 A가 남편 몰래 내연남 B를 집으로 불러들여 바람을 피운 사건이었다. 남편 없는 사이 B가 집에 3회 들어온 것은 자기 아내의 동의가 있었기 때문인데 그런데도 남편 C가 B를 주거침입죄로 처벌해달라고 할 수 있는지가 쟁점이었다.

대법원은 1984년 재판에서 '평온하고 안전한 주거권은 공동생활을 하는 전원에게 누릴 권리가 있기 때문에 한 사람의 승낙이 있었어도 다른 거주자의 의사에 반해 주거권을 침해받는 경우에는 주거침입죄가 성립한다'고 판시했다.

이를 근거로 검찰은 상간남이 집에 들어가 범죄행위나 민사상 불법행위를 저질렀다면 아내의 승인이 있었더라도 '주거의 자유와 평온'에 대한 남편의 권리를 해친 것으로 보고 B를 주거침입죄로 기소했던 것이다.

반면 B의 변호인 측은 1984년과 달리 현재는 간통죄가 폐지되었는데 검찰이 간통죄를 우회적으로 형사 처벌하기 위한 편법으로 주거침입죄를 적용했다고 주장했다. 또 주거침입은 남편 C의 부재중에 이루어진 일이기 때문에 C가 실질적으로 평온을 침해 받은 바 없고, 과거 판례에 따라 공동거주자 전원으로부터 승낙을 받아야 한다면 셰어하우스 등 다양한 주거 형태가 등장하는 현실에서 타인의 집을 방문할 때마다 모든 거주자에게 일일이 동의를 다 받아야 한다는 말이냐며 검찰 주장을 되받아쳤다.

두 번째 사건의 쟁점은 함께 거주하던 사람도 주거침입죄로 처벌할 수 있느냐 하는 것이었다. 이 사건의 요지는, 부부싸움을 하고 집을 나간 남편 D가 있었다. D는 한 달여 뒤에 자신의 부모와 함께 집에 돌아왔으나 아내가 문을 열어주지 않자 잠금장치를 부수고 들어왔다가 주거침입죄로 재판에 넘겨졌다.

이 사건에서 검찰 측은 '공동거주자인 가사도우미의 방에 집주인이 무단으로 침입할 경우 주거침입죄가 아니라고 할 수 있느냐?'고 주장했고, 피고인 D의 변호인 측은 주거침입죄의 핵심은 타인이 자신의 주거를 침입하는 것인데 남편은 타인이 아니고 공동거주자이므로 애당초 주거침입 자체가 성립할 수 없다고 항변했다. 덧붙이자면 사회 통념상 부부는 이혼, 혹은 배우자 중 한 명이 법원으로부터 접근금지 명령을 받은 특수 상황 등이 아니라면 부부의 공동 공간에 자유롭게 출입할 수 있는 동의가 있는 것으로 봐야 한다는 것이다.

두 사건 다 공교롭게도 1심은 유죄로, 2심은 모두 무죄로 판단했다.

미국 뉴욕주의 경우, 거주자의 의사에 반해 타인 집에 들어가 단순하게 상대방의 평온을 침해한 정도에 그치면 경범죄인 trespass로, 후속 범죄행위라도 저지르게 되면 중범죄인 burglary 등으로 처벌하고 있다. 아직까진 불륜 문제로 주거침입죄를 적용한 사례는 발견되지 않지만 별거 부부간의 주거침입죄 적용 사례는 많다. 이때 법원에선 집에 대한 부부의 법적 권리인 소유권과 주거권을 분리하여 주거권에 중점을 두고 사건을 심리한다. 달리 말해 배우자 중 한 명이 법원으로부터 접근금지명령을 받았거나 가출 후 오랜 시간이 경과한 상황이라면 주택 소유권과 별개로 주거권이 축소되어 법원의 허락이나 상대방의 동의 없이 다시 집에 돌아올 수 없다고 보는 식이다.

부부는 너무 가까운 나머지 '무촌'이라고도 하고 TV의 유머코너 같은 데선 우스꽝스럽게 '평생 원수'라고 표현하기도 한다. 과연 한국 대법원은 2건의 부부간 주거침입 사건에 대해 어떻게 결론을 내릴지 귀추가 주목된다. (2021.7.7.)

결과: 대법원은 부부 중 한 명의 동의를 받아 집에 들어간 불륜남은 무단침입이 아니고, 부부 싸움 뒤 부모와 함께 돌아온 남편 역시 주거침입죄로 처벌할 수 없다고 판결했다.

Korean Legal Cases

⚖️

Domestic Criminal Trespass and Burglary

With quarantine and work-from-home arrangements during the COVID-19 pandemic, married couples are spending more time together than ever before. I hear people jokingly say they're fighting with their spouse more often. On June 16, the Supreme Court of Korea made national headlines by conducting a public hearing on two domestic criminal trespass cases.

The first case involved a wife who was having a secret extramarital affair. She invited her boyfriend over three times while her husband was not home. Although the boyfriend entered the house with the wife's permission, the issue was whether the husband could still ask the boyfriend to be charged with criminal trespass.

In 1984, the Supreme Court of Korea held that "the right to peace and quiet in the home belongs to every resident who lives there. Thus, even if there is consent by one of the occupants, criminal trespass may be committed against another if that person's right to peace and quiet is violated."

Based on this precedent, the prosecutor argued that the boyfriend is guilty of criminal trespass even though he entered with the wife's permission because he violated the husband's right to peace and quiet through his wrongdoing while inside the home.

On the other hand, the defendant pointed out that unlike in 1984, adultery is no longer a crime. He argued that the prosecution was indirectly prosecuting adultery through this charge. Furthermore, the defendant maintained that he did not commit trespass because the husband's actual peace and quiet was not disturbed because he was not present. The defense also asked the Supreme Court to revisit the standard given various living arrangements these days. If someone was visiting a friend who lives in a shared house, the defendant emphasized that it would not make sense for the visitor to obtain consent from every roommate.

The second case posed the question of whether the spouse who left the marital home may be charged with burglary. In this case, the husband left the house after an argument. He returned one month later with his parents. When the wife did not open the door, he broke the door lock and was arrested for burglary.

The prosecution argued that the husband committed burglary even though they acknowledged that it was the marital home. The prosecution defended their position by positing rhetorically whether it would not be breaking and entering for the landlord to enter a live-in nanny's room without permission. The defendant contended that he was not a stranger, which is at the heart of the case when dealing with burglary. Under the traditional standard, the defendant claimed that a spouse has implicit permission to enter the marital home unless they are divorced or there is an active stay-away order.

In both cases, the defendants were found guilty after trial, but the appeals court vacated their convictions.

In New York, entering someone else's private property without permission or authority and disturbing the peace constitutes a misdemeanor crime of trespass. If they commit a criminal act while inside, it's a burglary, a felony. So far, in New York, no one has been charged with burglary for going into their lover's house unbeknownst to the lover's marital partner. However, there have been numerous cases where separated couples have complained of trespass against their partner. The court separates one's ownership interest from a possessory interest in such cases. In other words, regardless of their ownership interest, if one of the partners got a stay-away order from the court or hasn't been home for a long time, they may no longer have the possessory interest and cannot return without the court's permission or the other person's consent.

The spouse can be so close and yet, so distant sometimes. It remains to be seen how the Supreme Court of Korea will decide these two cases. (2021.7.7.)

Outcome: The Supreme Court ruled that the boyfriend who entered with the wife's permission couldn't be guilty of trespass. Similarly, the husband who returned with his parents after leaving the marital home was found not guilty.

공소시효의 명암

1986년 9월부터 1991년 4월까지 경기도 화성시(당시는 군이었음) 일대에서 부녀자 10명이 강간, 살해당하는 끔찍한 사건이 발생했다. '살인의 추억'(봉준호 감독)이라는 영화로 만들어져 우리에게도 익숙한 이른바 화성연쇄살인사건 이야기다.

5년여 동안 같은 지역에서 잔인하게 반복된 범행으로 인근 주민뿐 아니라 전 국민을 공포의 도가니로 몰아넣었던 이 사건에 연인원 205만여 명의 경찰력이 동원되어 지문대조 4만, 그중 2만 명을 수사했지만 수십 년간 진범이 명쾌하게 잡히지 않아 강력범죄 사상 최악의 영구 미제 사건으로 남는 듯했다.

오랜 답보상태에 머물던 사건은 DNA 해독기술의 발달과 함께 이를 기반으로 한 신원정보 자료 등이 축적됨으로써 2019년 드디어 실마리가 풀리기 시작했다. 당시 피해자의 증거물에서 채취했던 DNA가, 자신의 처제를 성폭행하고 살해한 죄로 구속돼 무기수로 25년째 복역 중인 이○○(57세)의 것과 일치한다는 결과가 나왔기 때문이다. 범죄혐의를 부인하던 이 씨는 프로파일러 등을 동원한 경찰의 끈질긴 대면조사 끝에 14건의 살인과 9건의 강간사건 등 그간 밝혀지지 않은 사건까지 모두 자신이 저질렀음을 자백했다.

하지만 그의 자백 내용을 경찰이 사실 확인까지 했음에도 불구하고 공소시효가 만료되어 기소는 불가능하다. 범행 당시 법으로는 살인죄의 경우 공소시효가 15년이라 지난 2001~2006년 사이에 모든 사건에 대한 시효가 만료되었기 때문이다. 이후 강력범죄자를 엄벌하자는 사회적 분위기가 조성되어 2007년 15년에서 25년으로 공소시효가 한 차례 연장되었고, 2015년에는 살인죄에 대한 공소시효가 완전히 폐지됐지만 형벌불소급의 대원칙에 따라 이 씨에게는 해당되지 않는다.

이처럼 시효란 형사사건에서의 범죄 행위나, 민사사건에서 손해가 발생하여 법원에 기소 또는 소송을 청구할 수 있는 권리가 있음에도 불구하고 일정 기간 그 권리를 행사하지 않으면 자동 소멸되는 제도를 말한다. 보통 사건 발생일로부터 유효기간을 계산하지만 피해자가 미성년으로 신고를 하지 못하는 성폭력 사건에선 피해자가 성년이 된 날부터, 또는 피해가 이미 발생했지만 피해자가 미처 발견하지 못했다면 발견한 날로부터 시작되기도 한다.

고대 그리스에서 '프로소송꾼'들의 소송 남발을 막기 위해 처음 도입된 것으로 알려진 공소시효는 현대 법리에 의하면, 사건에 대한 당사자들의 기억이 부정확해짐에 따라 재판의 공정성을 담보할 수 없고, 오랜 시간 증거물 보존에 따른 어려움과 공적 비용이 발생하며, 가해자와 피해자의 생활안정도 보장해주어야 하고, 시간의 경과로 인한 사회적 관심 희석 등을 그 필요성으로 내세운다.

그러나 최근의 세계적 추세는 증거물 보관기술의 발달과 아울러 DNA 검사나 CC-TV 같은 각종 과학적 뒷받침도 가능해져 한국과 마찬가지로 강간이나 살인 등 강력 범죄에 대해서는 공소시효를 배제하는 분위기이다.

그 예로 미국 캘리포니아주의 경우, 원로 유명 코미디언 '빌 코스비'가 반세기에 걸쳐 60여 명의 여성을 성추행 또는 성폭행했다는 의혹이 제기됐음에도 불구하고 공소시효 만료로 기소를 피해가자 이 사건을 계기로 2016년 강간에 대한 공소시효를 폐지했다.

그 외의 공소시효는 주의 법에 따라, 또는 범죄행위의 경중에 따라 유효기간이 각각 다르다. 뉴욕주에서 대부분의 경범죄는 사건 발생일로부터 2년, 중범죄는 5년이고, 캘리포니아에서는 경범죄 1년, 중범죄는 3년의 공소시효를 적용하고 있다.

또 똑같은 행위를 두고도 형사사건으로 접근하는지 아니면 민사사건으로 접근하는지에 따라 시효가 달리 적용된다. 예컨대, A가 뉴욕주에서 중범죄에 해당하는 폭행죄를 저질렀다면 형사사건의 공소시효는 5년이지만, 폭행죄로 인한 치료비 등을 A에게 청구할 수 있는 민사사건의 소멸시효는 1년밖에 되지 않는다. "정의에는 유효기간이 없다"는 법언이 있긴 하지만 일상 대부분의 사건에선 정의에도 유효기간이 있는 셈이다. (2021.8.18.)

Korean Legal Cases

Pros and Cons of Statute of Limitations

From September 1986 to April 1991, a series of horrific rapes and murders of women occurred in Hwasung-si, Gyeonggi-do. It was called the Hwasung serial murders in the newspapers. Director Bong Joon-ho later made Memories of Murder, loosely based on these incidents. To catch the perpetrator, more than 2.05 million police officers were mobilized each year. The investigation also included comparing 40,000 fingerprints and investigating 20,000 suspects. However, the murderer evaded the police for decades. It remained Korea's biggest mystery in the history of violent crimes.

The old mystery began to crack in 2019 with advances in DNA technology and the accumulation of DNA profiles in the police database. The DNA profile developed from a victim matched Lee, 57, who was serving a 25-year sentence for raping and murdering his sister-in-law. Lee denied his involvement, but ultimately confessed to 14 murders and eight rapes after face-to-face interrogations by the police and profilers.

However, even with his confession, he evaded prosecution as the statute of limitations had run out. At the time of these crimes, the statute of limitations for homicide was 15 years. As such, they expired between 2001 and 2006. Since then, based on broad social support for more severe punishment for violent crimes, the statute of limitations was extended to 25 years in 2007 and was eliminated for homicide cases. However, under the legal principle that bans ex post facto – a legal concept stating that a person may not be punished retroactively based on a new law – these changes do not apply to Lee.

As the case highlights, the statute of limitations extinguishes the right to prosecute or file a civil lawsuit if it is not exercised within a specified period. Generally, it starts to run from the date of the incident, but in sexual assault cases involving minor children, it runs from the date the child reaches maturity. In other cases, it can run from the date the damage is discovered.

The statute of limitations was first introduced in ancient Greece to prevent excessive lawsuits by "sycophants." Today, it is justified as a way to guarantee a fair trial as witnesses' memories fade and evidence gets lost with the passing of time. There is also the issue of spending public funds to preserve the evidence for a prolonged period. Equally as important, there's an interest in providing closure to the victims, and the perpetrators. Society's attention to the case also diminishes with time.

However, the recent international trend is to eliminate the statute of limitation for violent crimes like murder and rape, as in the case of Korea. The technological advancements have made the preservation of evidence or obtaining scientific evidence like DNA or video surveillance footage much cheaper. Another benefit is that they are not affected by human memory, either.

Similarly to Korea, California also eliminated the statute of limitations for rape in 2016 when well-known comedian Bill Cosby evaded criminal prosecution even though there were allegations that he sexually assaulted or harassed approximately 60 women over 50 years.

The period of the statute of limitation varies depending on the state and severity of the crime. For instance, in New York, the statute of limitation for misdemeanors is two years and five years for most felonies. In California, it's one year for misdemeanors and three years for most felonies.

Moreover, it changes depending on whether it's civil or criminal. For example, the criminal statute of limitation for felony assault is five years. However, for the same act, the time to bring a civil lawsuit is only one year. Although some say, "justice doesn't expire," there is an expiration date for most cases. (2021.8.18.)

⚖️ 에필로그(번역 작업을 끝내고 나서…)

3년간 누적된 나의 칼럼을 책으로 묶는 일이야 거의 출판사의 몫이라고 하더라도, 이를 영어로 번역하는 일이 또 한 권의 책을 내는 것만큼 쉽지 않은 과정이었음을 독백 삼아 털어놓고자 한다. 처음엔 대수롭잖게 여기고 번역에 착수했다. 왜냐하면 텍사스 주립대 학부 시절 매일 3만 부 정도 발간되는 학보 'The Daily Texan'의 수석칼럼니스트와 이어서 포드햄 로스쿨에서도 학보 'International Law Journal'의 에디터 경험이 있고, 지금도 계속 판결문 등을 영어로 써와 나름 믿는 구석이 있기 때문이었다.

그러나 난생처음으로 해본, 그것도 변화무상하고 난해하기 이를 데 없는(?) 한국말을 영어로 옮기는 작업은 이와는 별개의 영역임을 절감했다. 번역가들이 '번역을 제2의 창작'이라고 내세우던 이유를 알게 됐다.

예전엔 전혀 몰랐던 사실로 칼럼을 시작하면서 온몸으로 느낀 것은 우리말의 어휘가 참으로 풍부하고 표현법이 다양하다는 것이고, 문제는 그만큼 어법과 문법도 만만치 않다는 점이었다.

예컨대 보조용언이니, '으' 탈락 현상이니, '~대'와 '~데'의 차이점, 의존명사, 사이시옷 등의 맞춤법에서부터 띄어쓰기와 겹받침 단어, 외래어 표기법 등도 잠깐 방심하면 틀리기 십상이다. 한국어 어원의 70% 정도가 한자에서 유래하였다고 하니 한자를 배우지 않은 우리 세대에겐 동음이의어, 사자성어에다 존댓말 문제까지 더해지면 머리가 혼란스럽다. 특히 내 칼럼의 경우 수시로 법률 영어가 등장하는가 하면 한국과 미국의 소송 체계와 행정기관 직제 등의 차이에서 오는 명칭과 용어의 혼동으로 문장이 뒤엉킬 때가 부지기수였다.

그렇다면 미국에서 중·고등학교와 대학, 로스쿨을 거쳐 바이링구얼이 된 나에게 영어는 쉬운 언어일까? 이것도 절대 장담할 수 없다는 걸 이번 번역과정에서 새삼 알게 됐다. 어느 나라 말이든 생활 언어를 떠나 한 수준 높은 글을 제대로 구사하려면 모두 녹록하지 않은 법. 번역 문제도 원래 뜻을 왜곡되지 않게 전달하려면 의역이 필수적인데 이도 마찬가지였다. 결론은 책 한 권 만들 수준에 이르기 위해서는 쉼 없이 공부하고 노력하는 수밖에 없고, 인생살이에서 공짜로 되는 게 하나도 없다는 점이다.

본론으로 돌아와 왜 굳이 한글 칼럼을 영어로 다시 옮기려 했는지 그 이유도 고백한다. 처음에는, 프롤로그에서 밝혔던 것처럼, 한국 독자들을 위한 배려에서 출발하였다. 그 배려의 동기는 이렇다. 나는 학부 시절, 방학 때면 한국에 나가 토익학원에서 영어 강사를 했다. 그렇게 하면 왕복 항공료를 제하고도 제법 학비를 벌어올 수 있기 때문이었다. 오갈 때마다 한국의 변한 모습을 보는 것은 덤으로 얻는 소득이었다.

내가 한국을 떠날 때가 온통 '세계화 드라이브'로 조기유학이 붐을 이루던 때였다면 몇 년이 지나 성년이 되어 다시 학원 강사로 나갈 즈음의 한국은 그야말로 '영어가 바로 계급장'인 시대라고 해도 과언이 아니었다. 직장인이 대부분이었던 나의 수강생들은 퇴근길 파김치가 된 몸으로 집에도 가지 못하고 학원으로 와 강사 입만 주시하고 있었다. 영어는 입사시험, 승진시험 등에서 신분 상승의 사다리로 그들의 발목을 잡고 있었기 때문이었다. 프롤로그에서 적시한 것처럼 '한국의 지성인들은 하루라도 영어를 가까이하지 않으면 경쟁에서 낙오될 것 같은 분리불안을 느끼지 않을 수 없다'는 것도 그때 안 사실이다.

그래서 기왕에 미국을 알기 위해 나의 한글 칼럼을 읽은 마당에 거기서 조금만 더 나아가 영어로 문장을 익히고 리스닝 공부까지 할 수 있다면 그것은 아주 유용한 공부 방법이 될 것이라는 게 나의 계산이었다.

이런 선의를 가지고 덥석 발을 담그긴 했으나 복잡하고 긴 한글 문장 하나를 두고도 낑낑대는 빈도가 잦아지고, 이렇게 옮긴 문장이 책으로 내놓아도 될 만큼 제대로된 영어인지 자신감이 떨어지기 시작했다. 이 무모한 일을 계속해야 하는지 수시로 회의가 밀려올 무렵 나의 초심을 다잡아 준 '회초리'가 바로 다음의 두 번째 이유다.

즉 우리 아이들과의 훗날 모습이 번쩍 떠올랐던 것이다. 이민 1세대 못지않게 열심히 살아온 조기 유학생 출신 1·5세대 아빠의 인생 궤적을 이 기회에 이민 2세대 우리 셋 아이들에게 온전히 전해주고 싶었던 것이다. 교포라면 어느 집이나 마찬가지겠지만, 이민 2세들은 공동생활을 하게 되는 학교에 입학하면서부터 급속도로 영어를 습득하는 반면 그 속도에 반비례하여 모국어를 까먹기 시작한다.

이를 염려하신 가친은 "한국말을 잊지 않기 위해서라도 방학만 되면 무조건 애들만 비행기 태워 한국으로 보내라"고 늘 입버릇처럼 말씀하시지만 코로나-19로 벌써 3년째 한국행이 멈춰 섰고, 부모님의 왕래도 끊어졌다. 그 사이 하루가 다르게 커가는 애들은 거의 한국말을 다 까먹어 이제 한국말로 밥상머리 교육을 하는 것은 우리 부부의 꿈이 되고 말았다. 안타깝고 서글프지만 이건 팩트고 현실이다. 나는 그래도 중2 때 건너와 이나마 바이링구얼로 버텨냈지만 우리 아이들에게 나 정도의 한국말 실력을 기대하기는 무리일 것이다.

그래서 이참에 영어로 옮겨두지 않으면 이 책이 아이들에겐 천덕꾸러기 이삿짐밖에 되지 않을 것이고, 영어로 옮겨둠으로써 비로소 책에 생기가 돌아 미국에서 온갖 차별과 어려움을 겪어내고 최소한 신문에 고정 칼럼을 쓸 정도로 성공한 아빠의 흔적을 아이들도 공감하고 장차 우리 집 가보로 대물림이 될 것으로 생각되었던 것이다. 조금 힘들더라도 마저 끝을 보자고 마음을 다잡았던 두 번째 이유다.

마지막 이유로는, 영어로 옮겨놓으면 내 책이 우리 아이들 같은 북미권 이민 2세들과 외국인들을 위한 한국어 교재로도 활용이 가능하다는 점이다. 6·25전쟁이 발발할 당시만 해도 세계 최빈국이었던 우리 대한민국이 이제는 당당하게 세계 10대 경제 강국의 반열에까지 오르게 되었다. 정말 감격스럽고 격세지감을 느낀다.

이 같은 경제적 위상에 걸맞게 'BTS'와 '기생충', '오징어게임'에 이어 바로 얼마 전에는 세계 3대 영화제의 하나인 '칸 영화제'에서 '헤어질 결심'과 '브로커'가 나란히 큰상을 동시에 수상하는 등 우리의 문화적 영향력도 무시할 수 없는 단계까지 진입하였다. 한국교포의 한 사람으로서 가슴 뿌듯하고 고마운 일이다.

세계는 각종 SNS를 통로로 급속하게 글로벌화하고 있는 가운데 이제 우리 한국어도 아시아 변방의 로컬 언어가 아니라 하나의 글로벌 주류 매체로, 하나의 문화 코드로 등장하였다는 점이다.

그 방증으로 북미에서나 유럽에서나 중동에서, 동남아에서도 이제 한국어를 배우려는 사람들이 많이 늘었다. 또 서울은 어느새 국제도시가 되어 세계 각국에서 온 외국인들로 넘치고, 이들 중에는 한국어를 곧잘 하는 사람도 많다. 이들에게 나의 책이 한국 서점의 매대에 있든, 미국이나 인터넷 공간의 서점에 있든 언젠가 영어를 통해 고급 한국어를 배우려는 학습교재로 선택되는 날이 있으리라 기대한다. 이런 목적도 염두에 두고 그만큼 영어 교정을 꼼꼼하게 거쳤으니 이 책은 고급 영어 필사 교재로 내놓아도 손색이 없다고 자부한다.

이렇게나마 프롤로그에서 미처 하지 못했던 속사정을 털어놓고 나니 좀 위안이 되고 스스로 보상을 받은 느낌이다. 독자께서도 널리 공감해주신다면 더할 나위 없이 고맙겠다. 아무튼 부족한 내 책을 선택해 주신 데 대해 다시 한번 깊은 감사의 말씀을 전하고 싶다.

뉴욕에서 손경락

영어 녹음 듣기

⚖️ Epilogue(After finishing translation···)

Translating three years' worth of my columns from Korean into English was a process as difficult as putting together another book. At first, I did not think much of it. As a college student at the University of Texas at Austin, I worked as a senior columnist for The Daily Texan, which had a daily circulation of 30,000 copies. I continued my writing as an editor of the International Law Journal at Fordham Law School, and then, as a court attorney writing judicial decisions. These experiences made me confident that translating columns would not be too challenging.

However, as I was translating for the first time, I realized that translating Korean into English, with their different syntax and cultural expressions, was something quite different than writing. I learned why professional translators say that the art of translating is 'the second creation.'

Writing columns in Korean helped me to realize that the Korean language has a large vocabulary and allows one to express thoughts in various ways. Consequently, word usage and grammar are very tricky.

For example, if I am not paying close attention, it is easy to make an error with auxiliary verbs, when to delete 'eu (으)', the difference between '~dae(대)' and '~de(데)', dependent nouns, when to use (or not use) the sai siot (사이 시옷), spacing of words, and correct spelling of words with double consonants and

409

loanwords. In addition, approximately 70% of Korean vocabulary is derived from Chinese characters. It is even more confusing to think about homonyms, Chinese idioms and honorifics, especially growing up as a part of the generation that did not learn Chinese characters in school. Making it even more complicated, my columns often contained English legal terms, which, when translated, would take on a different meaning because of the difference between the Korean and American legal and government systems. This would result in the meaning of my sentences being unclear or being difficult to understand.

On the opposite side of the coin, was English easy for me as someone who went to middle school, high school, college, and law school in America? The answer that I realized during the translation process is a resounding "no!" I learned that it is very difficult to write in Korean or English at a higher level than having a normal, daily conversation. Translation was just as difficult because it was important to convey the meaning of the original text without distorting or losing it. In the end, I realized that, in order to write in Korean or English at a level that is appropriate for a book, I must continue to study and practice writing. As some say, nothing comes easy in life.

But I digress. Here are the reasons why I wanted to translate my columns into English. At first, as I mentioned in the prologue, it was to add value to readers in Korea. To provide some context, when I was in college, I used to go to Korea and teach TOEIC during the summer vacations. I was able to earn my airfare and then some for my tuition. As an added bonus, it was good to visit Korea and see it changing over the years.

When I left Korea as a teenager, a huge wave of globalization had engulfed the entire country. Students were leaving en masse to study abroad. When I returned as a TOEIC instructor a few years later, English aptitude was a symbol of one's achievements. Most of my students were office workers. They would drag their tired bodies to come straight from work to my class and look blankly at my mouth without being able to go home. That is because the English language stood as a gatekeeper to their dream jobs or promotions at work. As I pointed out in the prologue, I realized that Korean intellectuals inevitably feel separation anxiety from the English language. If they do not do something related to it, even for a day, it made them fear falling behind the competition.

Since my column's readers in Korea have a desire to learn more about America in the first place, I thought that it would be even more beneficial if they can use the same content to learn English and practice their listening skills.

I took on the project without much thought as I believed my good intentions would carry me to the finish line. However, as I struggled with translating a long Korean sentence, for example, or as I began to doubt whether my English was good enough, I felt discouraged and found myself asking whether I should continue in this endeavor.

In the middle of such self-doubt, the second reason was the stick and the rod that gave me the necessary push to return to my original goal. It was a flash forward to my future with my three children. I wanted to teach them, all of whom are second-generation Korean-Americans, about my life as a 1.5-generation Korean-American, and how I struggled in this land just as much as first-generation Korean-Americans. The same phenomenon probably repeats itself in every Korean-American household. Second-generation children rapidly pick up English once they start school and get immersed in the school community, usually at the expense of losing their ability to speak Korean.

My father was concerned about this, and he would always tell me to send the kids to Korea on every vacation so as not to forget the language. However, because of the Covid-19 pandemic, we have not visited Korea in the last three years nor have my parents visited us. All the same, my children are growing day by day, and they have almost completely forgotten Korean, devasting my wife and I's dream of teaching them valuable life lessons at the dinner table in Korean. It is upsetting and regrettable, but it is also the reality and an inescapable fact. Having come to America during my second year in middle school (eighth grade in America), I was fortunate enough to become bilingual. But it would be unreasonable to expect my children to attain the same level of proficiency in both languages.

As such, I reached the conclusion that if my work is not translated, they will only be meaningless pile of newspapers, and I should take this opportunity to translate them into English so that my children can understand that their father overcame discrimination and other adversities to become, among others, a regular contributor of legal columns. I thought that it could give us a shared experience upon which we can continue to build our parent-child relationship. Perhaps they could even get passed down to my children's children. This was the second reason why I wanted to finish the book in spite of the difficulties that I mentioned earlier.

Finally, once translated into English, my book could also be used to teach Korean to second-generation Korean-Americans like my children or anyone else who wishes to learn the language. Korea was one of the poorest countries at the Korean War's outbreak. Now, it is one of the top 10 economic powers in the world. I am proud, and I also feel a sense of astonishment about how much things have changed in such a short period of time.

'*The Daily Texan*' 수석 칼럼니스트 시절(텍사스.2005)
Working on a story as a senior columnist at the Daily Texan (Texas)

In addition to economic affluence, we have also attained cultural influence as demonstrated through, for instance, BTS, Parasite, and Squid Game, and recent international recognition at the Cannes Film Festival for Decision to Leave and Broker. Cannes is, of course, one of the three most influential film festivals in the world. As a member of the diaspora, I feel proud and grateful.

With rapid globalization through different social media networks, Korean is no longer a foreign language on the fringes of the world. Rather, it is at the center of global mainstream media and a significant cultural code.

We can see the transformation. An increasing number of people wish to learn Korean from North America to Europe, from the Middle East to Southeast Asia. Seoul is an international city brimming with travelers from all over the world, many of whom are already fluent in Korean. For those who wish to learn more advanced Korean, I hope that my book could be helpful as a textbook, whether someone finds it on the bookshelf in Korea or at an online store in the United States. I have proofread the English translation with such a purpose in mind. I am also confident that this book could be helpful as a high-level English transcription workbook for those who learn better by writing.

It comforts and reassures me to explain the reasons behind my decision to translate the columns. I want readers to understand my intentions. Finally, I want to express my most heartfelt gratitude to you once again for choosing my book, despite its limitations.

K.R. Mark Son
From New York

Torture won't be forgotten

Friday, August 5, 2005

By Mark Son
Daily Texan Columnist

> As Sen. John McCain, R-Ariz., a former POW said, "This isn't about who they are. This is about who we are."

The Daily Texan 시절 썼던 칼럼
A column that I wrote for the Daily Texan

FORDHAM
INTERNATIONAL
LAW JOURNAL

Volume 33		2009-2010

BOARD OF EDITORS

JUSTIN D'ALOIA
Editor-in-Chief

BRANDON SHERR
Managing Editor

JARED LIMBACH	FRANKLIN MATRANGA	LIZ SHURA
Senior Articles Editor	*Executive Notes & Articles Editor*	*Writing & Research Editor*
CARLOS F. PEREZ	ROXANA AZIZI	ALI SHARIAT
Business & Articles Editor	*Notes & Articles Editor*	*Symposium Editor*
AMAL BOUHABIB	LAURA DEROSSI	LAURA FISHER
Notes & Articles Editor	*Notes & Articles Editor*	*Notes & Articles Editor*
CHARITY MAURER	KRISTEN O'CONNOR	KYUNG-RAK MARK SON
Notes & Articles Editor	*Notes & Articles Editor*	*Notes & Articles Editor*

ANDREW WACHTENHEIM
Notes & Articles Editor

ASSOCIATE EDITORS

MARINA ANDREWS	ITRIA CASSANDRA BENITO	POUYA GHARAVI
NOUSHIN KETABI	MONICA LAI	ELENA POLEGANOVA
JOSHUA SIEGEL	MARKUS SZTEINBERG	ANDREW CHAN WOLINSKY
	JI ZHANG	

STAFF

AMY E. ABBANDONDELO	DOMNA ANTONIADIS	SEAN BALKAN
NICHOLAS R. BARTILT	JENNA M. BEATRICE	ELIZABETH A. BENDER
EDUARD CADMUS	ALLISON K. CHANDLER	JULIE CHO
GENEVIEVE COHOON	THOMAS A. COURNOYER	ERIC DAWSON
CRISTINE M. DELANEY	ALEXIS DIAZ	SAMARA LAUREN GELLER
JASON GOLDSTOFF	CARLEY ANN GROOBMAN	ANARIA HASAN
SASHA HOLGUIN	MEGAN E. HORN	JULIA HAEYOUNG KIM
ALICIA KRAVITZ	JIWON KWAK	MICHAEL LANDIS
MICHAEL KANGKOOK LEIGH	JUSTINA K. LOPEZ	MARGARET MAIGRET
KRISTIN MARLOWE	SARAH MATARI	ERIK MORALES
CHELSEA MULLARNEY	PATRICK STEIGER NAGLER	SHERI G. NENTIN
MELISSA PAQUETTE	ASHLEY C. POPE	JENNIFER E. POPE
MATTHEW F. PUTORTI	PRIYA RAVISHANKAR	RENEE REEKIE
LAURA REIPINGER	AARON C. RETTER	DAVID SALHANICK
CHRISTINE S. SEO	TOVA B. SIMPSON	BOJAN STEFANOVIC
RYAN SYLVESTER	PHILIP TAYLOR	ELINA TURETSKAYA
ROBERT PATRICK VACCHIANO	ARIA VAUGHAN	MARIE T. VAZ
SERENA WHITE	RACHEL T. WU	JOHN DONGYUAL YI
	MICHAEL ZOLDAN	

INTERNATIONAL GRADUATE FELLOWS

ROWENA DUNGCA	KATIA FACH GOMEZ	ROBERTA KIRITSIS
ASHWINI KUMAR	URIM LEKAJ	LUCAS J. MINKOWSKI
ROXANA POPESCU		HANDSDEEP SINGH

FACULTY ADVISORS

JOSEPH C. SWEENEY	ROGER J. GOEBEL
Professor of Law, Fordham University	*Professor of Law, Fordham University*

포드햄대 'International Law Journal' 에디터 시절
2009-2010 Masthead for the Fordham International Law Journal

조기 유학생 출신 바이링구얼 뉴욕 손변의 재밌는 미국법 이야기

지 은 이 | 손경락
만 든 이 | 최수경
만 든 곳 | 글마당 앤 아이디얼북스

(출판등록 제2022-000073호)

만 든 날 | 2023년 04월 01일
펴 낸 날 | 2023년 04월 07일
주   소 | 서울시 종로구 인사동길 49 (안녕인사동 4F 403)
전   화 | 02. 786. 4284
팩   스 | 02. 6280. 9003
이 메 일 | www.idealbooks.kr
　　　　　 madang52@naver.com

ISBN 979 -11- 978822 - 6 - 5(03340)

값 23,000원